# *Prelude to harmony on a community theme*

### Health care insurance policies in the Six and Britain

# Prelude to harmony on a community theme

## Health care insurance policies in the Six and Britain

JOZEF Van LANGENDONCK

Introduced and edited by
GORDON FORSYTH

Published for the
Nuffield Provincial Hospitals Trust
by the Oxford University Press
London   New York   Toronto
1975

*Published for the*
Nuffield Provincial Hospitals Trust
3 Prince Albert Road, London NW1 7SP
*by*
Oxford University Press, Ely House, London W1

GLASGOW  NEW YORK  TORONTO  MELBOURNE  WELLINGTON  CAPE TOWN
SALISBURY  IBADAN  NAIROBI  DAR ES SALAAM  LUSAKA  ADDIS ABABA
BOMBAY  CALCUTTA  MADRAS  KARACHI  LAHORE  DACCA
KUALA LUMPUR  SINGAPORE  HONG KONG  TOKYO

© The Nuffield Provincial Hospitals Trust 1975

*Editorial Board*
Lord Cohen of Birkenhead, CH, DSC, MD, FRCP
Sir Edgar T. Williams, CB, CBE, DSO, DL
Gordon McLachlan, CBE

ISBN 0 19 721387 1

*Designed by Bernard Crossland*
Printed in Great Britain
by Burgess & Son (Abingdon) Ltd
Abingdon, Oxfordshire

The main text is based on a translation
of the updated version of
*De Harmonisering van de Sociale Verzekering*
*voor Gezondheidszorgen in de EEG* by
JOZEF Van LANGENDONCK
*Professor of Social Security*
*Director of the Institute of European*
*Health Services Research, University of Leuven*

The English text edited and introduced
with an essay on the theme by
GORDON FORSYTH
*Reader in Social Administration*
*University of Manchester*

# CONTENTS

Preface ix

Acknowledgements xiii

Introduction: *A British descant on the theme*
GORDON FORSYTH 1

Foreword 39

## PART ONE
## COMMON ASPECTS

1. Health insurance, its concept and scope 45
   Concept, 45. Scope, 48. Quantitative importance, 50.

2. Financing social health insurance 53

3. The benefits of social health insurance and access to them 57
   Extent of benefits, 57. No limitation in time, 59. Official lists, 60. Cases of exclusion, 62. Registration with an insurance organization, 63. Previous permission of the insurance institution, 66.

4. Relations with suppliers of care 68
   Independent status, 68. Agreements, 71. Institutional framework, 73. Ratification by government, 74. Contents, 77. Imposing tariffs, 81. Paying for services, 82. List of services, 82. Payment for supervision in the hospital, 84. Private room in hospital, 85. Free choice, 86. Clinical freedom, 88. References, 91.

## PART TWO
## MAJOR DIFFERENCES

5. Structure, organization, and area of application 97
   Structure, 97. Forms of insurance, 97. Independent schemes, 98. Organization, 99. Field of application, 101. Primary field of application, 101. Secondary field of application, 104.

## 6. Financing   106

Contribution by employers and workers in the general scheme for wage-earners, 106. Premiums for self-employed people and farmers, 112. State contribution, 114.

## 7. The services   117

The form of the benefits, 117. The prices of medical services, 121. Conditions for obtaining benefits, 123. Qualifying period and minimum premium, 123. Partial payment by patients, 127.

## 8. Relations with suppliers   133

The operation of the agreement system, 133. One or more levels of agreement, 133. Nature of agreements, 135. Extent of agreements, 137. Duration of the agreement, 139. Remuneration, 140. Payment form, 141. Calculation of payment, 143. Adaptation of remuneration to price rises, 146. References, 147.

## PART THREE
## CONVERGING AND DIVERGING PATHS

## 9. Evolution of social insurance as an institution   153

The future of the insurance principle, 153. Field of application, 157. Organization, 162. Unification or diversification of insurance, 162. Centralization and decentralization, 166. Public or private administration, 168.

## 10. Evolution of financing   171

Growing financial strain, 171. Increase in contribution rates, 173. Form of the premium, 174. Evolution towards national solidarity, 177. The future model of financing, 179.

## 11. Evolution of insurance benefits   183

The type of benefits, 183. Extent of insurance protection, 190. The duration of benefit, 195. Conditions for admission to benefits, 196. Partial payment by the insured, 196. Qualifying period, 202.

## 12. Evolution of relations to suppliers   206

The principles, 206. Free choice of supplier . . ., 207. . . . And rationalization of supply, 212. Clinical freedom and control, 214. Payment of suppliers, 221. Budgeting of the payments, 228. Agreements between insurance and suppliers, 231. The legal status of agreements, 231. The role of public authorities, 242. References, 251.

PART FOUR
# TOWARDS HARMONIZATION

13. Proposals 263
    Nature, field of application, structure, 263. Insurance or health service?, 263. Field of application, 264. Special systems, 266. Financing, 267. Services, 269. Extent of services, 269. Degree of protection, 270. Type of benefits, 272. Limitations imposed on benefits, 274. Conditions required for obtaining services, 276. Relations with care suppliers, 278. Free choice of supplier, 278. Clinical freedom and medical control, 279. Paying the supplier, 281. The system of agreements, 283. Form of the agreement, 283. Approval by government, 284. Measures in the absence of agreements, 285.

14. The way ahead 287
    Action nationally, 287. Belgium, 287. Germany, 289. France, 290. Italy, 292. Luxemburg, 293. Netherlands, 294. Britain, 295. Requirements at the European level, 296. Procedures stipulated in the treaties, 296. Action of the community organizations outside the procedures stipulated in the treaties, 298. Action by national authorities, 300. References, 302.

# PREFACE

JAN E. BLANPAIN MD
*Chairman of the Institute for
European Health Services Research*

When historians in generations to come endeavour to pass judgements on the era in which Europe started to unify, they will undoubtedly, through the telescoping effect of time past, perceive with greater perspective and appreciation the uniqueness of the fundamental and irreversible changes the continent with its centuries of rich and varied history is currently experiencing. It is indeed probable that we, who are in the midst of this unparalleled drawing together of a cluster of nations who have been fighting among each other for centuries, realize insufficiently the importance and ultimate consequences of Europe's moving towards being an actual entity. Towards that goal, the steps taken as yet are doubtless minimal, hampered as they are by setbacks and crises great and small. Yet it can hardly be denied that the European Community is slowly but gradually evolving in a positive way, affecting standards of living, economic affairs, commerce and trade, and challenging both the leadership of all the countries concerned and their peoples to forge and foster conditions, structures and common values through which a European identity and life-style will eventually emerge in a harmonization of all the various cultures and heritages of the Member-countries.

Harmonization as a mechanism to encourage more naturally the balanced and adaptive interaction of social systems which have evolved severally throughout history is a deliberate choice as a way towards the eventual unification of Europe. It is vastly preferable to the drive towards a soulless uniformity, which would almost certainly result, by blending and seeking common denominators, in the loss of the uniqueness and richness in variety which is the Europe of today. It does, however, call for mutual respect and understanding, and intimate knowledge of why individual systems evolved into their existing forms.

The Treaty of Rome which governs the process towards a more unified Europe, although mainly concerned with economics, includes important harmonizing provisions in the social sphere, two of which have direct bearing on health care. Thus, there is a provision for the free circulation and establishment of health workers, in particular of physicians, within the borders of the Community. This provision becomes effective in 1976. It has also a second important stipulation in regard to the harmonization of social security including health insurance, and the first steps have already been taken.

By their nature and in implications both provisions are bound to attract the interest of scholars, for both must be subjected to the systematic rigorous evaluation and analysis which is a precedent to the deep understanding for the changes which must eventually lead towards fulfilment of the Treaty's objectives.

This book is fundamentally an updating and revision of Dr Van Langendonck's original doctoral work *De Harmonisering van de Sociale Verzekering voor Gezondheidszorgen in de EEG*. With its firm base of references and analysis it is a concrete and substantial contribution towards an understanding of trends and the development of future social policy in the health insurance field. It may be of interest to note that his well-documented analysis is part of a systematic effort at Leuven University on the part of several scholars who since the early 1960s have been focusing their attention on the health care scene against a broad European perspective. There are several factors involved in the fostering of this development which culminated in 1972 in the creation of the Institute for European Health Services Research at the University. Commitment to the European cause, a strong tradition in Belgium has undoubtedly been a major factor in this focus. The fact that the EEC headquarters are in Brussels and the presence of the expanding physical token of a dream becoming reality, has encouraged and made feasible the strategy for EEC-centred research on social policy in general, and health services in particular.

This strategy has proved to be sound in view of the inadequacy of the narrow concept of a purely economic market, and the consequent rapidly increasing interest in EEC-wide studies on medical demography, health care costs, hospital systems, etc. This interest has not been confined to the 'Six' founding member countries, but has quickened in the prospective member countries and to a great extent also in North America. In particular in the USA, scholarly interest in European health services has had an expression in governmental initiatives to know more about Europe's experience, in prospect of the likelihood of legislation on national health insurance.

In 1972, all these elements and considerations led several departments at Leuven University covering the fields of hospital administration, social legislation, medical sociology, health economics, health facilities engineering, and community psychiatry, to create a multidepartmental consortium to undertake health services research, focused primarily on the EEC countries as a group. The development of the Institute was boosted by the enlargement in 1973 of the European Community through the accession of Great Britain, Denmark, and Ireland. In particular the prospective membership of Great Britain spurred interest in, and launched studies on health services on both sides of the channel. In the UK, concern over the harmonization of the National Health Service with indirectly financed continental health care systems, was a matter of some moment, while on the continent interest in the unique social experiment of Great Britain was quickened by the prospect of linking up with it.

The Nuffield Provincial Hospitals Trust with its long-standing commitment to health care issues in general and health services research in particular has had a unique role in guiding, sponsoring, and focusing some of the research efforts of the Institute for European Health Services Research. The Trust's Secretary, Gordon McLachlan, sensed the importance of Dr Van Langendonck's work and the Trustees readily agreed to publish an updated English version which will considerably enlarge the audience for Dr Van Langendonck's scholarly treatise. In addition the idea of commissioning Gordon Forsyth to produce an introductory chapter on the UK and to edit and revise the other chapters for the English edition was Mr McLachlan's; and it will contribute I am certain to the chances of eventual harmonization by the common factors it distinguishes and the perspective it brings. It might also be appropriate to note that further moves are planned to add to the literature of health services in Europe. The Nuffield Provincial Hospitals Trust in 1973 commissioned the Institute to carry out a survey of health services research in certain EEC countries. The report of this particular survey covering Belgium, West Germany, France, and the Netherlands is being planned as a forthcoming Trust publication, and together with the existing literature on health services research and development in English, notably the *Portfolios for Health*[1] and *Positions, Movements, and Directions,*[2] will it is hoped provide a substantial base of knowledge.

Another book likely in early 1976 is from a major study in progress evaluating hospital legislation in the nine member countries of the EEC. Dr Van Langendonck's book hopefully is thus the overture of a series of basic volumes likely to stimulate the rapidly developing forum on European health affairs.

*University of Leuven*
*May 1975*

1. McLachlan, G. (ed.) (1971). *Portfolio for Health, Problems and Progress in Medical Care,* Sixth Series; (1973) *Portfolio for Health 2, Problems and Progress in Medical Care,* Eighth Series (Oxford University Press for the Nuffield Provincial Hospitals Trust).

2. McLachlan, G. (ed.) (1974). *Positions, Movements, and Directions in Health Services Research.* Papers and proceedings of a meeting held at Hertford College, Oxford (Oxford University Press for the Nuffield Provincial Hospitals Trust).

# ACKNOWLEDGEMENTS

It is fair to inform the reader that this book is a revised and reduced version of a doctoral thesis promoted by Professor Roger Dillemans of the Law School at the Catholic University of Leuven. It was written in close co-operation with the members of the Institute of Social Security, which is part of the Institute of European Health Services Research at this university.

Translating the text into English was a task which far exceeded my capabilities. I therefore owe many thanks to Mrs Ann Pattyn and Miss Sonia McKay who helped me greatly in producing a version English readers could understand. This was to enable Dr Gordon Forsyth to rewrite the thesis into acceptable English. He also rearranged part of the text and agreed to write an introductory chapter on the position of the British health service in the EEC, accounting for the fact that since my original manuscript was completed Britain entered the Community. I should say that this book is more Mr Forsyth's than mine, except for the many errors and misjudgements.

I am also very much indebted to the Nuffield Provincial Hospitals Trust, and to its Secretary, Mr Gordon McLachlan, for financing the publication.

Finally I wish to repeat what I said in the first edition concerning the important role my wife played in the realization of this book. I am very grateful for her daily uninterrupted support.

*Leuven*
*31 December 1974*

INTRODUCTION

# A British descant on the theme

GORDON FORSYTH

Dr Van Langendonck's admirable study of the social health insurance situation in the European Economic Community was written before the accession of Britain, Denmark, and the Republic of Ireland in 1973. His interesting proposal for the future harmonization of social policy in the provision of health services could therefore proceed from the common denominator of the founding Six in this field: the insurance principle, with defined services available on certain conditions in return for the payment of specified premiums. In Britain the insurance principle in publicly financed health services was abandoned in 1948 when the National Health Service was established on the principle of finance through general taxation and entitlement to medical services depending on residence, the need for treatment, and no other qualifying condition.

Clearly there is a major divergence in principle between Britain and the Six in the way health services are financed and organized. In practice the differences are less sharp but they are still pronounced and the proposals for harmonization merit attention in the light of British entry. We may not of course stay within the Community. If we do the NHS is bound to be affected sooner or later. For practical purposes the Community at present is little more than a Common Agricultural Policy. As regards entitlement to health services a measure of harmonization is already in operation and there is the immediate prospect of mutual recognition of medical degrees and qualifications, in accordance with the requirement for the free mobility of labour. The Treaty of Accession has transferred legislative authority in an extensive range of economic and social matters from 'the Queen in Parliament' to the institutions of the Community (particularly the Council of Ministers and the Commission) and as the Community progresses towards full economic and monetary union pressure may develop for the harmonization of taxation and tax systems. With so much uncertain there would be little profit in speculating here about what will happen and how the NHS might be affected. Decisions have to be taken in a political and social context; there are conflicts of interest as well as of attitude; rational choice is therefore not always possible. This applies to the NHS as much as any of the other European systems. Within the Community influence will not be in one direction only. It may be that the health services of the future Europe will follow the British model rather than the existing European systems.

It is relevant therefore in this introduction to attempt to consider where the balance of advantage lies between the NHS and the future developments in the founding Six as outlined by Dr Van Langendonck, not in any spirit of narrow chauvinism but mindful of the severe strains the NHS is experiencing and recognizing too that the various systems are no more than differential responses to the common problems of advanced industrial societies.

**Entitlement to benefit**

On Britain's accession to the EEC in January 1973 British citizens became subject to the Community's regulations on social security. An immediate advantage was that retirement pensioners, widows receiving a National Insurance pension, employed persons and their dependants became entitled, when visiting any of the Common Market countries for holiday or business purposes, to receive medical treatment on the same terms and conditions as nationals of the country they were visiting. The intention of the regulation was to facilitate the free mobility of temporary labour rather than holiday tourism. For long-term migrant labour the applicable legislation is that of the country in which they are employed. Temporary visitors (less than twelve months) are the responsibility of their own government. The member-states might be expected to work on a 'knock for knock' basis to avoid administrative cost but in fact there are annual settlements, with member-states paying for entitled persons on the basis of average per capita cost in the country where treatment is given.

It might appear churlish to cavil at this practical expression of European unity; but entitlement to medical benefits while visiting one of our Common Market partners is not universal. The self-employed and the non-employed and their dependants are excluded and if taken ill must rely on their own financial means or take out private insurance to cover the period of their stay. The point may seem trivial but it is none the less worth recording that in terms of eligibility for socially financed health services the British people have been divided in a way they have not been divided for over a quarter of a century.

As a result of this provision some British tourists will by now know at first hand how financially and administratively complicated illness can be across the Channel. If he knows about the arrangement, perhaps from his travel agent or other source, the traveller must before leaving the UK obtain a Certificate of Entitlement (form E111) available after completing the relevant application form at a local office of the DHSS or Employment Exchange. If illness occurs during the visit the procedure to follow varies somewhat between country and country. Generally it is advisable first to contact a local office of the responsible health insurance authority before consulting a doctor, although in Belgium, France, and Luxemburg failure to go through proper channels is less likely to cause the patient problems than in Germany, Italy, and the Netherlands.

In France and Luxemburg there are single national insurance authorities (France has two other systems and Luxemburg eight others for various occupational classes but the British tourist has in each case to deal with a national control authority) while in Belgium there are six, five of them being Friendly Societies (including Liberal, Socialist, and Non-Party). The patient can, however, go to any doctor. In Luxemburg the doctor's charges will be refunded at the local insurance office on presentation of receipts and E111 but the patient will have to pay a small part of the cost of drugs. Payments by the patient will be greater in

France and Belgium and there is uncertainty about the amount. The patient will pay at least 30 per cent of the fees in France and 25 per cent in Belgium but the refund rates are based on fee schedules which the doctor may exceed, the excess being paid entirely by the patient. In Italy and the Netherlands there are no charges either for doctors' services or drugs while in Germany there are small charges for drugs but not for medical services. This only applies, however, if the doctor consulted operates within the sickness insurance scheme. It is therefore important to contact a local sickness insurance office particularly in Italy.

Hospital treatment (third class) is free in all the Common Market countries except France and Belgium provided authorization is obtained from the appropriate sickness insurance authority. Major surgery is free in France, otherwise the patient pays 20 per cent of the costs. Part of the cost must be paid in Belgium and insurance authorities will advise where treatment can be obtained on the most favourable terms. In Italy it is essential to choose a hospital which has concluded an agreement with INAM: Istituto Nazionale per L'Assicurazione Contro le Malattie. In all countries where refundable charges are made reimbursement must be obtained before returning to the UK.

Provided he has E111, knows the correct procedure, and follows it the British tourist if taken ill on the continent will find little at which to grumble. Services are mostly free or at least heavily subsidized and if he finds the administrative process of securing benefits complicated and cumbersome in comparison with the stark simplicity of the NHS he will no doubt reflect that after all he is a foreigner and must expect to fill in some forms. Further reflection will remind him that he is receiving treatment on the same terms and conditions as nationals of the country he is visiting. The sick tourist finds life much simpler in Denmark and the Irish Republic. In Denmark a British passport is normally enough for free or fully reimbursed medical treatment and prescribed drugs at a reduced rate and in Ireland the tourist simply needs to sign a simple declaration to a GP that he is an employed person and British subject normally resident in the United Kingdom. In both these countries it is necessary to go to a GP who participates in the health service scheme, just as it is in Britain. Names of available practitioners are obtainable from local councils in Denmark and eight area health boards in the Irish Republic.

In some respects the British tourist is better off than nationals of the country he visits. In the Netherlands for example, although all residents are covered by a general scheme for particularly heavy costs, employees earning above a wage-ceiling are excluded from membership of other subsidized health insurance systems. The visitor's entitlement is established by E111 but the French or Belgian national must satisfy further qualifying conditions. These are not too onerous in France: he must have worked 200 hours during the three months preceding the date of treatment or 120 hours during the preceding month; but in Belgium there are three conditions: six months' membership of the scheme, including 120 days of actual work, proof of payment of minimum contributions, and proof that the illness is covered by the insurance. It is clear from Dr Van Langendonck's study that in terms of coverage the difference between countries is marginal; but the issue is not whether 90 or 100 per cent of the population is entitled to benefit but the way in which those entitled obtain their rights. Claims for full or partial reimbursement, arguments with doctors about the cost of every item of service, disputes with sick funds about eligibility: all these are reflected in high administrative costs which the NHS has avoided by making the service universally available. Since 1948 foreign nationals visiting Britain have been entitled to use the NHS on the same terms and conditions as the resident British (the exception being those coming here deliberately to seek hospital in-patient care for an existing condition). This open-ended commitment is justified by the fact that the administrative expense of recovering costs would be high in relation to the amount recovered and that the provision has been used as a springboard to negotiate reciprocal arrangements with other countries (notably the Scandinavian countries, Yugoslavia, and Romania). International co-operation in this field precedes the EEC by many years.

Pragmatism determined the characteristics of the NHS far more than political ideology and it was the waste and inefficiency of compulsory insurance which led to the abandonment of the insurance principle.

## Finance and organization
### EVOLUTION OF THE NHS

Thirty years elapsed before Britain emulated the German example of 1883 and brought into operation in 1913 a limited provision of health care based on compulsory insurance. After another thirty-five years pluralism was replaced by a near State monopoly and extensive compulsory insurance was replaced by finance through general taxation. Significantly the reorganization which took place in 1974, twenty-six years after the establishment of the NHS, affected the administrative structure, not the financial basis. The process of change has been adaptive and pragmatic throughout, and the systems have had ample time to demonstrate their weaknesses and strengths. A broad perspective shows that the course of evolution has been towards greater central control over resource allocation to health care, initially over the global amount allocated, later over the way resources are used. Hospital costs have been the main concern and increasingly it became apparent that to control expenditure on health care (either to increase or restrain) it is necessary to plan and control hospital services, and that to control hospital services it is necessary to plan and control other services which affect the use of hospitals.

The tendency towards greater public control over hospital costs has also been a feature of the European systems, though it is doubtful whether this has yet extended to the determinant factors external to the hospital. Even where hospitals are not owned by public authorities public control is exercised through capital grants or the power to withhold approval for capital development. Hospital current expenditure is an acute problem in all industrial countries and for much the same reasons: increased technology is increasingly making hospitals labour-intensive and vulnerable to inflation at an accelerating rate. In the European systems, charges at voluntary hospitals are based on daily rates imposed by governments after negotiation and deficits are the cause of frequent crises. Subsidies by public authorities are used to finance the funds' deficits, although France and Germany try to uphold the principle that the funds should be self-supporting.

In Britain compulsory and voluntary insurance scarcely affected hospital resources at all and never approached providing the comprehensive range of services offered by the insurance systems of the founding Six at the present time. At the end of the Second World War, when the NHS was being planned, half the British population (twenty-four million people) were compulsorily insured under the National (Health) Insurance Act 1911. Originally the Act applied to manual workers earning less than £160 per annum but extensions brought in other groups, such as agricultural and horticultural workers, domestic staff in institutions and clubs, and white-collar workers; in 1942 the wage-ceiling was raised to £450. Despite its extensions in coverage, however, the system still reflected the limited nature of its aims and its administrative system reflected the conflict of interests which surrounded its inception. At the end of the nineteenth century Charles Booth and Seebohm Rowntree had demonstrated the extent and causes of primary poverty, the impact of interruption of income through the 'social contingencies' of old age, unemployment, death, or sickness of the breadwinner. Their findings suggested specific social policies to a Liberal government, in the first decade of this century, anxious to find new sources of electoral support and aware of a recently enfranchised working-class. Hence non-contributory Old Age Pensions, Labour Exchanges, and National Health Insurance. Within the health insurance provision however the emphasis was not on combating illness itself but preventing the poverty illness caused. The main concern was to provide cash benefits during absence from work through sickness. A government actuary's report in 1910 noted that there was no need to include wives as it was only the breadwinner's illness which caused income loss and in 1945 the retired and dependent wives and children of insured workers were still excluded from the medical benefits offered by the scheme.

The insurance principle was the necessary basis of the 1911 legislation to accommodate the élite of the artisan class who believed in individual responsibility and who had for generations developed and sustained a system of voluntary insurance and mutual aid to provide for the social contingencies. A wide range of cash benefits and medical services were provided by a diverse array of friendly societies, many of which were trades unions, offering their members sick pay, death grants to cover funeral expenses, treatment by GPs, and in some cases making sizeable grants to voluntary hospitals in return for admitting their members without charge. The friendly societies were bound to be affected by government intervention in health insurance and it was the interplay between government, friendly societies, and their natural enemies, the doctors and commercial insurance, which created the administrative system which in turn led the insurance principle itself into such disrepute that no place for it could be found in the National Health Service.

Unlike the health insurance systems of the founding six European countries today the compulsory insurance scheme of 1911 was based not on a percentage of wages but on a flat-rate basis between employee, employer, and government. The Act created two separate administrative agencies, local insurance committees and approved societies. Local insurance committees, which in 1948 became local executive councils and in 1974 family practitioner committees with essentially unchanged functions whatever the name, represented a triumph for the doctors over the friendly societies. The friendly societies needed GPs to certify that claims for sickness payments were genuine and they employed them both for this purpose and to provide treatment and drugs. The societies' interest was to reduce costs and contributions (many were near insolvency) and in 1905 the British Medical Association had reported on the wage-depressing and other effects of contract practice. To the BMA the 1911 scheme meant nationally negotiated fees and local insurance committees, with associated local medical committees to investigate breaches of discipline, meant freedom from control by the friendly societies. Separation of the administration of medical benefits from that of cash benefits was one of the concessions won by the BMA during the negotiations which accompanied the preparation of the 1911 legislation.

Approved societies, or rather the conditions under which a

society could be approved under the 1911 Act for the provision of cash benefits, represented a triumph for the commercial insurance interests. Commercial insurance was not interested or involved in the provision of cash or direct medical benefits during sickness absence from work; but funeral policies were the main source of the commercial insurance firms' income. Their interest in State intervention therefore was to ensure that death grants and widows' benefits would not be provided and that they would be able to provide sick pay on the same terms as the friendly societies, to avoid competition over funeral policies which the non-profit societies offered at much more favourable rates. The powerful commercial insurance companies therefore saw to it that they could be approved under the Act. Although not permitted directly to profit approved societies could recover administrative costs and the commercial insurance companies could safely offer salaries to the many additional door-to-door canvassers they recruited who could promote commercial policies while paying out sick pay. Not infrequently sick pay was used to maintain premiums on commercial policies and there was much exploitation of the fear of a pauper's funeral. Immediately before the Second World War the British system of compulsory insurance offered the poorest benefits and had the highest administrative costs of any compulsory system in Europe.

The system never made available the additional health care benefits provided for under the Act. In certain circumstances an insured worker could receive care in hospital and convalescent home, dental and ophthalmic treatment, and other services, depending on how much the approved society had in surplus after paying sickness absence cash benefits. As the scheme operated on a flat-rate contributory basis each society had the same per capita income; but many societies, particularly the trades unions, concentrated on particular occupations and industries and expenditure on cash benefits varied with the morbidity experience of the membership. Consequently their ability to finance the additional benefits varied too and those most in need of services were least likely to get them. In 1939 for example, when the scheme covered 17 million workers, only 1·6 million could have had the cost of a stay in hospital paid under compulsory insurance.

Hospitals derived little therefore from compulsory insurance and increasingly ran into deficit. The voluntary hospitals continued to depend on donations and patients' fees but they maintained their charitable tradition and patients without means were not turned away or discharged. In the open wards of the voluntary hospitals doctors' services were also given free of charge. In the absence of necessary pressures voluntary prepayment insurance did not develop extensively as it did in the United States. Municipal authorities also provided hospital care for their residents. Some of the more progressive authorities provided general acute hospitals under permissive legislation of 1929 but usually municipal hospitals were for specific groups or conditions: tuberculosis, infectious diseases, maternity, or the aged, indigent poor. Municipal authorities were responsible only for their own residents and locational barriers restricted access on the part of patients, while rivalries and jealousies between authorities themselves, and between local government and voluntary hospitals, brought poor co-ordination, duplication, and waste.

The problem of the hospitals was recognized in 1920 in the Dawson Report (1). Apart from wishing to avoid duplication of hospital services by creating regional planning authorities the Dawson Committee wanted to integrate curative and preventive medicine through health centres. Moreover if the standards of the voluntary hospitals were to be raised they must be associated with teaching hospitals. Efforts were made voluntarily to co-ordinate hospital planning on a regional basis but it took the prospect of the Second World War to bring home the obvious fact that the hospitals were simply not equipped to cope with the expected air-raid casualties. Under the Emergency Medical Service the State controlled the hospital system. A regional pathological laboratory service was created, based on the twelve provincial hospital groups associated with medical schools which, outside London, were virtually the only voluntary hospitals with pathological laboratories. The National Health Service Act of 1946 transferred ownership of all hospitals to the State. Public financing was necessary to give effect to the general reform of social security outlined in the Beveridge Report (2) which insisted that an adequate health service free at the time of use was a necessary prerequisite to a social security system. An extension of the 1911 Act to cover the whole nation would not have sufficed because the system failed to separate the financing of sick pay from that of direct health care and the insurance principle was by now in general disrepute where health services were concerned. Funds might have been channelled through local government, which owned most of the hospitals anyway, but the medical profession would not join the hospital service if it were owned by local government, and the structure of local government was not geared to the regional basis which hospital planning required. Thus in 1946 regional hospital boards and group management committees emerged to provide hospitals and services as agents of the responsible central government Minister. These non-elective *ad hoc* authorities were the only new administrative agencies created by the NHS. Local insurance committees became local executive councils and local government health and welfare authorities retained responsibilities for public health and domiciliary support services. In 1974 both health and local government service administrative structures were reorganized partly to promote greater efficiency in the use of resources. Regional and area health authorities replaced the hospital boards and management committees and some services and staff were transferred between local government and the former hospital authorities. Health and local government authorities were made geographically coterminous at the area level and were placed under a statutory obligation to collaborate with each other in comprehensive health services planning.

SOURCES OF FINANCE AND RESOURCE ALLOCATION

In comparison with other Common Market countries Britain is a modest spender on health service, although the difference is generally less than 1·5 per cent of the gross national product. Indeed Abel-Smith (3) in a study for the WHO showed that in 1961 Britain spent a smaller proportion of the GNP on health services than any country at a comparable stage of development outside eastern Europe and Simanis (4) shows that in 1968 the relative position had not changed. As Abel-Smith was careful to point out, different levels of expenditure between countries reflect differential wage levels between the health professions and differing combinations of resources. In maternity, for example, costs are bound to differ according to whether midwives, GPs or specialist obstetricians, hospitals or the patients' homes are involved. The highest-spending countries do not always achieve the best results in terms of staff and facilities provided and the question of the benefits derived from expenditure is entirely open. Infant mortality is sometimes higher in countries which allocate relatively high proportions of national resources to health care than in countries which spend less; but infant mortality reflects living standards in general, and is affected by many factors in addition to health services.

Accelerating health care costs, particularly hospital costs, are as much a cause for concern to those who have to find the resources in Britain as in other countries. At least the British system of central control means that health service resources are determined in relation to the resources available for other essential public services as well as in relation to the general state of the economy. In the EEC countries there has been a marked movement towards greater direct or indirect public control over hospital and other health service costs. Britain has gone further than the rest have so far, unquestionably because the threat of war enforced a political will which was lacking before, and the fact that Britain is marginally a lower spender may be seen as a virtue of strict centralized control over finance, at least in the eyes of public authorities if not in the eyes of those who work within health services.

Sources of finance for the NHS are dominated by general taxation: some 80 per cent of the resources come in the form of Exchequer grants; in the systems of the founding Six the role of general revenues varies but is generally less pronounced. In Belgium government subsidies account for 40 per cent of the insurance scheme costs and 15-20 per cent in Italy and the Netherlands. General revenues play only a minor role in the other three. In general the European systems rely on insurance premiums on an earnings-related basis and in effect they represent earmarked taxes on income. The NHS derives very little from compulsory insurance. In 1973 the National Insurance Fund contributed only £237 million to the NHS, about 8 per cent of the £2,995 million spent on the service in that year. Originally it was thought that this source would provide 20 per cent of the costs but it has never been more than 15 per cent and has declined steadily over the years. The flat-rate contributions by the employee represent about 0·4 per cent of the average wage and payment by the employer about 0·2 per cent of the gross wages and salaries bill. In the European systems the employer pays more than the employee for health insurance. Employees, as Dr Van Langendonck's estimates suggest, pay from 2 to 5 per cent of their gross earnings (in Italy little more than 0·1 per cent) but the employer in Italy pays over 12 per cent, in France 9 per cent, and between 1 and 5 per cent in the other four countries. Should the British employer also pay more for health services? Harmonization of taxation and tax systems has not yet been an issue within the Community since the period 1956–62 but in the past it has been suggested by European industrialists that the low demands made on British industry by social security in general represent a form of export subsidy. It is true that in the founding Six general social security contributions, and the employer's share in them constitute a much more important component of taxation than in Britain. In 1971 for example social security contributions accounted for only 14 per cent of total taxes in Britain and the employers' contribution only 7 per cent. The comparable figures for the Six were: Belgium 30 per cent (employers 20 per cent), France 41 per cent (30 per cent), Germany 32 per cent (18 per cent), Luxemburg 29 per cent (16 per cent), the Netherlands 37 per cent (18 per cent), and Italy 39 per cent (almost all by the employer). These figures, however, relate to social security in general; Dr Van Langendonck's estimates of the burden of payments to health services carried by employers suggest that the founding Six are far from comparable and that it is the French and Italian employer who is most affected. Moreover, the British employer can argue that he makes a bigger contribution to general taxation than his European counterparts: in 1971 taxes on corporations in Britain were, as a percentage of total taxation, 30 per cent higher than in France, 60 per cent higher than in Italy, and twice as high as in Germany. Again as percentages of total taxation, taxes on incomes and expenditure were higher in Britain than the EEC countries.

The small share in NHS financing accounted for by social security contributions is something of a historical anachronism since payment of the contribution confers no right to benefits. In practice the sum available to the NHS from this source is taken as given, in other words earmarked taxation. In considering how much to make available to the NHS the Treasury by convention ignores this source, estimates the yield from direct charges to patients at the time of use and undertakes to find the rest. Charges to patients therefore do not add to the resources available to the NHS, they ease the burden on the Exchequer since the Treasury will normally reduce the contribution from general revenues in the light of increased trading income to the NHS. An exception to this practice occurred in 1970 when by special agreement a third of the increased income from increased charges was made available to the NHS and formed the basis of increased expenditure on facilities for geriatric and mental illness patients. Charges are not particularly significant as a source of revenue, varying from 2 to 5 per cent of total NHS expenditure. The British patient is in much the same position as the insured German, Dutchman, Italian, or Dane. Small fixed charges for drugs, half the cost of dental treatment up to a fixed maximum, but no charges for hospital and general medical services. Many people are exempt from charges: the retired, children, and expectant mothers, those receiving means-tested cash assistance, and those suffering from one of a variety of chronic diseases. The motive for introducing or increasing charges has varied. Charges for dental treatment, when first introduced in 1951, undoubtedly were intended to act as a deterrent to adults acquiring or renewing dentures. With a shortage of dentists adults were in effect competing with children and expectant mothers seeking conservative dental treatment. With charges and exemptions there has been a marked shift towards conservative treatment for children. Prescription charges have been introduced, abolished, and reintroduced by Labour

## Introduction

governments (the present Labour government is committed to their abolition again) and increased by Conservative governments. The motive seems to have been to maintain a small source of income although on one occasion it was suggested that the measure was necessary to signify the government's determination to restrain public expenditure in the midst of an external payments crisis. It is perhaps significant that dental and prescription charges involve little or no administrative cost: dentists are paid by item of service and chemists on the basis of the drugs prescribed, and the onus of collecting charges can therefore be put on the provider, the public authorities merely deducting the appropriate sums from their payments to him. There is no doubt that under Treasury pressure both Labour and Conservative governments have contemplated new charges. The limiting factors of high administrative costs in relation to the amount collected, given the necessarily exempt groups, have as much as objections in principle prevented the application of charges to consultations and home visits by family doctors or to hospital services for meals or other 'hotel' costs. Charges are less costly to collect where reimbursement of the patient operates, or where doctors are paid by item of service. Within the EEC reimbursement applies mainly to Belgium and France, and in Luxemburg to the funds catering for salaried employees. Direct payment by funds on behalf of the insured is more common in the other countries as is payment of the doctor by salary or capitation fee. Had British doctors been paid by item of service rather than salary or capitation fee then the British patient might also have had to pay small charges for doctors' services.

Another form of direct charge to patients is for use of private pay beds in NHS hospitals. In 1972 this produced a mere £17 million. Private pay beds have become an emotive issue to an extent far beyond that justified by their numerical importance. Occupants of private pay beds pay the full average weekly cost according to the type of hospital in which they stay (London or provincial, teaching or non-teaching) and make their own arrangement for paying the specialist who treats them. Earnings from private practice in effect have eased two awkward problems for the

NHS. They have helped to sustain an income differential between GPs and specialists which the NHS itself has found increasingly difficult and embarrassing to maintain; and secondly they have allowed the NHS to employ specialist surgeons without at the same time having to pay a full market rate for non-surgical specialists. Private practice therefore, both within and outside the NHS, has to be seen as part of the relationship between the NHS and the providers of care and treatment. In many ways private practice in Britain can be regarded, though on a smaller and far less socially divisive scale, as the equivalent of the German and Dutch doctors' attempt to protect their income by insisting on the exclusion of those above certain income levels from the protection of compulsory insurance, and the French and Belgian doctors' resistance to third-party payment and insistence on the freedom to charge more than the fees listed in schedules.

### Relations with providers

A former Minister of Health (5) commented: 'The universal Exchequer financing of the service endows everyone providing as well as using it with a vested interest in denigrating it.' In fact expressions of dissatisfaction with the NHS have tended to come from the providers rather than the users. The NHS is the largest single employer of labour in the country and those working for or under contract with it are subject to wide variation in quality and in income distribution. At one end of the scale half the hospital specialists earn at least four times the national average earnings for adult male manual workers in manufacturing industry (including overtime and bonus payments). GPs on average earn three times this reference wage, and hospital doctors in training receive on joining the service from medical school about 10 per cent more and in the top training grade about two and a half times the reference wage. At the other end most nurses receive less than the national average wage and many ancillary workers (porters, cleaners, kitchen staff, and so on) are among the poorest paid workers in the country. At regular intervals doctors have been in dispute with the government over their pay (a situation not unknown in the other EEC countries) and recently industrial action has been taken by some nurses, technicians, and ancillary staff. The difficulty of maintaining income in the face of inflation has been particularly acute since 1970 given the fact of an accelerating rate of price inflation and incomes policies which have affected the labour-intensive public services (education as well as health) far more severely than the private sector or the nationalized industries.

To be fair to the British Medical Association and other spokesmen for the profession they have not confined their complaints about inadequate resources to their own rewards and in 1974, when £110 million was cut from NHS allocation as part of a general cut-back in public expenditure, the BMA pressed for an extra £900 million to be injected to raise the level of facilities and services. The difficulty is that public authorities already spend nearly half the GNP in Britain, a shift to a markedly higher tax plateau does not seem politically feasible, economic growth alternates between the sluggish and the stagnant, any growth there is will have to be set against massive external deficit, and all the public services are inadequate: the police are seriously under strength for example, social workers carry an average caseload of over sixty cases at any one time, there are enough residential homes for only 2 per cent of the elderly population, and 40 per cent of the retired population live in houses lacking an indoor flush lavatory. While wages and salaries in health and other public services are freely and collectively negotiated at the national level the amount made available for current expenditure on goods and services and for capital development is determined by the central government. Doctors and health authorities cannot therefore themselves add to the resources available.

In the absence of objective criteria to determine priorities decisions on resource allocation tend to be political, and taken by those accountable to Parliament for the services they administer. Although Parliament votes money annually, in practice the Government allocates funds on a rolling five-year basis, annually surveying public expenditure for the next five years. The basis of these surveys is an annual report from the Public Expenditure Survey Committee, a committee of Treasury officials and finance officers from the main spending departments (Defence, Environment, Health, etc.). The report shows the financial implications of maintaining existing programmes and allowances for new ones and in the light of the latest estimate of the future economic outlook in general the cabinet allocates funds between the various public activities. The system is in effect a control mechanism working back through departments and an estimating and information system working upwards. The amount available for the NHS is at once related to the economic state of the country and to the demands of other competing but necessary public services. By deliberate choice expenditure on health services is allowed to rise at a faster rate than that for public expenditure in general: the plan for 1971–2 to 1976–7 envisaged an average annual growth rate in public expenditure of 2·5 per cent in real terms but a rate of 4·8 per cent for Health and Personal Social Services (6). The next annual survey (7) in a worsening economic climate, envisaged public expenditure for the period 1972–3 to 1977–8 rising at an average annual rate of 2·0 per cent and Health and Personal Social Services at 4·6 per cent. Hospitals' current expenditure on goods and services was to be much the same in both surveys, rising at about 3·5 per cent per annum, despite a reduction of £110 million imposed in December 1973. Hospital and health authorities under this system work within budgets imposed from above, which are never exceeded, based on estimates and requests from below which are never met in full. Wage and salary increases are treated separately and are usually given through supplementary estimates approved by Parliament. Hospital and health authorities are not themselves responsible for finding the money they spend and this in itself is liable to focus attention on shortcomings of the service and inadequacy of resources. Moreover public accountability has meant that any unspent funds could not be carried over from one year to the next. Under the reorganized structure of 1974 authorities will be able to carry funds over, and use capital monies for current purposes and vice-versa, but it is clear that these flexible arrangements will operate within very narrow limits. Apart from tight financial control the relationships between the central department and hospital and other health

## Introduction

authorities have been remarkably non-directive. For example no advice on how to deal with patients' complaints was issued until 1966: nearly two decades after the NHS began and only in 1968 was a centrally based Hospital Advisory Service established to visit hospitals and advise on standards of care, and the system is advisory without executive powers. While in many instances a more positively directive approach was desirable and possible it should be noted that at the regional and area level administrators are not civil servants of the Crown, as those in the central department are, but are employees of the regional and area health authorities. Their training, work-experience, and career patterns are therefore essentially different from those of the central civil servants and apart from medically qualified administrators few in the centre have working experience at the local operational levels. The health authorities themselves act as agents of the responsible Minister but they comprise voluntary members of the public nominated for their personal qualities. Some voluntary members are doctors and others are also members of local government authorities, elective authorities responsible for a wide range of public services including Personal Social Services. Relationships between the central department and local government authorities are conditioned by the fact that they are authorities in their own right, subject to Parliament rather than the government, and to their own electors. They raise much of their own resources from local taxation and although 60 per cent of their expenditure comes from the central government 90 per cent of the government aid is in block grant form, not tied to specific services, to respect the local authorities' autonomy and avoid detailed accounting to the central authority. Apart from hospitals relations with providers of drugs and with the medical profession are most relevant to the harmonization issue. Apart from small prescription charges successive governments have used two approaches to limit drug costs: sanctions against GPs for overprescribing and direct negotiations with the pharmaceutical industry over prices. If a family doctor in his prescribing cost persistently exceeds the average of his colleagues in the area by more than 25 per cent he is at risk to a complaint being made to a committee representing all doctors in his area. Where appropriate his peers can recommend (and there is an appeal procedure to the national level) that he be warned or that remuneration be withheld from him. Very few doctors are in fact disciplined but it is assumed that the system keeps most doctors aware of the need to exercise economy in prescribing. Chemists are in contract with local NHS authorities to dispense drugs prescribed by family doctors. They are paid the net ingredient cost plus 25 per cent mark-up with small allowances for containers and for their services. They have no discretion over prices which are negotiated at the national level between manufacturers and the central department. Drug costs have been remarkably stable during the lifetime of the NHS. In 1951 they accounted for 8·8 per cent of total expenditure and in 1972 8·6 per cent. Although not entirely satisfactory the price negotiating system must have contributed to this stability. The system has to operate in a situation where the British pharmaceutical industry has only 30 per cent of the market and wishes to maintain a high investment rate and profit margins to sustain the search for new products, and spends more on direct advertising to the profession than it spends on research. Given the existing structure of the industry direct promotion, though much criticized and certainly expensive, is probably necessary if manufacturers are to recover development costs quickly in a competitive market. In the past manufacturers of new drugs of proven therapeutic value have been allowed three years in which to recover development costs before negotiating a price but increasingly the tendency has been for price negotiation to occur earlier and on the basis of increasingly detailed information. The 1949 Patents Act gives certain protection to the interests of the Crown and on one occasion has been used to reduce the price of an antibiotic subject to international patent of an American manufacturer who had refused to co-operate in the price reduction scheme. Recently too the Monopolies Commission has intervened and on its advice the government ordered a reduction in the price of two drugs sold by a Swiss-based firm to its British subsidiary. Under a centrally based Medicines Commission surveillance is kept over the cost and safety of drugs. It has developed since the thalidomide tragedy a decade ago but administratively is still a spare apparatus (compared, for example, with the US Food and Drugs Administration) and like all aspects of the NHS draws on the voluntary services of doctors, pharmacologists, and so on.

As for relationship between the NHS and the medical profession the ex-Minister who commented on the denigrating effect of universal Exchequer financing observed: 'the nationalized service makes money the sole terminology of intercourse between profession and government' (8). No cynicism was intended and indeed it is inevitable that as the State has made itself responsible for the provision of a service adequate to the needs of every individual the profession should direct to that quarter its dissatisfaction with both its own rewards and the adequacy of the available services. Relations with the profession however are more complex than this. Although the central department has maintained tight control over the global NHS spending it has been less successful in influencing the way resources have been used. Within hospitals (as in all countries the main consumers of resources) general acute hospitals have fared much better in resource allocation than those catering for the chronic sick and mentally ill and handicapped. Some of the costly facilities and procedures provided in hospitals have been questioned as to their true effectiveness (9); for example treatment in coronary care units may be no more effective than domiciliary management (10). In the NHS public accountability extends far beyond mere finance and successive ministers have had to account for individual cases of inadequate or bad treatment which ultimately arise through poor staffing and facilities in the long-stay institutions. Over the years successive ministers have tried to redress the imbalance between the 'cure' sector and the 'care' sector and have found it difficult. The fault does not lie entirely with the medical profession (which always reflects wider community attitudes anyway) but within the profession geriatrics and psychiatry enjoy a lower prestige than the general acute specialties and to some extent at least the profession has projected its own values and priorities on to the NHS because it is necessarily and closely involved in the administration of the service at all levels.

At regional and area level there are now statutory medical committees. They have no executive powers but must be consulted by health authorities (who are not of course obliged to accept their advice or confine their consultative process to the statutory bodies). At the district level hospital medical advisory committees developed on a voluntary basis soon after the inception of the NHS and rendered some valuable service to group management committees. Unlike many European hospitals there is no medical directorate in British hospitals. Senior specialists are of equal status and medical administration is a matter for collective responsibility. New machinery was recommended in 1967 to improve the organization of medical work in hospitals and provide for collective review of clinical policy (11). The response was varied but substantial and while not wholly successful (12) at least encouraging. Rather than meeting in one large single body specialists are organized in divisions of related specialties, with a small elective executive committee. The involvement of GPs in the divisional machinery has been inadequate and under the 1974 reorganization a new device has been adopted. District management teams, whose decisions are to be based on consensus, will include administrative, finance, nursing officer, and medical administrative staff and also one specialist and one GP, drawn from the divisional system in hospital and from the local medical committee in general practice, through a district medical committee which gives equal representation to both branches of medicine. At the district level too specialists and family doctors are to join nurses and social workers in health care planning teams covering five patient need areas: geriatrics, mental illness, mental handicap, maternity and child care, and general acute. It is hoped ultimately that this system will relate budget estimates to the solving of problems by those who perceive them at the local level.

It is apparent from this that the relationships between the NHS and the providers of services go far beyond a dialogue about earnings. Obviously there are common features in all systems so far as the profession's role in hospitals is concerned but compared with the other EEC countries the profession's role in the NHS is infinitely more organized.

Doctors' remuneration has been the cause of much dispute in Britain, as it has in other European countries. About 68 per cent of British doctors belong to the BMA but there is some dual membership with other representative associations whose policies often conflict with those of the BMA. The BMA itself tries to represent the profession as a whole and this task is often made difficult by innate and perhaps inevitable conflicts within the profession. The most difficult to reconcile are those between GPs and specialists, between the older established specialists who have reached the top grade in the hospital service and younger specialists in training who are trying to climb the hierarchy created by the NHS, and between senior specialists associated with prestigious teaching centres and those working in provincial non-teaching hospitals. The absence of a common interest has sometimes led to the formation outside the BMA of small groups trying to represent sectional interests and has always made it difficult for the Association to apply effective sanctions against the government. Crises over pay have been more apparent than real and threats to withdraw from the NHS have lacked conviction given the absence of something to withdraw into. An attempt to organize a viable alternative for general practice in 1965 foundered through lack of support from both doctors and the general public. A new system of paying family doctors made general practice more attractive financially and this itself led to unrest among specialists. The idea has been floated of specialists forming an agency to hire specialists to hospital authorities but apart from administrative problems, doubts about the present generous superannuation scheme, and uncertainty about how many specialists would cooperate, there would of necessity still have to be a dialogue at the national level between the government and the profession about money. There are no blank cheques on public funds, here or in the founding Six. The German system is a case in point, with an association of sick funds' doctors paying its members with money received from the funds. German doctors complain that their income is too low and depend on fees from those excluded from social insurance by the earnings ceiling.

The BMA provides the officially recognized machinery for

negotiating the terms and conditions of service for NHS doctors. There are separate committees for hospital medical staff and general medical practitioners. Contracts are nationally standard but entered into individually, between regional authorities and senior specialists, area authorities and junior hospital staff, and family practitioner committees and GPs. Apart from those of consultant rank hospital doctors are employed on a whole-time salaried basis. Consultant specialists can either work whole-time or part-time. The week is divided into eleven notional sessions and most work maximum part-time or nine-elevenths. They are paid a proportion of an age-related incremental salary scale appropriate to the proportion of the week worked. Only part-time consultants may engage in private practice. Maximum part-timers can be required to work a tenth session unpaid. This dates from 1969, a much-resented concession by the specialists' leaders in return for the NHS not insisting on preference being given to whole-timers when making new consultant appointments. A consultant must work at least six sessions to be eligible for consideration to receive a distinction award. These awards are available to about 40 per cent of the consultants and involve substantial additions to salaries (about 1 per cent can double their income). As with salaries the awards are related to the proportion of the week worked. They were intended to serve several purposes: rewarding research, encouraging distinguished specialists to work in the NHS if only part-time, allowing specialists to earn high incomes in provincial towns with little or no private practice and in consequence promoting a better geographical distribution of specialist skills, and less explicitly, maintaining an income differential between specialists and GPs. Dr Van Langendonck notes that during the 1960s changes in some of the European fee schedules tended to favour medical services relative to surgical. The situations are not strictly comparable but in Britain in this period the average net income for GPs rose by 103 per cent compared with an increase of 62 per cent in the specialists' maximum salary and distinction award (13). Financially specialist practice is still more rewarding than general practice. At 1971–2 prices computed career earnings for specialists were £238,000 (whole-time) and

£277,000 (maximum part-time) compared with £204,000 for GPs (14). These earnings are from all sources, including private practice. In the same year it is estimated that the average GP earned £350 from non-public sources and the average maximum part-time specialist £2,375 from private practice. A new contract for consultant specialists was being negotiated in 1974 and progress on it became delayed by the new government's decision to remove private practice from NHS hospitals.

Private practice is not at all extensive in Britain. In 1972 less than 3 per cent of the population (some two million people) were voluntarily insured against the costs of hospital and specialist care (15). Payments for private care amounted to about £27 million compared with £3,000 million NHS current expenditure. Doctors do not always respect the fee schedules suggested by the insurance schemes and of the total private spending patients paid £2·5 million. While specialist physicians received only £850,000, surgeons and anaesthetists received £7·6 million. Private practice therefore essentially means private surgical practice.

Although only 1 per cent of NHS hospital beds are set aside for private pay purposes they represent by far the majority of acceptable facilities for private practice in the country. In many parts of the country they represent the only facilities available and given the removal of private beds from NHS hospitals many surgeons would become dependent on their NHS salary. The government was prepared to compensate for the loss of private earnings and make whole-time NHS work more attractive but this itself raised awkward issues. The NHS pays the same salary scales irrespective of specialty while private fees predominantly go to surgeons and anaesthetists. Compensation in the form of increased salaries would have to be substantial if surgeons were to be compensated adequately (some earn two or three times the NHS salary) and applied to all specialties if the principle of inter-parallelism was to continue. Greatly increased salaries for consultants though would not go unnoticed by GPs and the struggle over differentials would be renewed. An option considered was to add a fee-for-service element to the salary system thereby allowing a covert departure from the inter-parallelism principle but this would create a differential between those in clinical practice and those in clinical teaching. Moreover payment by item of service for surgeons particularly can result in an excess of elective procedures.

The pragmatists who shaped the NHS recognized that the public hospital service would suffer if the top specialists were driven into private clinics and nursing homes. Thus a limited amount of private accommodation in public hospitals was conceded. Ill-feeling developed over waiting-lists for admission to public wards culminating in the dispute of 1974. About half a million people are on the lists, predominantly for non-urgent elective surgery and it is argued that private patients should not be able to avoid waiting. The removal of private pay beds from the NHS would not of course prevent those with means securing earlier non-urgent surgery outside the NHS and the release of 1 per cent of NHS beds would hardly reduce the waiting period. Waiting-lists are inflated by duplication and inefficient management but some waiting is inevitable as in the absence of a monetary nexus waiting-lists represent the necessary balance between supply and demand.

It is unfortunate that concern over a relatively minor inequality should sour relations with a section of the profession when so much depends on the profession's co-operation in making the NHS more effective. Many part-time consultants play a full part in the administration of the service at all levels and a better atmosphere is needed if progress is to be made towards redressing the greater inequality between the 'cure' and 'care' sectors.

Private general practice hardly exists at all in Britain. About 5 per cent of family doctors have 100 or more private patients, a third have none at all, and the rest rarely more than 20 each (16). Private patients face the full cost of drugs and the GP, lacking control over hospital beds, finds it difficult to offer the private patient anything markedly different from the service he offers his NHS patient. Family doctors are independent contractors with family practitioner committees. In effect they are paid by salary, the size of the salary being determined to a considerable extent by the number of patients registered. Before the inception of the NHS there were fears that a salaried service might be imposed and in

1949 an Amendment Act prohibited this. In 1966, following unrest within the profession against its leadership, another amendment allowed GPs to opt for payment by capitation, salary, or fee-for-service. In fact no real progress was made in discussions about the last two methods and family doctors are still paid by a combination of all three, although fees-for-service play little part. There are fixed payments to reflect those expenses which do not vary with list size, direct reimbursement for rent and rates of practice premises, 70 per cent of the salaries of ancillary staff employed, extra sums for length of service (conditional upon attendance at a fixed number of refresher courses), capitation fees (higher for patient aged over 65) and several other items. There are extra fixed payments for those in group practice and for practice in under-doctored areas. Unlike the hospital service the NHS has enjoyed little success in promoting a better geographical distribution of family doctors, partly because the monetary inducements to relocation have been low in relation to the earnings of GPs wherever they practice. Item of service payments relate to services in pursuit of public policy: generally they are low, the intention being not so much to encourage particular services as to compensate those already providing them. Since 1966 the GPs contract has been based on a five and a half day week in that an extra allowance, supplementary capitation fees, and specific fees for night calls are also paid to those available for 'out of hours' work. In reality, however, the individual GP is still responsible for a twenty-four-hour service and can restrict demands on his time only by making arrangements with colleagues or a commercial deputizing service. Almost a third of GPs use deputizing services (17) although there is much variation in different parts of the country. Family practitioner committees' approval is required and again there is wide variation between committees as to the extent to which they allow these services to be used. However the committees do not seem to have a legal right to check on the effectiveness of their control and as public money indirectly finances these services a responsibility vacuum seems to have developed.

The earnings of all types of doctor within the NHS are nationally negotiated. Confrontation over pay between the profession and the central department is no longer direct. During the first decade of the NHS adjudication by a High Court judge and a Royal Commission became necessary to resolve the vexed question of adjusting pay levels to inflation. The present machinery was created in 1960 and has not really succeeded in making the question less public or controversial (18). The profession and the central departments submit evidence to an independent Review Body, which reports annually and considers doctors' and dentists' remuneration in comparison with those of other professions. The Review Body advises the Prime Minister direct and he is supposed normally to accept its advice unless there are obvious and compelling reasons to the contrary. In 1965 the profession threatened resignation unless the Review Body was abolished (it was not), in 1970 the Review Body resigned because the Prime Minister did not accept its advice and the profession threatened sanctions if the Review Body were not re-established (it was but with a different membership) and in 1974 the Chairman resigned because his independence was questioned by the profession. All this suggests that the Review Body has in fact been impartial.

The trouble is that the Review Body was established just before successive governments began to rely on statutory incomes policies, usually abandoned as a general election grew near. When policies were statutory the Review Body abided by the rules, and though the profession grumbled there was no trouble. The difficulties and protests have come when incomes policies have not been statutory, as in 1970 and 1974. Even so three public disputes, none causing disruption of the service, in the fourteen years of the present machinery is not a bad record and the index-linking method used in some European systems has little to commend it as differentials cannot be rigid either within the profession or between the profession and other occupations seeking manpower.

## The future

Medical care is not simply a question of organizing the financing of services but also of organizing the services themselves and involving the health professions in organizing and reviewing the effectiveness of services. The need for such involvement becomes apparent when we consider that about a third of the radiation hazard to which people are exposed is generated by the health professions (19). Moreover in mammography in the past a radiation dosage was used of 8 rads per breast per examination (modern techniques have allowed a reduction by a factor of 10 or more) but at this former level it is possible that repeated annual examination (perhaps over fifteen years) may have induced more cancer than was cured through early detection (20). The point is sharpened by the finding that a number of commonly used investigative procedures are as yet unproven as to their effectiveness (21). Ethically it is hard for a doctor to withhold services he thinks *might* help, even when his income is not affected (as in salaried or capitation systems). There is no doubt that the NHS gives the best value for money of any system in the western world (22) and it involves the profession in organizing services as much as any system and far more than most. How does the system stand in relation to the future of European systems as depicted by Dr Van Langendonck on the basis of skilfully observed trends?

Universal coverage, with entitlement divorced from the payment of premiums, no restrictions or conditions such as minimum payments or waiting-periods: these are already characteristics of the NHS and in the founding Six coverage is already sufficiently extensive to suggest that universality of coverage is feasible. In Germany however, and to a lesser extent in the Netherlands, removal of the wage-ceiling would raise questions about the level of medical remuneration within compulsory insurance, since fees from the excluded wealthy are said to compensate for poor insurance rewards. The creation of a single fund in each country would certainly reduce administrative costs, particularly in France and Belgium, but one wonders about the resistance likely to be encountered from those professionally engaged in the administration of the variety of special schemes and voluntary funds. The projected system of financing is not radically different in principle from that of the Six now: contributions as a fixed proportion of income, with some government subsidy and some payment by the patient. Payments by patients would, however, be restricted to charges for drugs and appliances and therefore much less than in countries such as France and Belgium where reimbursement covers 75 or 80 per cent of agreed fees but where many doctors charge more than the agreed rates. While the future role of charges is little different from their role in the NHS now the principle source of finance under the proposed harmonization implies important practical differences from the system used to finance the NHS. Premiums related to income are in effect taxes on income but they represent earmarked taxation. Earmarked taxes tend not to be popular with governments because they imply a certain rigidity. In any case an earmarked tax implies that the service to be financed necessarily has greater priority than other services. In our present state of knowledge can we honestly claim that personal health services have a greater priority than education, residential care of the aged, housing the homeless, ending the bad, insanitary housing which inflates the demand for hospital care, or any other demand on the community's resources? Moreover as the only agency really capable of collecting income-related premiums from the self-employed as well as the employed is the internal revenue authority in each country this might as well be done by that authority directly rather than through a fund or funds. There are other considerations too. A tax fixed as a proportion of income is less redistributive than a tax system which is proportionate and progressive. An income limit, below which premiums need not be paid, looks attractive but such devices can produce marked disincentive effects around the income limit: a man might rise above the limit, have to pay the health tax and be worse off than he was before. In any case as some role is left for government financing from general revenue it follows that the government would ultimately decide the level of resources to be made available and a single source of income under compulsion would seem administratively simpler and cheaper. Given this decisive role by government it would follow that negotiations over remuneration would be pursued nationally and would involve the government. Contracts and agreements with the medical profession might just as well be offered by the government as by a fund or funds.

Control of the cost of medical services through budgets, setting norms for the provision of services, prescriptions, use of hospitals, and so on with professional review of performance and questioning of deviant behaviour is not yet extensive in this country although there are elements. A GP may for example be fined for persistent over-prescribing. In hospitals there are cases where medical executive committees have been given responsibility for all medical and nursing expenditure within a budget. The divisional system is supposed to provide for the review of clinical policy and in some cases statistics have been used to compare specialists with each other on the basis of average stay in hospital for particular diagnoses and procedures. Differences indicated by statistics are not always true and when they are not always on the specialist's initiative but related to the beds and theatre time he is allocated (23). It might be wiser to let the desired approach evolve through understanding and professional perception rather than through laws. As it is there is growing interest in Britain in medical audit and review of professional activity and one response to the problem of financing the NHS was a conference organized by the profession to consider such questions as: are all pathological tests necessary, a restricted list of NHS drugs, can the use of hospitals be reduced and medical tasks delegated?

In most respects therefore the NHS already has the cardinal features of the suggested future European system. In fact the NHS is closer to the future European system than the founding Six are now. Some will not achieve adjustment easily attainable; France for example will find it hard to introduce direct payment of doctors, ending reimbursement and the practice of extra billing. The referral system, firmly established in Britain, is to be generalized but payment systems are not. It is, of course, politically realistic to accept that in the final analysis medical professions themselves decide how they are paid and cling to the form they are used to. There is a trend towards salaried systems in hospitals but in general practice only Britain, the Netherlands, and Italy feature capitation payment. The point is that a referral system is not compatible with the fee-for-service system common in four of the Six. If a GP refers he is losing fees: if he enters partnership with a specialist then both have a vested interest in unnecessary referral and greater emphasis is placed on the need for control systems to focus on abuse rather than quality of care.

There is nothing in the existing EEC provisions for the harmonization of social policy to require changes in the working of the NHS. The Commission's directives are binding on member states as to their effect, not the way that effect is achieved administratively. In the long run changes in health care systems might have to be initiated by member-states on their own initiative if serious distortions in the level of service are caused by gross imbalances in the movement within Europe of doctors and other staff. Obviously medical professions will advance the threat of emigration as a reason for obtaining higher pay without suffering the inconvenience of actually going, assuming that doctors in other countries are better off and that mutual recognition of qualifications will in fact make movement easy. The BMA has raised the spectre of emigration with the Review Body (25) and is surveying medical earnings in the member states. Anxiety has also been expressed about a decline in standards of care if foreign doctors are admitted to practice in this country.

Differences in earnings are meaningless: differences in real living standards will be the determining factor. The EEC has shown little real interest so far in regional economic policy and indeed such policies are inconsistent with the Community's competitive philosophy. Gross imbalances in living standards may develop and large numbers of doctors may try to move. Although migration of workers within Europe so far, despite existing differences in living standards, has not been extensive and largely between Italy and Germany, the same may not be true of medicine. It would be idle to speculate here about future differences in living standards and their impact. However mutual recognition may not open as many doors as might be supposed. Equally fears about the quality of foreign doctors coming here may be exaggerated.

The founding Six made little progress with mutual recognition of medical qualifications before the enlargement of the Community in 1973. The draft directives proposed six years of basic training in university with at least 5,500 hours of instruction. Postgraduate diplomas for mutual recognition of specialist qualifications were to be based on training in appropriate centres of from three to five years according to the specialty. Only thirteen specialties were to be recognized in all member-states and another thirteen in some of the states. For example thoracic surgery and vascular surgery would be recognized only in Belgium and Italy, cardiology and rheumatology would be recognized everywhere except Germany and so on. Quality of training did not apparently matter.

By convention new entrants to the EEC can join discussions on existing questions the year before their membership begins and representatives of the British government joined negotiations of the medical directives in 1972. Arrangements for licensing and training are quite different in this country (including the Irish Republic) from those in the other member states. Not that the founding Six are at all uniform. In Italy it is possible to qualify in medicine without ever having laid hands on a patient. In Germany, under new laws to become effective by 1978 in all parts of the Federal Republic, training will consist of six years, including a year's internship and residence in a university hospital, after which a degree will be granted. Faculties will draw on a national bank of questions for examination purposes. At present there are 4,500 places in medical schools and normally about 21,000 applicants for them. Selection is on the basis of high school record. Since 1968 four years' graduate training are required before a doctor can legally describe himself as a GP. There are no postgraduate specialist examinations in Germany but the Medical Association will not grant a specialist diploma until the candidate has spent the stipulated period working with an approved teacher. The teacher is approved and not the hospital. France places less emphasis on practical training. Each year about 30,000 enrol in universities for the seven-year medical course but available facilities allow only a third to proceed to the second year. Hospital work becomes more pronounced over the last three years and in the final year the student accepts responsibility for patients. A thesis has then to be defended and with his degree the doctor is entitled to practice.

Specialist recognition is by the Ordre Nationale des Médicins on the basis of certificates available in one of two ways, one setting very high standards, the other less certain.

In the United Kingdom the right to practice depends on registration by the General Medical Council. The GMC is responsible for the five-year undergraduate curriculum in medical schools and the one-year postgraduate training in approved hospitals. Specialist training is provided in hospitals approved by medical corporations or Royal colleges who are also the examining authorities. Strictly there are no legally required specialist qualifications but by long custom nobody can proceed far in British hospitals without being a fellow or member of the appropriate Royal college. A central committee for postgraduate medical education tries to promote more uniformity in training. Membership or fellowship of a Royal college does not guarantee access to independent specialist practice within the NHS. This requires appointment to the consultant grade. There have been attempts to introduce career grades below that of consultant but the profession has always resisted and the career grade is still that of consultant. The time normally taken to achieve consultant status is longer in all specialties than the periods indicated in the Commission's draft directives as they stood in 1972. At present three years' postgraduate training is recommended before entry into general practice but is not yet obligatory. In 1968 a Royal Commission on Medical Education proposed a system for all clinicians of an additional five years' postgraduate training, consisting of three years' general and flexible training, followed by vocational (specialist) registration, and another two years as hospital specialist or assistant principal in general practice.

Faced with the prospect of increased costs to introduce vocational registration the GMC proposed a small annual fee (£5) for doctors to stay on its register. The profession used the occasion to force an official inquiry into the structure and functions of the GMC. A report was expected at the end of 1974. There were various motives behind the demand for an inquiry. The GMC controls professional discipline and can suspend doctors for 'serious professional misconduct'. This can include conviction in ordinary courts, breaches of NHS discipline, adultery, alcoholism and so on. Some medical spokesmen object to the double jeopardy in which doctors may be placed and to sanctions against conduct which is for others tolerated in a permissive age. More important though was the profession's desire for control over access to practice in this country, especially with the EEC in view, and perhaps the government's desire to exercise more influence over the profession.

The GMC is an independent statutory authority, subject to Parliament and governed by Medical Acts, not the government. It is therefore independent of the NHS although the NHS provides the training hospitals and the government finances the medical schools. The GMC is also independent of the BMA since only 11 of the 47 Council members are directly elected by the profession. Another 8 are nominated by the Crown through the Privy Council, 18 from the medical schools and teaching hospitals, and 10 from the Royal colleges: although the GMC has no responsibility for postgraduate training. The arrangement at least separates the wage-negotiation function from that of registration and training. Undergraduate and specialist training could be brought under one umbrella by creating two subcommittees under the GMC. There is something to be said for government representation; but it must be appreciated that the business of medical schools and the Royal colleges is to train doctors and not simply to staff the NHS.

Whatever the future structure of the GMC its tasks will not be ended by mutual recognition of degrees. In 1972 negotiations over the draft directives turned to the question of quality of training. A European GMC was not thought possible in view of the universities' traditional independence in some member-states. However an Advisory Committee has been suggested with powers to collect information about teaching conditions and courses. The final composition of the committee was still not known at the end of 1974. Nominees (one from each member-state) representing medical associations and committees of university principals were not apparently acceptable to the Commission without representation of governments, which the professions found hard to swallow. Moreover the professions sought to concentrate in the first instance on basic training while the Commission wanted the advisory committee to tackle specialist training as well.

Meanwhile it seems clear that any doctor admitted to Britain will be 'deemed to have registered' with the GMC and will therefore be subject to the same code of discipline as British doctors. As the draft directives stood at the end of 1974 they did not apply to public service employees but to self-employed doctors. It may therefore not be easy for British doctors to join public hospitals in France (where specialists and medical teachers are civil servants) or the many German teaching hospitals. Access to general practice in the Netherlands and Germany requires three or four years' training and acceptance by a sick fund or an association of sick fund physicians. Similarly doctors from Europe coming here will need to be acceptable to a regional or area health authority or a family practitioner committee. There is a loophole here in that in designated areas there is no power to stop a doctor setting up in NHS practice. Lord Hill caused a DHSS official some embarrassment when he raised this point during a Select Committee of the Lords' hearing on the directives and was told the last words on the matter had still to be spoken (26). The directives made no language requirement (the GMC announced in 1974 that in future a working knowledge of English would be required) but in the under-doctored north, even if family practitioner committees cannot prevent a foreign doctor setting up in practice the citizens of Wigan and Widnes are not likely to register with anyone who cannot communicate with them. One suspects that the movement, if there is any, will be from Italy; and the medical services of the north may depend on the culture of southern Europe rather than southern Asia. We must wait and see.

## REFERENCES

1. MINISTRY OF HEALTH, *Interim Report of the Consultative Committee on Medical and Allied Services* (London: HMSO, 1920).
2. *Social Insurance and Allied Services*, Cmd. 6404 (London: HMSO, 1942).
3. ABEL-SMITH, B., *An International Study of Health Expenditure*, General Paper no. 32 (Geneva: WHO, 1967).
4. SIMANIS, J. G., *Soc. Sec. Admin. Bull.* **33** (Washington DC, 1970), 1.

5. POWELL, J. ENOCH, *A New Look at Medicine and Politics* (London: Pitman Medical, 1966).
6. *Public Expenditure to 1976-77*, Cmnd. 5178 (London: HMSO, 1972).
7. *Public Expenditure to 1977-78*, Cmnd. 5519 (London: HMSO, 1973).
8. POWELL, J. ENOCH, op. cit.
9. COCHRANE, A. L., *Effectiveness and Efficiency*, Rock Carling Monograph (London: Nuffield Provincial Hospitals Trust, 1972).
10. MATHER, H. G., et al., *Br. med. J.* **3** (1971), 334.
11. MINISTRY OF HEALTH, *First Report of the Joint Working Party in the Organisation of Medical Work in Hospitals* (London: HMSO, 1967).
12. MCLACHLAN, G. (ed.), *In Low Gear?* Occasional Hundreds 2 (Oxford University Press for the Nuffield Provincial Hospitals Trust, 1971).
13. *Br. med. J.* **4**, suppl. 5 (1970).
14. REVIEW BODY ON DOCTORS' AND DENTISTS' REMUNERATION, *Fourth Report*, Cmnd. 5644 (London: HMSO, 1974).
15. LEE DONALDSON ASSOCIATES, *U.K. Private Medical Care: Provident Schemes Statistics 1972* (London: Lee Donaldson Associates, 1973).
16. CARTWRIGHT, A., *Patients and Their Doctors* (London: Routledge & Kegan Paul, 1967).
17. WILLIAMS, B. T., and KNOWLEDEN, J., 'General practitioner deputising services', *Br. med. J.* **1**, suppl. 9 (1974).
18. For a general review of relations between the profession and the NHS, see FORSYTH, G., *Doctors and State Medicine* (2nd edn) (London: Pitman Medical, 1973).
19. MCKEOWN, T., Personal communication.
20. —— Personal communication.
21. MCLACHLAN, G. (ed.), *Screening in Medical Care: Reviewing the Evidence* (Oxford University Press for the Nuffield Provincial Hospitals Trust, 1968).
22. See, for example, MAXWELL, R., *Health Care: The Growing Dilemma* (New York: McKinsey & Co. Inc., 1974); and STARK MURRAY, D., *Medical Care: Who Gets the Best Service?* (London: Fabian Society, 1971).
23. FORSYTH, G. et al., 'Planning in practice: a half-term report', in McLachlan, G. (ed.), *Problems and Progress in Medical Care*, Fourth Series (Oxford University Press for the Nuffield Provincial Hospitals Trust, 1970).
24. 'New alternatives in the N.H.S.', *Br. med. J.* **4** (1974), 272-8, 327-32, 389-96.
25. REVIEW BODY ON DOCTORS' AND DENTISTS' REMUNERATION, *Fourth Report*, Cmnd. 5644 (London: HMSO, 1974).
26. SELECT COMMITTEE OF THE HOUSE OF LORDS ON THE EUROPEAN COMMUNITIES, *Eighth Report* (London: HMSO, 1974).

# FOREWORD

Economic integration cannot be an end in itself: Establishing a common market and, later, an economic and monetary union, only makes sense if there is an ultimate social goal; namely the improvement of the life condition for people in general. The national governments could hardly accept measures decided by the authorities of the Community if they were not assumed to serve the well-being of their people. Stiffening competition depresses both wages and employment. Therefore workers and unions can only accept a common market if there exists a social policy which respects their chief ambitions, namely rising living standards, control of unemployment, maintenance and improvement of social benefits, and extension of economic democracy. Finally disparities between social provisions influence economic integration itself: they hinder the free mobility of labour, and free provision of services and the free flow of capital. Economic integration in Europe cannot exist without social integration.

National social legislations can be integrated in one of two principal ways: *co-ordination* and *harmonization*. In general terms, co-ordination fits existing national laws and regulations together whereas harmonization changes and converges these laws and regulations. The importance of harmonization increases on the international level, as international mobility of labour and services increases. Obviously the European Common Market which seeks explicitly to stimulate these two aspects of mobility, will have to focus attention on the harmonization problem.

*Social security* holds a very special place in social legislation. Unlike most fields of social law which are centred on labour in commercial and industrial enterprises, social security has a broader field of application, sometimes even covering the whole population. It consists much more of a set of institutions, which are charged with the provision of certain public services. It may be superfluous to underline here the importance of social security in our society; suffice to point out that some 20 per cent of the national income is spent on social security in the European Economic Community. Moreover social security has become an essential element of social order. It responds to one of the most fundamental needs of man: the need for security and safety.

*Harmonization of social security in the European Community* has already been the subject of many studies and plans. The institutions of the EEC started the process by organizing a European Conference on Social Security in 1962. As a result of that conference the Community Commission drafted a general plan to harmonize social security. However, the harmonization programme was seen as too theoretical for practical application by the Council of Ministers. Harmonization therefore comes about slowly and reluctantly. The problem is partly that social security as a whole is too broad a field for research aimed at harmonization. Much study has to be done in each sector of social security before a global harmonization plan can be developed. This study of health insurance is intended to contribute to that task.

Apart from personal interest there are good reasons for starting with *social health insurance*. First of all, insurance has an important position within health care as a whole, and hence, within the economic and social policies of each country. In fact social insurance has withdrawn health care largely from the free market economy. Then there are strong tendencies for converging development in this sector as will be shown in this study. Therefore, the harmonization task will perhaps be less difficult than in other sectors. All citizens have fundamentally the same need for health care, while the structures of medical care (medical professions and care institutions) are not essentially different. The harmonization of the way to obtain and finance medical care cannot really cause insurmountable difficulties in countries with after all a similar social-economic situation and structure. Moreover there is the rapid development of medical science which poses new problems in the organizational and financial field and sharpens the need for insurance for all population groups. Thus, in the end it will be inevitable that all concerned countries review the problems associated with the distribution of medical services. They will have to prepare radical reforms in existing systems.

Such a situation offers a unique historical opportunity for harmonization *in the progress* as article 117 of the treaty says.

The *intention* of this study is to investigate the possibilities and difficulties of social harmonization within the EEC, in one specific sector of social security, namely social health care insurance.

Part One sets out the common features of the health insurance systems in the six founding nations as they were in 1972. Part Two reviews the major differences. Thus we obtain a black and white picture of the present situation in the EEC. Harmonization requires not only knowledge and comparison but also forecast. Plans have to be directed towards the future, rather than the present. Therefore in Part Three, the evolution of the main elements of the different national systems is analysed. The tendencies are compared with each other from their origin until the present. This dynamic comparison shows a number of converging and diverging trends: these are brought together to create an ideal image of future health care insurance, on which a common harmonization policy can be based. Finally Part Four sets out a detailed harmonization plan, showing for each country the measures implied by the proposed plan.

With this structure repetition is inevitable and unavoidable. Perhaps the reader will not merely forgive repetition but actually welcome it: the subject matter is intrinsically complex and made more so because six countries are dealt with. Each look into the future is a speculation. The proposed harmonization plan only has value as a personal idea, for a harmonization programme has to be aimed at a future notion of social security more than at the present converging tendencies. With this study we hope to make a contribution to the debate about this important and inevitable point of action in European integration.

# PART ONE

## COMMON ASPECTS

# I
# Health insurance: its concept and scope

### Concept

By its very nature, social insurance for health care occurs in three forms (1): public subsidy for private provision, compulsory membership of self-managed insurance schemes, and national health service under direct government responsibility. In the Western world the three forms occur simultaneously. But in all six founding countries of the EEC the provision for health care appears mainly in the second form, namely compulsory insurance. In the Netherlands, compulsory insurance for heavy medical risks applies to the whole population, and half the population is compulsorily insured for current care as well. In France, Belgium, and Luxemburg compulsory insurance has been extended over the years to practically the total population, under different forms. The obligation to be insured is less general in Italy and Germany but it can be said that the majority are mandatorily covered: 86·2 per cent in Italy and although no official figure exists for Germany 75 per cent would be a reasonable estimate (2). The figure is high enough in both cases to talk in terms of a predominant compulsory insurance.

An important characteristic of this insurance is its incorporation in the whole system of social insurance or social security. Essentially health care comes under the generally accepted definition of social security, as stated in the Convention no. 102 of the ILO. Formally insurance for health care is a part of the code of social insurance in France, Germany, and Luxemburg. In Belgium it comes under the financial superstructure of the National Office for Social Security of Workers and the National Office for Social Insurance of the Self-Employed.

At first sight it appears that in the Netherlands and in Italy health care insurance does not belong to the system of social insurance: provisions are based on separate legislation, with separate executive and maintenance bodies. No code of social security exists in Italy or in the Netherlands. Italian health insurance is mainly administered by the *Istituto Nazionale per l'Assicurazione contro le Malattie* (INAM) (National Institute for Insurance against Illness) whereas the classic branches of social security are managed by the *Istituto Nazionale della Previdenza Sociale* (INPS) (National Institute for Social Security). Dutch health insurance is managed by sickness funds, while the normal social insurance for workers (with the exception of family allowances) is managed by 'bedrijfsverenigingen' or 'industrial associations'. Nevertheless, in both countries health insurance is, in general, considered as a part of social insurance or social security. It comes under the same ministerial department: in the Netherlands, the *Ministry of Social Affairs and Public Health*; in Italy, the *Ministero del lavoro e della sicurezza sociale* (Ministry of Labour and Social Security). In manuals, tracts, and official reports on social insurance or social security, insurance for health care is invariably treated as an integral part of that field (3).

The conclusion is therefore that in each of the six countries health care is based on compulsory insurance within the framework of a general system of social security. This is a very important statement. It means that a fundamentally solid basis of congruence exists between what are, in other respects, such different systems.

In none of these countries however has compulsory insurance been allowed to monopolize the financing and organizing of health care. In all the countries considered, care is also associated with other types of provision, such as limited kinds of public health services and with voluntary and private insurance. In most countries, not only in Europe, the army has a military health service of its own. In most countries preventive care is a government concern, social insurance mainly dealing only with curative care (4). Social insurance has a limited role in preventive care in Belgium and Italy; but in the other countries it deals with prevention only in a very small degree. In all the countries of the original EEC *voluntary* health insurance plays a part. This can consist of giving extra benefits to the compulsorily insured, but it can also bring those exempt from compulsory insurance within the social security scheme. In all the countries it is noticeable that a place is also left for private health insurance whether commercial or non-profitmaking. The importance of this varies from country to country (5).

Thus the nature of health coverage is strikingly similar. Health care in these six countries is supplied mainly through a compulsory insurance within the framework of social security, complemented by limited public health services, systems of voluntary insurance and private provision.

The systems of the continent are united also by their common, and very old, concept of health insurance. They began long before the 'Beveridge Revolution' or were at least supported by a tradition preceding universalist conceptions. They all directly or indirectly originated from, or were mainly influenced by the legislation which Bismarck introduced in 1883 and which led to the classical concept of *social insurance*. In this concept defined benefits are supplied to a limited group of contributors and beneficiaries by using the insurance technique. The size of the provision is related to the amount of the contribution (6).

In all countries of the original EEC the basic idea of social insurance for health care is still that of the classic (Bismarckian) approach. In each of these countries care is, in the first place, supplied to groups of indicated contributors. Their family and persons in their charge are considered to be covered by the same contribution.

The concept of social insurance has gradually evolved since Bismarck's time. New ideas about social security emerged in the period between the two world wars: especially the Anglo-American concept (often called after the famous Beveridge Report) which regards social security as a set of measures to protect all citizens against want.

This new line of thought exercised strong influence on health insurance in Europe, especially after the Second World War (7). In most of the countries protection against medical costs is also given to groups of persons who do not contribute or who do not work. In this way, almost all the inhabitants of Belgium and France are compulsorily insured or can voluntarily join the compulsory insurance for health care, while in all countries medical care is given to those disabled by war service. In most countries too medical care is given to different categories of handicapped people. In the Netherlands, protection against heavy medical risks is even extended to the total resident population.

The concept of social insurance for health care in the six countries of the EEC can therefore be described as classical compulsory social insurance of the Bismarck type, with concessions which benefit certain groups such as students and handicapped people, who do not pay contributions as they are not gainfully employed.

## Scope

The scope of health insurance regulations in the Six is defined in terms of those obliged to contribute and in terms of those eligible for benefits or for repayment of medical costs under insurance. In all countries the group of beneficiaries is related to the group of contributors. The person who should contribute (even if he is exempt from the contribution for some reason) is considered to confer the right to services for the non-contributing persons dependent on him. Consequently, the application of the regulations is described by defining first the compulsorily insured and then the benefiting dependants of a compulsorily insured person. There is only one exception to this rule. The general insurance for special medical care costs in the Netherlands applies directly to all inhabitants of the country. Another exception is forthcoming: the Italian government introduced in parliament in August 1974 a proposal for a national health service.

Much common ground is seen where the basic field of application of health insurance is concerned. Generally all workmen and employees of private enterprises in trade and industry (agriculture, fishery, navigation, and aviation included) come under social security provisions which include insurance for health care. They are all obliged to contribute and all the members of their family and persons in their charge are entitled to receive services.

Only one important exception has to be made: the German and the Dutch law set a wage limit, the latter for all workers, the former for employees (except mining and navigation) only. There is no obligation to be insured over this limit and consequently no entitlement for the next of kin.

There are other people, besides workers in the private sector, who generally are obliged to be insured, even if they are exempt from contribution: those who have a right to a pension as ex-workers in the private sector—except for the Netherlands, where compulsory insurance always ends at retirement age; those who temporarily or permanently do not work because of incapacity, provided that they worked in the past and had been obliged to be insured; and those unemployed who meet the requirements of the legislation on unemployed insurance. The technique of the various regulations can be different for this last category: in some countries the unemployed are classified as obligatorily insured people. This applies in the Netherlands, Belgium, Germany, and Italy. In France and Luxemburg the insured is considered to retain his status as employed during periods of unemployment.

Apprentices in trade, industry, or agriculture are always protected, even if they do not earn a wage. However, they are considered as compulsorily insured in some countries (Luxemburg, Germany, the Netherlands, and Italy), and as dependants with a right to services in France and Belgium.

A number of special groups of workers are expressly mentioned as compulsorily insured: homeworkers and domestic staff (in all six states), commercial representatives and agents, musicians, showbusiness artists, and interim workers.

The conscript is also protected in all countries. He retains his rights as insured (for himself and for his family) during the period of his active military service. This rule has lost its point in Luxemburg with the Act of 29 June 1967, abolishing military service.

The secondary field of application in the six countries is also very similar in several respects. In all systems the members of the family are largely considered as co-insured. This applies in all

## TABLE I
### Health insurance coverage, 1970[1]

|  | Total population (1,000) | Insured for medical (1,000) | % |
|---|---|---|---|
| Belgium | 9,684 | 9,587 | 99·0 |
| Germany | 61,566 | 55,000 | 89·3 |
| France | —[2] | —[2] | 98·0 |
| Italy | 54,683 | 48,749 | 86·8 |
| Luxemburg | 339 | 336 | 98·9 |
| Netherlands | 13,119 | 9,900 | 75·5 |

1. Compulsory and voluntary social insurance.   2. Not available.

*Source:* Commission des Communautés Européennes, *Rapport sur la situation sociale dans la Communauté en 1971*, Brussels, 1972, table 10, p. 325; *1974*, table VII, pp. 242–3.

compulsory systems to the wife of the insured and also, in certain circumstances to the husband of the female insured.

The workers' children are also insured free of charge until they reach a certain age, differing from country to country. This applies in all systems to legally recognized natural and adopted children and in most systems to children who are simply in the custody of the insured. In all systems the age limit is raised for children who are studying, who are under a contract of apprenticeship, and for handicapped children.

Certain important differences appear in the precise description of co-insured people or persons in charge. These differences will be dealt with later.

The field of application of social health insurance for social groups other than employees in the private sector, such as public servants and the self-employed, is not as congruent. The striking differences which can be indicated are also discussed later.

### Quantitative importance

The total number of people insured for health care compared with the total population of the countries concerned is shown in Table 1.

These figures show that in all EEC countries most people are insured for medical care. Only the Netherlands is the exception

TABLE 2
Part of social insurance in total expenditure for
health care, 1970, in national currencies (millions)

|  | Belgium | Germany | France | Italy | Luxemburg | Netherlands |
|---|---|---|---|---|---|---|
| Health care benefits of social insurance | 36,526 | 21,969 | 31,570 | 2,301[1] | 1,266 | 4,390 |
| Total health care expenditure | 51,789 | 35,674 | 48,434 | 2,584[1] | 1,860 | 5,395 |
| Percentage | 70·5 | 61·9 | 65·0 | 88·9 | 69·1 | 81·4 |

1. Billions of lire.

Source: Statistical Office of the EEC.

with 75 per cent. This figure is misleading. Under the General Insurance for Special Medical Care Costs the Dutch population is 100 per cent insured for heavy medical risks, so that the figure of 75 per cent only relates to 'normal' medical care. Another rider is that the hospital reform in Italy extends voluntary social insurance for hospital care to all inhabitants, as from 1 January 1975, as a preparation to the imminent establishment of a national health service.

In the six countries health insurance plays an extremely important role with regard to the provision and consumption of health care. A key indicator of its importance is the contribution to total health care costs (Table 2).

In 1965 for example the costs of health services provided under social security amounted to 76 per cent of total personal health expenditure in Italy, 66 per cent in Belgium, 59 per cent in the Netherlands, 57 per cent in Germany, 56 per cent in Luxemburg, and 55 per cent in France (8).

Compared with countries outside the EEC the figures are both high and uniform. A study by the World Health Organization in 1961 (9) collected data for a number of countries; it appears that generally social insurance only accounts for 1·7–12·2 per cent of the costs of health care (in countries with social insurance). Canada had a high figure of 29·6 per cent. Only Yugoslavia reached a level which is similar to that of the EEC: 77 per cent.

There is similarity too in the burden of health care in the total expenses of the social security systems.

The relation of expenses for health care under social security to the total costs of social security ranges from 16·9 to 26·1 per cent, and does not vary much in the six countries. Surrounding countries have the following figures: Denmark: 10·1 per cent; Norway: 21·5 per cent; Switzerland: 16·1 per cent; Yugoslavia: 30·2 per cent (10).

If the relation found for the original EEC countries is sometimes lower than in nearby countries, the reason for this lower proportion is not a lower importance of health care costs in the EEC countries, but on the contrary, a relatively smaller total expenditure on social security in countries outside the Six (11). In short social health insurance displays a strikingly similar pattern in the Six in scope, concept, and financial weight.

# 2
# Financing social health insurance

There are three sources of finance for health care: the resources of the family, compulsory savings, and public funds.

On this point the six systems are similar: first because compulsory savings, as a source of finance, are emphasized in every country; secondly, no method of finance is excluded in any of these systems.

Compulsory savings in every system and in all countries take the form of compulsory contributions by the insured. Nearly all social security systems in the Six are predominantly financed by these contributions ranging from 65 to 90 per cent. The spread is somewhat wider for maternity (60–99·6 per cent). At any rate the share of contributions is predominant in all cases. There is only one exception: in the Italian schemes for farmers and craftsmen, where for basic insurance government subsidies seem to be far larger than the contributions (12).

Payments by the insured himself, and subsidies by the government, exist in each of the European systems in addition to compulsory contributions by the insured. Their share in the total finance differs from country to country. It will be discussed in Part Two.

Despite differences in the arrangements for premium payment by the several systems and countries common traits are apparent, especially in the systems for wage-earners in the private sector, as opposed to the systems for public servants and those for the self-employed.

They concern both the method of premium calculation and of imposition.

In almost every case, the contributions consist of a percentage of the wage of the employee. An interesting exception was introduced in 1968 in France, where part of the contribution became calculated on the premium for the compulsory automobile insurance. In some cases it will be calculated upon a fictitious or fixed wage. The contribution can be a fixed amount in some special cases, such as for students in Belgium and France. The percentage is in all countries calculated on the gross wage, including the advantages *in natura*, before the deduction of taxes.

No contribution is payable on earnings over a ceiling. The use of ceilings for the calculation of premiums is only unknown in Italy. In France a small part of the premium (3 per cent) is imposed on the total wage, without taking account of a ceiling and in Luxemburg the contributions of white-collar workers and public servants are calculated from a minimum.

The contribution consists of an employer's part and an employee's part in all countries. The exception is the Dutch general insurance for special medical care costs: in the Dutch general insurance schemes there is one contribution, payable by all insured or by their employers. The relative shares of employer and employee differ from country to country (13), as indeed does the amount of the contribution.

The same contribution technique, as for employees, is used in the schemes for officials and public servants, where they exist. The premium is a percentage of the wage, with a ceiling. It is divided into a contribution from the insured and a contribution from the public authority which is the employer.

There is even a certain unity in the financing systems for self-employed, in those countries where they have social insurance for health care. Usually this insurance is financed by fixed monthly or quarterly premiums, supplemented by governmental subsidies. A scale of fixed premiums is predominantly used, the insured being divided into income classes. However, self-employed in the Netherlands and Belgium pay a premium for health care as a percentage of their income. In Belgium it is the result of a recent reform; and in the Netherlands it concerns the General Law on Special Medical Care Costs, the general insurance covering only long-term intramural treatment.

The contribution is considered as a familial one in nearly all the systems of compulsory insurance. This means that one premium payment confers rights to care for the worker and for his family and dependants. The exception is the Italian scheme for the craftsmen and small merchants and also the French scheme for farmers. In the latter scheme, however, in certain circumstances the wife and children of the insured can be exempted from contribution. In the systems of voluntary insurance the premium is due per insured, but there usually is no contribution or only a small one for children under a certain age.

So, in general, it can be said that there is a broad consensus about the contribution arrangements for social insurance for health care. The systems for employees and public servants are everywhere to a large extent maintained by premiums deducted from the wages, plus employers' contributions. They are a percentage of the wages calculated on a wage ceiling. The systems for self-employed are largely (except in the Netherlands and Belgium) financed with fixed premiums, more or less related to the income of the insured.

Only one kind of government subsidy is common to all the European countries: the payment by the government of the premium for persons who cannot normally pay it themselves. The Dutch sickness funds insurance attains this by way of premium reduction regulations for voluntarily insured people and through the insurance for aged people. The Belgian government takes to its account insurance for the unemployed. The government pays for health insurance of retired farmers and part of the insurance for miners in Germany and part of all social insurance contributions in the south of Italy. Of the same nature is the governmental intervention in the premiums of pensioners, children, students, and disabled in Luxemburg, in the systems for self-employed in Italy and for farmers in Luxemburg, France, and Italy.

On the other hand, the government also grants fixed subsidies to some systems of insurance. Typical examples are the fixed amount of 475 million fl. per year for the Dutch General Insurance for Special Medical Care Costs, and the basic subsidies in the Belgian social insurance for health care: 27 per cent of the total planned expenses. The Italian government grants fixed subsidies as a temporary measure to several systems of insurance for health care.

In Belgium and Luxemburg, the government also intervenes in the cost of specific types of insurance activity, supposed to be of special interest to the community. In Belgium, the state supports 25 per cent of the day-price in hospital and 95 per cent of the expenses for 'social diseases' (ie cancer, tuberculosis, mental illness, poliomyelitis, and congenital diseases and deformities). In Luxemburg it pays for maternity care (except in pathologic cases), hospital care for mental illness, tuberculosis, cancer, and poliomyelitis, all expenses for congenital diseases and deformities. In addition, the Luxemburg government also supports all medical expenses occasioned by motor-car accidents not covered by insurance and by sports accidents, and it pays for half the administration cost of the medical control services, as well as for the full wages of medical control officers (14).

A third type of government intervention is the last resort method: the government pays for the possible deficits of the funds. This was the case in Belgium before the reform of 1963. The French reform in 1967 sharpened the financial responsibility of the funds: every governmental intervention is excluded. In Germany, the local communities and industries which own a 'Krankenkasse' are still legally obliged to cover the deficit when the premium reaches the legal limit (15). The deficits in the Italian systems are in fact always covered by additional governmental subsidies (16). The same phenomenon threatens Belgium and other countries, and soon the increasing costs of medical care will have passed beyond the bounds of mere premium increases.

In all the systems part of the costs of medical care is paid by the patients at the time of use. These independent payments occur in different forms and have a differing level of importance in every country. They will be considered later.

# 3

# *The benefits of social health insurance and access to them*

### Extent of benefits

No element of social insurance is more important for the insured himself than his right to benefits. For most individuals the entitlement to health care benefits is a matter of much personal concern. Within the whole range of social insurance legislation he wants especially to know which are the benefits he has a right to and within what limits and under what conditions. Strong resistance to premium payment appears when the level of benefits is considered insufficient. This has been demonstrated in France in a convincing way (17). Every inequality in the range of benefits is considered as an important discrimination by the people concerned. Especially since the 1950s the principle of social equality has been supported by all social groups (18).

It is therefore a good augury that the benefits in the European systems of social health insurance are generally very similar. The differences are mainly in the area of their organization and financing. The points of likeness appear in the range of benefits, the limitations to benefits, and the conditions for obtaining them.

The similarity of medical benefits in the European systems appears first in their completeness. They are generally in accordance with the possibilities of medical science and technique in their present state. After a survey of the systems in the EEC and Britain, a serious and competent international comparative research concluded: 'Practically all curative medical provisions are taken care of or are repaid in all countries' (19).

With these statements about similarity in mind, it is interesting to read the legal texts and the regulations which describe the range of medical benefits. A comparison of these texts shows at first sight only diverging points. Nowhere is the same definition used, nor is the same division made, nor the same limits, specifications, or descriptions stated. Some legislations distinguish between the benefits of maternity insurance and those of the health insurance in general (France, Germany, Luxemburg: only for workers). Some systems only in general terms point out which kind of care is given by the insurance (Belgium and the Luxemburg systems for employees, officials, and self-employed). Other systems describe care in greater detail (the Netherlands, Germany, less in France, and in the Luxemburg system for workers). Italy in principle follows this line but the decree that would enforce a detailed description of medical benefits has not emerged for more than twenty-five years and probably never will. So Italy belongs in fact to the non-specific group.

Where some legislative systems are more precise in pointing out the medical benefits, this occurs in very different ways. Some countries describe the kind of people and institutions which are allowed to provide care to insured people. Others rather specify which types of care can be provided under which conditions. And in Germany the measure and the method of providing care in the most economic way is emphasized.

At the same time all these formal differences between legislations are not really important. What they have in common is that they indicate the insurance benefits in a general way. The details in the Dutch executive decrees, in the Belgian and French *nomenclature*, and in the German *Richtlinien* of the *Bundesausschuss der Artze und Krankenkassen*, aim to protect the rights of the insured rather than limit them. Chiapelli wrote this conclusion about the several legal systems in Italy: 'the different descriptions of the insurance object in all the systems is in fact not important because these differences do not have a substantial value and because a technical definition of the covered risks is absent in every legislation' (20). This can certainly be applied to the systems in the Six.

# The benefits of social health insurance

The content of the various legislations cannot indeed be considered as a technical description of the object of the insurance: neither the risk that is covered (the illness) nor the benefits in the framework of the insurance are the object of an exact legal definition. Only in Germany one finds in the manuals (not in the legislation) a definition of the term 'Krankheit' (illness) (21). Where the legislation indicates some types of benefit, this does not mean that all other types are excluded, but rather that the benefits mentioned are certainly not excluded. The rare exclusions are found mentioned in the comments, not in the law or regulations. The exclusion of thermal cures by the Dutch compulsory system, for instance, is not written in the decrees for execution of the law.

The classification of the medical benefits in the legislations is ultimately based upon the different forms in which the systems supply medical care for their members. The Belgian legislation is the only one to distinguish between 'magistral' preparations by the pharmacist and pharmaceutical specialties; this distinction is made because of a difference in price calculation and intervention of the insurance. For the same reason care in a sanatorium is mentioned apart in the Dutch sickness funds insurance while it is incorporated in the term hospital care in Belgium, Germany, etc. The same can be said for laboratory analyses in France and for many other points.

The only limitations and exclusions which are found in the texts relate to the amount and to the method of providing benefits and not to medical services. The insurance provides, in all countries, for the full range of available medical services.

All systems apply some limit to benefits. The most important of these are: limitation in time, limitation in the amounts payable by the insurance, limitation by an official list of providers or of products, and exclusion of intervention in some cases. Some of these elements are found in a similar way in the six systems. They can now be mentioned briefly.

## No limitation in time

There is a link between the systems in a negative sense: in general no limitation in time for medical care exists. The limitation to 365 days per illness-spell for hospital nursing in the Netherlands is of no real importance because after the 366th day hospital care is chargeable to the general insurance for heavy medical care costs; although in some cases the passing on from one scheme to the other has caused some difficulties (22). The Belgian and the French system have no limitation in time for benefits either in law or in practice. The reimbursements for an ongoing medical treatment can only be stopped after a certain time, when the person concerned ceases to be insured: in Belgium the benefits are cut off at the end of the quarter in which the insurance lapses; in France it is one month after the end of insurance.

In some countries the general system for wage-earners applies a limit for hospital care alone. This was the case in Germany, where the supply of hospital care was provided for the same period as sickness benefits which are set at a maximum of 78 weeks in the three years from the beginning of the illness. It has been abolished as from 1 October 1973.

In Luxemburg, hospital or sanatorium care in the scheme for blue-collar workers was limited to 26 weeks per spell of illness, extendable within three months; this was in line with the supply of sickness benefits. This has been abolished by the reform act of 2 May 1974.

A general limitation in time for medical benefits (that is 180 days per calendar year) still only exists in Italy. However, this limitation does not apply to insurance against tuberculosis, which is organized separately, nor for typical old-age illness. The INAM can decide that in the case of especially long or serious diseases the payment of benefits may be continued after the legal term is expired.

### Official lists

The commitment of the funds can be limited by the institution of an official list, outside which social insurance does not apply. Such lists can exist for techniques of diagnosis and treatment, for drugs and for persons and institutions.

There is no limited list for physicians' services in any European system. In France there exists a *general nomenclature of medical services* which sums up all medical services and determines their relative price, but this list does not have any limiting character. The Belgian *nomenclature*, which has the same function, is formally a restrictive list of insured services. However it is so comprehensive that it is not considered as a limitation of the right to health care benefits. Tariff-lists for medical treatment (by specialists) also exist in the other countries, but they are only used for the calculation of the fees, not for determining the right to benefits.

The situation is different in the area of drugs and appliances. In this field the insured has in general only a right to reimbursement or to free use of the products on the official list. As far as drugs are concerned, this is a typical result of the noticeable and still increasing growth of pharmaceutical consumption. A list of recognized drugs does not seem to exist in Germany; the physicians can prescribe for the insured any medicine they wish to. However, this freedom is limited in a very special way: namely the physicians are in general obliged not to exceed the amount needed in prescribing medicine. There exists a *Regelbetrag* for drugs, ie an average amount per year, to be agreed between the sickness funds and the union of fund physicians. If the average prescribing of one physician exceeds this *Regelbetrag,* he will have to justify his expensive prescriptions and his fees may be reduced.

The Dutch list, called *Regeling en Klapper* and drafted by a mixed central medical-pharmaceutical commission, not only contains the list of medicines which can be prescribed, but also severely regulates their prescription: a proprietary medicine (specialty) or a generic preparation is not allowed if it can be replaced by a cheaper one. Such products can only be prescribed on special permission by the fund. Strictly speaking this list is not legally binding and is only provisional until a definitive arrangement emerges. In practice it is always respected. Thus there is no need for legal sanction (23).

The French and Belgian lists of pharmaceutical specialties and aids and appliances are of a different nature than the nomenclature of medical services, even if they have often the same name. The list of reimbursable products is really restrictive: the product which does not appear on this list cannot be paid for by the insurance, not even if it is similar to a recognized product. If this list is not considered as a strong limitation of the freedom to prescribe, it is because the registration of products in the nomenclature is easily permitted, so that all useful and normally used products appear on this list.

The principle of limiting the right to prescription by an official list of medicines is being discussed in Italy, where a list exists and is in force in the systems managed by the INAM. It will be extended to all schemes in 1975. But it is so broad, that it hardly can be seen as a limitation of therapeutic liberty. The French nomenclature contains 'only' 8,000 products but the Italian has about 17,000 (24)! Luxemburg rejected its German model and introduced an official list. The conclusion may be that the prescription of medicines and related products in the European countries is generally limited by an official list of products. But it has to be added immediately that these lists are often very broad, so that freedom to prescribe may be most limited in the only country without an official list: Germany.

## Cases of exclusion

Health insurance benefits can also be limited in a totally different way, namely by considering situations which must and must not be covered. Social insurance could, in this way, give a definition of what is considered as illness and is not. This is not generally the case in Europe. But reservations are made with regard to some situations, where the need for medical care is deemed not to exist or is due to a fault of the insured himself.

All systems exclude from benefits every insured person who simulates an illness to obtain benefits by fraud or who himself deliberately causes his illness or injury. Differing with civil law, a serious negligence or imprudence is generally not regarded as fraud. Social and technical considerations justify this difference: most illnesses or injuries are in a way caused by the patient's negligence or imprudence to some degree. The general opinion is that for matters of health the insured person is not under a legal obligation to prevent risks (25). Nobody will be excluded from benefits for lung cancer because he has smoked.

Most systems however list some situations where the insured voluntarily endangers himself, so that the risk for the insurance is increased. Typical of these are participation in sporting competitions, disorderly and riotous behaviour, and the abuse of liquor and drugs. But judges are often very lenient towards the insured in these situations.

Insurance liability is generally refused when the insured can look elsewhere for a right to compensation, for example, if he has a legal claim for medical care against another public institution or a regulation for industrial accidents insurance, military health service, etc. This often also applies when a third party can be charged with liability for the condition of the patient (ie an accident).

## Registration with an insurance organization

In all systems the benefits are supplied by insurance organizations distinct (and often independent) from the State. Clearly a claimant should be registered with an organization. However the legal value of registration can be very different, depending upon the concept of insurance obligation.

One concept obliges the insured to join a sickness fund and to pay to it the necessary premiums. If they do not, then they will be penalized. Their membership of the insurance only starts on the day they have complied with their obligations.

Another concept asserts that everybody who fulfils the legal conditions is *ex lege* insured against medical care costs. However, if he joins belatedly he may have to pay his back premiums from the moment that they were legally due. These premiums may possibly be increased or linked with other sanctions. With this concept it is even possible that he can have the advantage of insurance for past episodes, unless excluded from them as a sanction.

An important common trait of the six systems is that the relationship between the insured and the insurance stems from the law governing the general conditions for compulsory insurance. In this way registration with an insurance organization is only a formality, even if necessary actually to obtain benefits.

Germany wrote this principle in to the terms of its law; the membership of the sickness funds starts on the first day of work which creates the obligation to become insured. The same applies in Luxemburg, to the system for blue-collar workers, where all workers are legally members of the regional funds, and, in the systems for white-collar workers, for government officials and free professions, where the law says that the insurance starts on the first day of actual entry into office. The Luxemburg legislation also provides an insurance *ex lege* for the self-employed. The law says that the insurance starts on the day of fulfilment of the conditions for its application.

The general system of health insurance for wage-earners in France has no such expedient rule, but the most authoritative comments, even those of semi-official character, place the matter beyond doubt: registration is considered as an administrative action following the acknowledgement of the eligibility for the social insurance and confirming it (26). The same interpretation is valid in the systems for independents: the insured has to join an insurance organization within a certain period, but his membership counts back to the moment that he fulfilled the conditions for insurance.

This too prevails in the recent system for self-employed farmers. The farmer has a right to insurance benefits from the day that he fulfils the legal conditions. Even if he has not registered or paid premiums, he can assert his right (in the future), provided that he pays his back premium.

The compulsorily insured in the Dutch sickness funds also belong *ex lege* to the insurance scheme from the day that they fulfil the requirements for compulsory insurance. The Sickness Funds Law does not compel workers to join a fund, but it directly declares them insured from the day on which they start work in an area covered by the law. But it states also that the insured who wants to make claims will have to register with a sickness fund. For the compulsorily insured this registration is retroactive to the date of his insurance obligation. The same does not apply to the members of the voluntary old-age insurance, they only enjoy their insurance rights from the week after their registration.

A similar arrangement exists in Italy for the compulsorily insured in the systems administered by the INAM. They are insured *ex lege* and not by their registration with an insurance organization. Chiapelli explicitly rejects the opposite opinion, which is sometimes advanced with regard to the family of the compulsorily insured (27). However, the farmworkers have a special arrangement in a different sense: they are only insured, still *opere legis*, from the establishment of their status as farmworkers, and not from the moment that they start to work as farmworkers. This official ruling appears in the publication of lists of farmworkers, drafted by special provincial and municipal commissions. One finds a similar arrangement for craftsmen: they have also to be registered in lists, drafted by provincial commissions ('*Commissioni provinciali dell'artigianato*') and approved by the sickness funds. The Supreme Court settled a dispute about the value of this registration in the sense that it is constitutive for insurance status, and not declarative, as has often been pretended. The compulsorily insured traders are in the same situation: they only obtain their compulsory insurance status by publication of their names on the lists, drafted by a commission with the complicated name of '*Commissioni provinciali per l'accertamento e la compilazione degli elenchi nominativi degli esercenti attività commerciali e dei respettivi familiari soggetti all'assicurazione obligatoria contro le malattie*'.

Only in Belgium is it not clear that the admission of the insured comes about *ex lege*. In fact, a waiting time is prescribed before there is a right to benefits. A certain number of premiums have to be paid during this waiting time, which implies the obligation to join an insurance institution. Yet a different interpretation is possible. There is, in the first place, the text of article 21 of the Compulsory Health and Invalidity Insurance Act, which says that those 'entitled to medical benefits under the conditions of the law are: . . .' (here follows an enumeration, without any reference to a premium payment). In the second place, a fixed jurisprudence of the Council of State calls the relationship between social insurance and the insured one of public law, which has its origin in the law itself and not in the relation to the employer or to an insurance organization (28).

In sum we can say that in Europe the principle is generally in force whereby benefits legally obtain from the moment the person concerned fulfils the legal conditions. Only in the Belgian arrangement is it not so clear. The Italian arrangements for self-employed and for farmworkers maintain the same principle, but insured status applies only after the fulfilment of another formality: the publication of name-lists in the occupations concerned.

### Previous permission of the insurance institution

It cannot be stated absolutely however that the previous permission of the insurance institution is a necessary condition for entitlement to medical benefits. On the contrary, insurance in all countries generally finances or reimburses medical care costs incurred when delivered by a recognized supplier on the initiative of the patient. The opposite is true, however, for some of the more expensive services. In these cases, except for emergencies, insurance will only apply after consent has been given for the treatment to commence.

In all the countries previous consent by the insurance medical control officer is required for admission to a hospital and for the supply of the more expensive expedients. But all countries also provide for urgent admission to hospital by allowing notice to be given to the insurance organization within a certain period, usually three days after the event.

In France previous permission is required for all services which bear the distinctive 'E' in the *nomenclature,* and for all services which are not mentioned in the *nomenclature*. Permission is considered as obtained when the insurance organization has not replied within ten days to the insured's application. However, the situation is the reverse for the supply of dentures: the fund's silence during the three weeks after the request means that the request is rejected. In the case of an urgent service the request is presented as soon as possible, and the urgency is mentioned.

A similar arrangement with some divergencies can be found in all the countries examined: the procedure may be somewhat different, the stress is laid more on the medical control or on the financial responsibility of the insurance organization, the scale of the services needing previous consent may be wider or narrower but it can in general be said that previous permission is required for every hospital admission, for all prostheses and important appliances, and for unusual services such as psychotherapy, logopedia, etc.

A special kind of preliminary measure, less restrictive, but very useful as a means of medical control, is to be found in the French system under the name *'bulletin d'information'*. This is a special form which has to be completed for services of a certain importance, which have the distinctive 'B' in the *nomenclature,* and for all services which are supplied in a series of ten units (except consultations and visits); in this way, the medical control department of the insurance institution is immediately informed but the rights of the insured are not limited. An analogous measure of supervision does not exist in the other systems.

# 4
# *Relations with suppliers of care*

The relations between social insurance and the suppliers of medical care (physicians, dentists, pharmacists, hospitals, and paramedical auxiliaries, but of course especially the physicians) constitute a special and difficult set of problems, which are characteristic of health care insurance. In this chapter those aspects of the problem which can be considered as common in Europe will be examined. The most important differences in the status of suppliers will be described in Part Two.

### Independent status

To avoid any misunderstanding, it has to be emphasized that our concern is only with the status of medical care suppliers *vis-à-vis the institutions of social insurance*. As a general conclusion it can be stated that it is strikingly similar in the European systems and this holds true for all groups of care suppliers.

This is firstly true for the hospitals (29). They are in all countries divided into two big groups: the public hospitals and the private institutions. There are more public than private hospitals in France and Italy, and more private hospitals in the other countries. The public hospitals belong to the State, to local governments, or to public bodies at a local level. The proportional division is also different in the several countries (predominantly state hospitals in France and Italy, hospitals of the Commissions for Public Assistance in Belgium, and municipal hospitals in the Netherlands and Germany) but the various categories are present everywhere. The private hospitals can be divided into profit and non-profit hospitals; the latter being mostly run by religious orders or by community-based boards of administrators.

It is especially important to note that the hospital services in all European countries are only in exceptional cases connected with the institutions of social insurance. These institutions have in all countries the right to establish their own hospitals, but very seldom does this occur (30). When it does it is mostly limited to outpatient clinics. The insured keeps his freedom to choose the institutions for care even if the insurance organizations provide their own services. In Germany where the funds can limit the free choice of hospital this is in fact not done (31). Thus the hospitals are organized as essentially independent of the insurance organizations.

Still fewer differences exist for pharmacists *vis-à-vis* the social insurance: they are everywhere predominantly independent from the insurance institutions, being considered either as belonging to the liberal professions or as independent traders. However, in some systems the insured can only go to a chemist who has concluded an agreement with his insurance institution: in the Netherlands the insured is registered on the list of his pharmacist, in Germany the funds can limit the choice of pharmacist; but this will not mean that the chemists lose their independent status as against the insurance institutions; it is a matter of freely concluded individual agreements of voluntary adherence to collective agreements. In exceptional cases the insurance institutions organize their own pharmaceutical service. This frequently happens in Belgium and is the rule in Italy within the network of direct benefits. In Italy it is expressly stated that the right of the insured to obtain free prescribed medicines is not limited (32).

The situation of physicians on the fundamental point of dependency or independence *vis-à-vis* insurance is similar in all the six countries; the insured are in most cases cared for by physicians who are not subject to the authority of the insurance institutions.

The type of practice is also very uniform: the free profession type of organization is predominant everywhere. This is true of practically all Belgian physicians, with the exception of some hospital physicians. It applies to about 50,000 German 'Niedergelassene Artze', as opposed to 38,651 hospital physicians and 10,268 physicians in public service or in research work (figures for

1973 [33]). Practically all the physicians in France work in the free profession type of practice with the exception of medical personnel in public hospitals, that is 5,102 full-time and 8,860 part-time staff, in a total of 67,800 physicans (figures for 1971 [34]). In Italy practically all hospital physicians are employed by the hospital but the majority of physicians are still in private practice outside the hospital (35). The situation in the Netherlands and in Luxemburg is similar to that in Belgium: physicians, including the greater proportion of hospital specialists, work as independent men.

It is especially important to point out that the physicians are only in very limited cases dependent on social insurance institutions. This occurs for instance, in the poly-clinics of the Belgian 'mutualiteiten', in certain Dutch industrial funds, in the Italian tuberculosis insurance, in some Italian industrial funds, and in the French systems for railway personnel and some transport companies. The most important exception is found in the numerous dispensaries of the Italian INAM.

The conclusion that the physicians, like the other suppliers of medical care, are generally independent of the insurance institutions is therefore justified. Health insurance has to count on the services of persons and institutions who are generally competent to supply medical care. Normally, insurance does not have its own medical organization, and if it does, it coexists with the medical services for non-insured persons which are also available for insurance members.

This does not mean that the medical services are fully equal for insured and for non-insured patients. Until recently in Germany and the Netherlands a number of physicians had separate waiting-rooms for both groups and still most doctors will advertise special consultation hours for insured patients (36). But at least they are *the same* doctors who take care of insured and non-insured (private) patients!

The six countries differ therefore from certain other European countries where social health insurance (in the form of a national health service) runs its own medical services. The national health service in the socialist countries, for instance, organizes complete medical services; the Secretary of State for Health and Social Security in Great Britain arranges complete specialist and hospital care within the framework of the National Health Service; in Sweden medical care is supplied by hospitals permanently staffed and by district medical officers under the authority of the county councils (37).

## Agreements

Existing international comparisons between the social security systems in the EEC countries show that social health insurance operates in all these countries by agreements between the insurance institutions and the suppliers of medical care (38). This has to be considered as an immediate and inevitable consequence of the description given above: since the institutions of social insurance do not have their own medical services, they have to rely upon the services of the existing physicians, hospitals, and other care suppliers (39).

However, the mere existence of these agreements is not the only element of relationship among the Six. Some other points of similarity are present. They concern mainly the method of concluding agreements (the partners in the agreement, the institutional framework), the requirement of ratification by government, the main outlines of the contents of agreements, and, an important element, their field of application.

The necessary agreements between the suppliers of care and the insurance institutions are, in each of the countries, concluded by unions of suppliers and by the higher bodies or unions of insurance organizations.

In France, conventions are agreed between the most representative professional unions of care suppliers and the health insurance funds; this is done at the national level for physicians and kinesitherapists and at the level of the *département* or of the territory of the *caisse primaire d'assurance maladie* for all other suppliers of care. In Belgium, the agreements or settlements are concluded between those unions of suppliers which are considered as representative and the national confederations of the insurance organizations. They meet as standing national commissions composed in equal parts of representatives of the care suppliers, and the insurance organizations.

The German sickness funds conclude agreements with the unions of physicians who work for them. These agreements are in force over the state but mainly dictated on the federal level by agreements between the federal union of funds' physicians *(Kassenärtzliche Bundesvereinigung)* and the federal organizations of health funds. The Dutch sickness funds conclude agreements with individual care suppliers. These agreements derive their content from national agreements, concluded between the unions of suppliers and the unions of sickness funds, under the general supervision of the Sickness Funds Council.

Italy originally applied a system of local or differentiated agreements between the different unions of suppliers and the several insurance institutions. However, because of the unsatisfactory nature of this procedure, the accent has been shifted to direct negotiations on a national level between the national confederation of the leagues of physicians and the Minister of Labour, who supervises all the institutions of social security. The result is not formally an agreement but a set of regulations concerning the relationship with the medical profession, issued by the INAM. In reality, however, this text reflects the agreement between the physicians and the government (40).

The agreements with suppliers in Luxemburg can also be concluded on the regional level. However, in fact agreements exist only on a national level, between the *Association des médecins et des médecins dentistes* and the associations of sickness funds.

Consequently, there are collective agreements in all countries, concluded between unions of suppliers and bodies or unions of insurance institutions on the regional or the national level (with a preference for the national level).

It has however to be stated that conformity at this point does not imply real similarities. The legal status of these collective agreements varies: the relations with the suppliers of care are in some countries (or for some systems) direct and binding by collective agreements (as in France, Germany, Luxemburg, partially in Belgium, and some systems in Italy); elsewhere, the collective agreements are only the framework for individual agreements (the Netherlands, partially Belgium, and some Italian schemes).

INSTITUTIONAL FRAMEWORK

Agreements are concluded mainly within an institutional framework, guaranteeing a permanent contact between the parties to the agreement.

The situation in Belgium is typical in this respect. The agreement of 25 June 1964 between the physicians and the government entrusted the conclusion of agreements to a public body called the *'medico-mutualistische commissie'*, composed equally of representatives of physicians and of the sickness funds. In France, the conventions must be approved on a departmental level by the *commissions régionales tripartites* and at a national level by the *Commission nationale tripartite* which is intended as 'a method of encounter and dialogue' between the parties concerned (41). Under the national convention for physicians and for kinesitherapists in every *département* a *commission médico-sociale paritaire* with equal representation of the funds and of the physicians, has to control the execution of the agreement. All problems concerning the relations between physicians and health insurance are examined by a *commission médico-sociale paritaire nationale*. The Sickness Funds Council plays the same role in agreements with the suppliers of care in the Dutch legislation. The concluded agreements are confirmed (after being approved by a commission) and their execution is supervised by the Sickness Funds Council. It is not composed exclusively of representatives of the care suppliers and the sickness funds, but they are well represented.

In Germany there exist commissions of physicians and sickness funds and of dentists and sickness funds on the level of the states and of the federation (*Landesausschüsse und Bundesausschüsse*). These commissions give directives for drafting the agreements. The regulations of both the funds and the unions of fund physicians have to contain provision for the directives of these commissions to be observed. If no agreement is reached, the arising conflict is not resolved by these commissions, but by a court of arbitration which is, however, very similar in its composition. In Luxemburg there is only a control body on the economic justification of medical services in the absence of an agreement. The function is taken by an arbitration committee following the German model.

The system of agreements in Italy works also within an institutional framework to supervise its execution and to deal with possible conflicts. Thus, the national agreement of 3 August 1966 established national commissions, composed of representatives of physicians, insurance institutions, workers, and employers, which will result in better co-operation between the insurance and care suppliers, and control committees with an equal representation of the INAM and of the care suppliers. These are charged with supervision at the provincial and national level, of the execution of agreements. Similar structures are established by the national agreement of 19 May 1972 between specialists and health insurance for practice in health insurance dispensaries.

This outline shows that the need is felt in all countries to bring the conclusion of agreements within an institutional framework for on-going contact between the parties and for supervision of the execution of agreements. However, this institutional framework is achieved in very different ways: in some countries one single body takes charge of the conclusion of agreements, their execution and supervision, in other countries these tasks are divided between several bodies. In some countries the institutional framework exists at the conclusion of agreements, in others at the approval or ratification stage. The institutions may work on a local, regional, or national level, or on several levels. They can be composed exclusively of representatives of the insurance institutions and of the care suppliers but can also have within them representatives of the employers and the trade unions and/or the government.

RATIFICATION BY GOVERNMENT

Health care supply is no longer the business only of doctors, hospitals, and other care suppliers, nor of the care suppliers and insurance institutions acting together; in modern society governments have an interest (42). This principle applies particularly to the relationship between suppliers and social insurance. Social insurance today has become the most important element of organization in medical practice and service (43), where once it did not affect them because of its small size. It is no surprise that (in principle free) agreements between the care suppliers and insurance-bodies are in each country subject to government ratification. Only Germany appears to be the exception.

A direct ratification can be required but it can also be indirectly implied through government supervision of a special body which controls the agreements.

*Direct* government ratification is required for agreements in Belgium and Italy. National settlements and the national or regional agreements in Belgium are only valid if they have been submitted for ratification and approved by the Minister of Social Affairs. Agreements in Italy are ratified by the competent public authority, which issues them in the form of a regulation. Only for the private hospitals are the agreements approved by an intermediate authority: the senior medical officer of the province or the region.

Ratification in other countries (France and the Netherlands) is granted by a public body, where the government and the parties to the agreement are represented. The French agreements are submitted for ratification to a regional three-party commission and ultimately to a *Commission nationale tripartite,* composed of representatives of the recognized care suppliers organizations, representatives of the highest executive bodies of the insurance institutions and representatives of the ministers of social affairs, agriculture (who controls the social security system for farmers), economic affairs, and finance. The commission may be differently composed according to the nature of the agreements to be discussed but it always includes one-third of representatives of the administration, one-third of representatives of the concerned professional groups, and one-third of representatives of the insurance institutions. The new national conventions for physicians and for kinesitherapists obey different rules. They are ratified directly by the government.

A similar structure is to be found in the Dutch *Sickness Funds Council,* which is also responsible for the ratification of agreements between the insurance and the so-called co-operators, the care suppliers. This council has a larger composition: its members are appointed by five partners, the government, the care suppliers, the sickness funds, the employers, and the employees, and for the supervision of the special medical care costs insurance it is expanded with members appointed by the insurance companies and by the civil service health insurance schemes. This council has indeed a wider area of activity: it is not only the structure for consultation between the parties but it is also considered the truly responsible arranger of the sickness funds insurance (44).

This ratification process is in fact not far removed from the situation in those countries where the government deals directly with the agreements. For the decision in these councils is in the main dependent on the attitude which government representatives assume during the deliberations. One may suppose that the opinions of the care suppliers and the insurance institutions and those of the employers and employees will cancel each other out. The supremacy of government representation in the councils is even expressly sanctioned by veto powers of the minister. This veto is exercised in the Netherlands by the Minister of Social Affairs and Public Health, who can send delegates to the council and to whom all the decisions of the council have to be communicated, and in France for suppliers other than physicians by a *comité interministériel,* composed of representatives of the ministers of social affairs, agriculture, economic affairs, and finance, presided over by a *Conseiller d'Etat* or a justice in the *Cour des Comptes.*

The situation in Luxemburg is rather similar to that in France and in the Netherlands, even if formally it is related to that in Germany. The *Code des assurances sociales,* which is the generally applicable system for blue-collar workers, provides that agreements with the care suppliers have to be ratified by a *Commission de Conciliation et d'Arbitrage.* The composition of this body recalls the French and Dutch ratification bodies: the president is a magistrate of the Court of Justice, who sits with two assessors, appointed by the minister; the commission co-opts two further members, representing the concerned group of care suppliers. The decision of this commission takes effect after ratification by the Minister of Labour and Social Affairs: he has the last word.

Although technically this arrangement is to be found in the legislation for blue-collar workers, it does apply to all systems of social insurance for health care in Luxemburg.

Only in Germany are agreements not presented to the government for ratification. The situation in Germany rather resembles that in Luxemburg: there are commissions of reconciliation and arbitration, here called *Schiedsamt,* but they only act in the absence of agreements, and not to supervise concluded agreements. Nevertheless it would be wrong to conclude that in Germany the partners to the agreement have complete freedom in contracting. Public supervision comes about in another stage of the negotiations: the unions of fund doctors and the sickness funds are obliged to write in their regulations that they have to conform to the directives, drafted by the *Landes- und Bundesausschüsse,* where physicians and sickness funds define rules for the supply of medical care. These directives concern, among other matters, both the contents of and the procedure to conclude agreements and have to be ratified by the federal Minister of Labour. These directives can be considered as collective agreements, which fix the principles of the relations between suppliers and carriers which local agreements only elaborate in greater detail. Thus Germany is not an exception after all: the collective agreements between the suppliers of care and the insurance institutions are subject to the ratification of the government and this in the same way as occurs in Belgium and Italy.

CONTENTS

The agreements between the suppliers of care and the social insurance are naturally very different in the various countries. The contents of the agreements may even within the same country be very different according to the groups involved. But the general object of these agreements is in a large measure the same. The most important group of agreements are those with the physicians.

The agreements first of all fix the tariffs of the medical fees. The agreements establish in all countries the amount of the tariffs.

The tariff form is prescribed in Belgium, in France, and in Luxemburg, by a *nomenclature* of the medical services. The agreements can only fix the tariff by attaching a certain value to the key-letters of this nomenclature. In the other countries the partners are free to fix within certain legal limits the form and the amount of the payment for medical services. In France these tariffs cannot exceed certain maxima, fixed by *interministerial* decree.

Under the new national convention of 1971 the tariffs for physicians and kinesitherapists are fixed by agreement between the suppliers and the ministers, to be renewed each year.

In the Netherlands the law only demands that the agreements contain regulations on some points, and that the supply of medical help is at least to the extent required by the law, and its executive decree. The German agreements are only required to 'guarantee' an efficient and sufficient medical care. The law further provides that the funds will free themselves of their obligations by paying to the union of physicians a lump sum fixed by certain agreed criteria. The INAM in Italy provides two systems of care benefits: the direct and indirect benefits. In the case of indirect benefits there is no link between the supplier and the insurance institution and so there is no agreement. The direct benefit system is not fixed by law, the payment of the suppliers being completely regulated by agreements.

Hospital care is an important exception. Here, the tariffs are generally fixed and supervised by the government. The insurance institutions do conclude agreements with the hospitals, but these deal mainly with problems other than the amount of the tariffs. The tariffs for hospitals in the Netherlands are fixed or supervised by the *Central Orgaan Ziekenhuistarieven*, established by the law on hospitals tariffs. In France these tariffs are fixed by decree for the public hospitals, by the *préfet* for public clinics of the public hospitals and by an agreement for private hospitals. However, these agreement tariffs need to be ratified by the *préfet* on advice of a special commission. In Belgium the price per day in hospital wards and the maximum supplement in a (semi-) private room are fixed by the minister under the hospital law. In Germany the day price is regulated per *Land* in the framework of federal rules. Nor are hospital prices freely determined in Italy; they are subject to government measures, which have existed since the prewar period and which are being adapted to suit forthcoming reform which seeks to integrate hospitals into a national health service. Hospital tariffs are determined by the board of administrators of each hospital institution, according to strict rules set by the hospital law. As of 1 January 1975 hospital care will be delivered directly by the regional authorities (Act of 17 August 1974, no. 386, art. 12).

The agreements do not only deal with the tariffs of the suppliers of care. They also cover the administrative formalities, the beginning and the duration of engagement, notice and renewal of agreements, limitations on the application of the agreed tariffs, supervision of compliance, and sanctions against breaches.

To this end the Dutch agreements provide administrative formalities for registration on the list of the family doctor and for transfer to another family doctor, for the settlement of fees, for the care of insured people when away from home, etc. The French agreements describe the administrative formalities to be fulfilled for every supply of medical services, the documents to be shown and forms to be used. The Italian settlements between the physicians and the INAM oblige the physicians to use the forms of the INAM for establishing incapacity to work, for consulting a specialist, for prescribing medicines, special examinations or hospital admission, etc. The Belgian agreements with physicans provide that the physician will give to the insured all the documents necessary for receipt of reimbursement by the insurance. The German agreements, especially the national agreements or *Mantelvertrage*, lay down those formalities which have to be fulfilled: the issue of sickness certificates, the keeping of records for all patients, etc. Finally the Luxemburg agreements have these administrative stipulations: the suppliers of care are obliged to deliver to the insured, free of cost, all administrative certificates which are necessary for the proper working of the insurance as long as this does not occupy too much of the doctor's time.

Similar, but not identical, stipulations about the field of application of the engagement (duration, cancellation, renewal) can be found in the texts of the agreement in the different systems and countries. It is especially important to look at the lines of similarity on the stipulations concerning the *supervision* of the working of the agreements and sanctions against non-execution.

The Belgian settlements with the physicians and dentists and also the agreements with other suppliers of care stipulate that the supervision of their performance be carried out by the relevant commission itself; under the agreement the insured can claim from the person who exceeds the tariffs, damages of three times the amount of the surplus, with a minimum of 500 BF. However, only the Councils of the *Orde van geneesheren* (League of Physicians) are competent to deal with abuses in the execution or prescription of services. The Dutch model agreements create supervisory commissions and judicial commissions to promote co-operation between the partners and to decide on complaints. They can blame the sickness funds or the physicians, oblige them to redress the injustice, and impose fines up to a maximum of 1,000 fl. (physicians) or 5,000 fl. (funds).

The French conventions necessarily refer to the legal arrangement, which provides that the commissions be equally representative in the *département* as well as at the national level. These commissions have to supervise the working of agreements. They can examine the reasons why a rate has been exceeded and oblige the supplier to return the surplus. They can issue warnings or accusations with or without publication, and they can even deny temporarily or definitively the right to supply care to be refunded by social insurance. Since the Act of 3 July 1971, this does not apply to physicians any more. Here the *commission médico-sociale paritaire* will propose to the health insurance fund to exclude a physician from health insurance practice. The Italian agreements with the medical profession also provide for the institution of supervisory bodies, composed equally of representatives of the INAM and of physicians. Their function is to improve the relationship between the physicians and the insurance institutions and to guarantee the proper execution of engagements; they can apply disciplinary measures, even exclude physicians who do not observe their obligations under insurance.

This also occurs in the Luxemburg agreements. These create a *Commission de surveillance* (commission of supervision) composed of two physicians, two delegates of the union of insurance funds, and an independent chairman. This commission can summon any physician accused of over-servicing or over-prescribing. Such physicians can be warned or found guilty. In serious cases they will be reported to the disciplinary authority, the *College médical*. The agreements between the German unions of fund doctors and their sickness funds arrange permanent agreement commissions (*Vertragsausschüsse*) which have to guarantee that the contract be executed in good faith. Other bodies are established by law: commissions on the level of the states and the federation are charged with fixing general directives for efficient and justified medical care and of improving relations between the suppliers of care and the sickness funds. The law also provides for commissions of arbitration whose duty it is to bring the parties to an arrangement when they cannot by themselves come to an understanding. The sanctions against the individual physicians are not within the competence of these bodies since the physicians have no direct relationship to the sickness fund, but only to the union of physicians.

This union establishes a supervisory commission, which checks the accounts of every physician to see if they are prescribing useless or exaggerated services and/or causing elaborate expenditures. The physician concerned is invited to justify himself. If he does not do so, a corresponding reduction of his fees or the repayment of certain expenses is ordered. Even his membership of the union can be withdrawn and consequently permission to take care of insured patients (45). This, however, is within the competence of a different commission, which also deals with admission to practise in the fund.

## IMPOSING TARIFFS

Reliance on a system of agreements creates problems when agreements for certain groups are lacking or when an existing agreement is not renewed. Most countries have responded similarly to this problem: in the absence of agreements official tariffs can be imposed. Naturally, this principle is elaborated in different ways in the different countries. The tariffs are, in some countries, directly fixed by the government (46), in other countries by a legal or conventional court of arbitration (47). They can be in force for the whole country or only for certain regions. The imposition of tariffs can be at the discretion of government, or it can be an obligation according to law from the moment that the agreement ceases to exist. In the latter case there is no gap in the protection of the insured people.

The situation is peculiar in the Netherlands and Italy. The Dutch minister can mediate between the partners in the absence of an agreement, but he has no actual powers to impose a solution; he could have this power on the basis of a general price-control legislation but this seems not to be used in the medical care field (48). In Italy no provision of any kind is to be found in the legislation or in the agreements; one relies on the goodwill of the partners.

## Paying for services

The actual payment of doctors will be dealt with later. However, it is worth noting common elements as they are particularly important for the development of a harmonious system. Three such factors are:

(a) The existence of a list for the payment of technical-medical services.

(b) Fixed payment for the supervision of patients admitted to a hospital.

(c) Freedom to charge supplementary fees to patients who have *special requirements* and particularly for patients who want a private room in hospital.

LIST OF SERVICES

In all countries there is a schedule of medical services supplied by specialists. Moreover, in a number of countries, such a list is used also for GPs and paramedical auxiliaries.

A schedule, in the sense used here, is a nominal list which covers all usual medical services, giving their price or an indication of their relative value. It is the basis of the whole system of supply of medical care under social insurance in these countries.

The Dutch model agreement between the unions of sickness funds and the national union of specialists contains eight groups of services. Each type of service is precisely described and numbered and specialist's fee is fixed together with that of the anaesthetist and possibly of the assistant. In tariff-group VIII (radiology and radiotherapy) the fee of the specialist and the compensations for expenditure are indicated separately.

The German schedule (*Gebührenordnung*) is somewhat less detailed. It is fixed by the government, just as in Belgium and in France, but it plays a very different role in the distribution of medical care. Each type of service is estimated in the 'Gebührenordnung' by a certain amount in Deutsche marks. However, this is not the amount paid to the physicians: at the quarterly settlement between the *Kassenärtzliche Vereinigung* and the individual physicians, the values of all supplied services are added and compared with the total amount which has been paid by the 'Krankenkasse' under the agreement. Finally, after the deduction of administrative expenses (and possible reductions for excessive prescriptions), the fees are set, proportionally raised or reduced according to the relationships between both amounts. Another 'Gebührenordnung', of a totally different nature, is in force for the *Ersatzkassen* and for the other funds which apply an over-all fee-for-service payment system. This tariff list indicates immediately the fee due for every service given. It is not imposed by the government, but is subject to negotiations between the physicians and the funds.

A list of services is in principle not needed in Italy for those specialists who supply care in dispensaries, directly managed by the insurance institutions. The specialists in these dispensaries are salaried. But it does exist for the purpose of paying them for their work outside office hours. Specialist help is also supplied outside the dispensaries by specialists under agreement. These are compensated per item of service according to a detailed tariff, which is very similar in structure to the French and Belgian schedules, the Dutch specialist tariff, and the German 'Gebührenordnung'. These tariffs are fixed by agreement between the insurance institutions and the physicians concerned.

The situation in Luxemburg is broadly similar to that in Belgium and France: the law enables the ministers of social affairs and public health to establish by common decree ('arrêté conjoint') a general schedule of medical services. But a very special feature is that as far as the employees and the officials are concerned a differential tariff is fixed by the agreement, according to the income class of the insured.

PAYMENT FOR SUPERVISION IN THE HOSPITAL

Generally doctors are paid composite fees or lump sums for supervising patients in hospital rather than by fee-for-service (49). In Germany and Italy the hospital physicians generally receive a salary for their work in the hospital. The hospital physicians ('Chefärtze', 'Oberärtze', and 'Assistenzärtze') in Germany are permanently attached to hospitals, both public and private. Their contract provides for the payment of a salary with the exception of treatment for patients in private rooms. Here they can charge fees. This system does not apply to the so-called 'Beleg-ärtze', who have no attachment to the hospital other than the right to admit their patients to certain beds. Their services are given in the same manner as for care outside the hospital. But the tariffs applying to the 'Beleg-ärtze' provide for lump-sum payments for care of hospitalized patients. These are settled in special agreements between the funds and the fund-physicians. Compensation of physicians in the Italian hospitals, public as well as private, is composed of a fixed and a variable part, the latter also calculated at a flat rate. The physician only charges fees for non-insured patients or for patients in private rooms. Both in Germany and in Italy those hospital physicians paid a fixed amount do not have a direct relationship with health insurance.

In the four other countries (the Netherlands, Belgium, Luxemburg, and France) hospital physicians are paid by salary only in public hosptials. In Belgium this is not entirely the case. Non-salaried hospital physicians are paid according to the tariffs of health insurance in the same way as the physicians who treat ambulant patients. But these tariffs invariably establish lump-sum payments per day for the observation of in-patients. These lump-sums appear in the Belgian schedule of medical services. The Dutch model-agreement between sickness funds and the specialist provides that hospital treatment for certain specialized cases is paid for at a fixed rate whereas some other specialist treatments are paid by a composite fee covering pre- and post-treatment care. In France, the medical supervision of hospital patients is paid by a fixed amount per patient and per day in the open wards of public hospitals and in the private institutions according to the fee schedule. The lump-sum compensation for care in a hospital is also arranged in Luxemburg where the law departs from the strong principle of payment per item of service (50).

In all these cases, the compensation for medical supervision in a hospital does not cover all those technical services which are mentioned separately in the schedules. Certain technical services can be cumulated with the lump-sum payments. But the principle of a fixed payment for hospital medical care is to some extent at least applicable everywhere.

PRIVATE ROOM IN HOSPITAL

In the various systems admission to a private room in hospital is considered a luxury, which will not be provided at the expense of social insurance. If the insured asks for a single room without any medical need for one, the difference in price between a private room and the common ward is paid by the insured himself. At the same time the physician will be entitled to exceed the health insurance rates in his fees. In most systems fees in excess of the hospital tariff are due when admission to a care-class higher than the lowest is sought. The extra charge varies with the required class. This is the situation in the Netherlands, Germany, Luxemburg, and France.

In principle in Germany, the funds should not pay anything if the patient chooses to be admitted to a private room. In reality the funds pay the cost of care in the common ward, and the insured pays the remainder (51).

The Belgian legislation provides that normally the hospital can only charge a supplement for special requirements if the patient wants a single bedroom. A two-bed room can involve a limited supplement, the amount of which is fixed by the government, if at least half of the number of beds in the institution are available for patients who want to be cared for in the normal way.

In Italy the practice is the same as in the Netherlands, Germany, France, and Luxemburg.

Admission to a private room is considered as a special requirement only if medically necessary and results in the application of higher fees if this requirement is not met. The Belgian agreement with the physicians provides this expressly (52). It is not clearly formulated in the French legislation but it can be included in the expression *les exigences particulières de l'assuré*; which is a justification for exceeding the agreed tariffs. Until recently, the choice of a private room in a hospital would certainly have been held as a sign of affluence which was also regarded as a motive for exceeding the agreement tariffs.

The Dutch legislation does not contain a positive definition of the right to exceed tariffs, neither do the agreements between specialists and sickness funds. However, it is generally accepted in practice that specialists charge their own fees for patients who are not in the lowest care class (53).

The German 'Krankenkassen' conclude agreements with hospitals whose medical staff are salaried. However there are the 'Belegärtze', who are not salaried but have beds at their disposal: they generally belong to the 'Kassenärztliche Vereinigung' and work within the conditions of the insurance. All hospital physicians collect their fee themselves from those patients who are admitted to the first- or second-class wards of the hospital.

The Luxemburg agreements also provide that tariffs may be exceeded when the patient has special requirements. The fees are, according to different formulae, adapted to the class of accommodation.

In Italy, as in Germany, where hospital physicians of the private as well as the public hospitals are salaried, the same situation prevails. The insured patient does in principle not pay the hospital: hospital tariffs include medical care, generally by way of a fixed lump-sum per day for medical services. However, private fees can be charged to patients who require a private room; private rooms though may not exceed a maximum of 10 per cent of the hospital beds.

## Free choice

The principle of free choice of supplier of care prevails in all six states based on the need for a relationship of trust between the physician and the patient.

This principle is not explicitly mentioned in the Belgian legislation, perhaps because it is considered self-evident. But it is expressly proclaimed in the national agreements between the sickness funds and certain groups of suppliers of care. It is still remarkable that the aspect of free choice is not mentioned in the national settlements with the most important groups: physicians, dentists, and hospitals. The important St John's agreement of 25 July 1964, which ended a serious conflict with the physicians and began the real enforcement of the law on health insurance, strangely omits mention of free choice. But the Minister of Social Affairs, E. Leburton, proclaimed it in Parliament on 18 June 1963.

The French legislation plainly states that each insured person has the free choice of supplier. The same can be said for Germany: the principle of free choice of physician and dentist is written into the law itself. There is one exception: the scheme for coal-miners, where a district medical officer is designated by the 'Knappschaftskrankenkasse'. The law in the Netherlands also states that the insured is left a free choice of persons and institutions who supply care under insurance.

Free choice in Luxemburg is not directly written in law; but one finds it confirmed in the competent comments of the chairman of the Luxemburg office of social insurance (54). The national agreements between the Italian physicians and the INAM stipulate expressly that the insured chooses freely between the physicians who figure on the insurance lists.

The similarity between the systems does not end here, for it should be added that this free choice is in fact also somewhat limited in all systems. These limitations can be of two kinds: in some systems free choice is only between physicians who have concluded an agreement with the insurance and who consequently appear on a panel. In other countries, the limitation is based on financial checks: it is more expensive for the insured when consulting a physician who has no contract with the insurance. The first kind of limitation is the most frequent: in the Netherlands, the insured has to choose a physician or a dentist who has made an agreement with the sickness fund; in Germany, free choice can only be made between physicians who are members of the union of fund-physicians; in Italy, insured persons can only choose freely among physicians who have registered as fund physicians by enrolling their name on a list for this purpose.

Financial restriction may be more important in practice for the insured: the lists of physicians in the fund are usually very extensive, whereas the chance of being treated by a physician at fund rates is relatively small in the countries which claim unlimited freedom of choice.

Such a financial limitation exists in France. In cases where the insured chooses a physician or a hospital not bound by agreement, and also if he has special requirements as specified by the *commission médico-sociale paritaire départementale* and still more if the physician is mentioned on the list of specially competent persons enjoying a permanent right to exceed the tariffs, in all these cases the insured will be financially penalized. An analogous situation exists in Belgium. The insured may be reimbursed up to the usual amount if he chooses a care supplier outside the agreement system, but he runs the risk of having to pay a higher fee. Moreover, even a physician who works under the agreement can freely fix his fee if the income of the insured is higher than 215,000 BF (16,000 BF added per dependant), and if the patient is admitted in a separate room in the hospital, or if he attends by appointment or has any other special requirements.

In sum the principle of free choice of physician is premised everywhere as an essential principle, but the exercise of this free choice undergoes a certain limitation in all systems, either by the institution of a list of physicians in the fund or by a system of agreements with financial checks.

### Clinical freedom
All European systems of health insurance take the same attitude to clinical freedom: physicians are asked to provide care in the

most economical way compatible with efficiency, and monitoring tries to reveal abuse.

The principle of therapeutic freedom is maintained in all systems. In Belgium, it is clearly formulated in the text of law itself, which says that the physician must judge in conscience and in full freedom about the care required (55).

The Italian national agreement with the physicians also states this very clearly: 'the physician works according to his science and his conscience' (56).

The prohibition of superfluous services is somewhat different in the various systems. The German law says: 'the medical care should be sufficient and efficacious; but it should not exceed necessity'. This formula is, in the German jurisprudence and doctrine, considered as basic to social health insurance (57). The Luxemburg legislation copies this text. The Dutch legislation says in the same way: 'The sickness funds take necessary measures to prevent unneeded services and expenses, which are above necessity.' A criterion to measure medical services is proposed for the enforcement of this law: 'medical care in amount is defined by what is usual among professional colleagues' (58).

France maintains a norm only for the prescription of drugs, prostheses, and other appliances. Examinations and treatment by the physician himself are not checked at all.

An analogous situation exists in Italy. There is no express limitation to the amount of services provided by the physicians and the hospitals and this is because the enforcement decree, which would decide upon the amount of health care benefits, has not been published since 1943. Chiappelli observed scornfully that Italy has celebrated the tenth, twentieth, and twenty-fifth anniversary of its absence (59). However there is a certain limitation in the prescription of medicine which results from the existence of a list of recognized medicines and by the rule that no expensive medicine should be prescribed if less expensive but as effective ones exist.

Nevertheless, the most liberal rule exists in Belgium where no limitation at all is placed on clinical freedom. This liberty is explicitly guaranteed by law. Yet the medical control officers of the sickness funds have competence to supervise the supply of medical care, but this competence is limited to the possibility of advising on the treatment given by the physician. This is seen as a means of improving the diagnosis or the therapy: but the physician is under no obligation to follow the advice.

All systems naturally try to avert abuses in medical care and prescriptions. Control mechanisms are organized in a different way in the various systems but they have one important element in common: the control of physicians is exercised exclusively by other physicians. In all systems special physicians are recruited for this purpose by the insurance agencies.

In all cases these controlling physicians work under the responsibility or supervision of a board which is also exclusively medical. In Belgium this is the board of the medical control department of the National Health Insurance Institution. In the Netherlands control is co-ordinated by a Foundation for Central Organization of Medical Control (CBS), set up in consultation between the organizations of insurance agencies. No actual authority on the controlling physicians is exercised but care is taken to co-ordinate the control activity locally.

The German system does not provide a body under the sickness fund but a special committee is set up within the groups of physicians themselves. These committees have the power to limit the fees of the physicians if the services or prescriptions are systematically excessive.

In France, for several years the medical control has been removed from the competence of the insurance agencies and organized as a national service under the authority of the 'Caisse Nationale d'assurance-maladie'. But there is a medical board ('Haut Comité Médical') which co-ordinates and directs the control. It also examines all national problems of medical control in social security. The board is exclusively composed of physicians assigned by decree.

In fact, the national convention between the physicians and the insurance has created a second type of medical control. The medical sections of the *commissions médico-sociales paritaires départementales* establish computer profiles of the individual physicians' practice and prescriptions. If his profile exceeds the average in an abnormal way, the practitioner will be required to justify. If he cannot, and the next profile does not show significant change, he may be reported to the *caisse* for exclusion.

In Luxemburg no special medical body is competent to deal with medical control. No real sanctions can however be taken against a physician unless the 'Collège Médical' is invoked. This 'Collège Médical' or medical board is the supreme authority on all medical obligations. In Italy, possible conflicts between the physicians and the insurance institutions on the subject of medical control as against doctors who are suspected of abuse, are judged exclusively by a provincial commission composed of physicians appointed by the government, the INAM, the employers, the employees, and the league of physicians. Appeal from its decisions to a central commission is possible.

## REFERENCES

1. BURNS, E. M., *Social Security and Public Policy* (New York, 1956), pp. 128–9. There is a fourth form: private insurance. It is not treated here, because it is not considered as part of social insurance. A contrary opinion is found in LINDEN, CHR., 'Die private Krankenversicherung versteht sich als Teil der Sozialversicherung', *Sozialer Fortschritt*, **7** (1969), 163–7.
2. These figures are different from Table 1 (p. 50) because they exclude the voluntarily insured.
3. For the Netherlands: VELDKAMP, G. M. J., *Inleiding tot de sociale verzekering* (Amsterdam, 1963); MANNOURY, J., *Hoofdtrekken van de Sociale Verzekering* (Alphen a.d. Rijn, 1967); DE GUASCO, R. A. F., VAN DER MEER, R. H., and HUIJ, J. A., *Het Sociaal Verzekeringsrecht in Nederland* (Alphen a.d. Rijn, 1971); for Italy: LEVI SANDRI, L., *Istituzioni di legislazione sociale* (Milan, 1966); FERRARI, G., and LAGONEGRO, G., *Le assicurazioni sociali* (Milan, 1971).
4. ROEMER, MILTON I., *L'Organisation des soins médicaux dans le cadre de la sécurité sociale* (Geneva, BIT, 1969), pp. 149–52.
5. FULCHER, D., *Medical Care Systems* (Geneva, BIT, 1974), pp. 23–36.
6. WANNAGAT, G., *Lehrbuch des Sozialversicherungsrechts*, Band I, (Tübingen, 1965), p. 73; NETTER, F., *La Sécurité sociale et ses principes* (Paris, 1959), p. 196.
7. DUPEYROUX, J. J., *Développement et tendances des régimes de sécurité sociale des pays membres des Communautés Européennes et de la Grande-Bretagne* (Luxemburg, ECSA, 1966), pp. 73–84.

8. VAN LANGENDONCK, J., *De Harmonisering van de Sociale Verzekering voor Gezondheidszorgen in de EEG* (Leuven, 1971), p. 154.
9. ABEL-SMITH, B., *An International Study of Health Expenditure* (Geneva, 1967), WHO Public Health Papers 32, table 8, 47.
10. INTERNATIONAL LABOUR OFFICE, *The Cost of Social Security, Seventh International Inquiry, 1964–1966* (Geneva, 1972), table 9, pp. 358–71.
11. LAURENT, A., 'La Sécurité sociale et l'évolution des sociétés', *Droit Social*, **4** (1967), 242.
12. COMMISSION DES COMMUNAUTES EUROPEENNES, *Indicateurs de sécurité sociale* (Brussels, EEC, 1969), p. 30; CONSIGLIO NAZIONALE DELL'ECONOMIA E DEL LAVORO, *I problemi dell'armonizzazione dei sistemi di sicurezza sociale dei paesi della C.E.E.* (Rome, 1969), table 25, pp. 62–63.
13. The difference between employers' and employees' contributions is largely theoretical; see BUREAU INTERNATIONAL DU TRAVAIL, *Les Aspects sociaux de la coopération économique européenne* (Geneva, BIT, 1956), p. 45; COPPINI, M. A., *Les Incidences économiques de la sécurité sociale* (Brussels, EEC).
14. Since the recent reform by the Act of 2 May 1974, *Mémorial* (Luxemburg), **33** (1974), 583–606.
15. BECKER, E., *Von der Sozialpolitik zur Sozialreform* (Recklingshausen, 1968), p. 98.
16. ROCCARDI, G., 'Il sistema dell'assicurazione malattia nel quadro della sicurezza sociale', *I problemi della sicurezza sociale* (Rome, 1970), **1**, 7–13; the most recent example is the *Decreto-legge* of 8 July 1974, converted into the law of 17 August 1974, providing for a government subsidy of 2,700 billion lire to cover the debts of health insurance institutions with the hospitals.
17. DUPEYROUX, J. J., *et al.*, 'L'Efficacité de la sécurité sociale, rapport français', *Annuaire 1970, de l'Institut Europeén de Sécurité Sociale* (Leuven, 1970), p. 144.
18. —— *Développement et tendances des régimes de sécurité sociale dans les pays membres des Communautés Européennes et de la Grande-Bretagne* (Luxemburg, ECSA, 1966), pp. 171–2.
19. ASSOCIATION INTERNATIONALE DE LA MUTUALITE, *Les Relations avec le corps médical* (Geneva, 1966), p. 3.
20. CHIAPPELLI, U., *L'assicurazione sociale di malattia* (Milan, 1969), p. 17.
21. JAEGER, C. H., *Krankheit des Arbeitnehmers* (Freiburg im Breisgau, 1968), pp. 18–23.
22. De sociale-verzekeringswetten, A.W.B.Z., Deventer, pp. 708–9; DE WIT, J., 'De geschiedenis van de ziekenfonds—en de algemene ziektekostenverzekering', *De groei van de sociale verzekering in Nederland* (Amsterdam, 1970), p. 154.
23. LEDEBOER, L. V., *Heden en verleden* ('s Gravenhage, 1973), p. 60.

# References

24. RIBETTES-TILHET, J., 'Médecins et sécurité sociale dans quelques pays d'Europe', *Droit social* (1964), pp. 649–50.
25. CHIAPPELLI, U., op. cit., p. 133.
26. UCANSS, *Guide de la sécurité sociale* (Paris, sd), part I, p. 81.
27. CHIAPPELLI, U., op. cit., pp. 111–12.
28. CREMER, R., op. cit., p. 371.
29. QUAETHOVEN, P., *Het statuut van de ziekenhuisgeneesheer in de lid-staten van de Europese Economische Gemeenschap* (Leuven, 1969), pp. 28, 104, 161, 218, 209, 284, 402.
30. ASSOCIATION INTERNATIONALE DE LA MUTUALITE, *Les Relations avec le corps médical* (Geneva, AIM, 1966), pp. 8–9.
31. SCHEWE, D., and NORDHORN, K., *Uebersichtüber die soziale Sicherung in Deutschland* (Bonn, Bundesministerium für Arbeit und Sozialordnung, 1970).
32. CHIAPPELLI, U., op. cit., p. 142.
33. FULCHER, D., *Medical Care Systems* (Geneva, BIT, 1974), pp. 74–75.
34. *Tableaux Santé et sécurité sociale*, Ministère d'état chargé des affaires sociales, Ministère de la santé publique (Paris, 1972), tables 6–9, pp. 124 and 162, 284.
35. EUROPEAN INSTITUTE FOR SOCIAL SECURITY, *Evolution and Financing of the Cost of Medical Care* (Leuven, EISS, 1972), pp. 351–2.
36. MANNOURY, J., *Hoofdtrekken van de sociale verzekering* (Alphen a.d. Rijn, 1967), pp. 123–4; KASTNER, F., *Monograph in the Organization of Medical Care within the Framework of Social Security* (Geneva, ILO, 1968), p. 65.
37. *Soins médicaux individuels et sécurité sociale* (OMS, Geneva, 1971), pp. 13–15; COPPINI, M. A., and ILLUMINATI, F., 'Les Relations entre les institutions de sécurité sociale et le corps médical', *Revue Internationale de Sécurité sociale* (Geneva, 1968), p. 280.
38. ASSOCIATION INTERNATIONALE DE LA MUTUALITE, op. cit., p. 13; COPPINI, M.A., and ILLUMINATI, F., op. cit., p. 221.
39. ROEMER, M. I., *L'Organisation des soins médicaux dans le cadre de la sécurité sociale* (Geneva, BIT, 1969), pp. 33 ff.; DEJARDIN, J., 'L'Organisation des soins médicaux dans la sécurité sociale', *Revue Internationale de Sécurité Sociale*, 3 (Geneva, 1968), 380–2.
40. *Il sistema assistenziale dell'INAM* (Rome, INAM, 1973), p. 15.
41. DUPEYROUX, J. J., 'La Sécurité sociale et les médecins', *Recueil Dalloz*, 31 (1960), 190–1.
42. LEENEN, H. J., *Sociale grondrechten en gezondheidszorg* (Hilversum, 1966). pp. 65–66; DOUBLET, J., 'Droits de l'homme et sécurité sociale', *Revue Internationale de sécurité sociale*, 4 (Geneva, 1968), 511–12.
43. NASCHOLD, F., *Kassenärzte und Krankenversicherungsreform* (Freiburg im Breisgau, 1967), p. 38.

44. MANNOURY, J., op. cit., p. 190.
45. JANTZ, K., 'Les Relations entre les médecins et l'assurance-maladie, en République Fédérale d'Allemagne', *Revue Française du Travail*, **1** (1965), 28–31.
46. Belgium: Act of 9 August 1963, art. 34, § 12; France: art. L. 259 and L. 260, *Code de la sécurité sociale*.
47. Germany: Reichsversicherungsordnung, § 368h and § 368i; Luxemburg: *Code des Assurances Sociales*, art. 308bis.
48. VELDKAMP, G. M. J., 'De plaats van de geneesheer in de wettelijke struktuur van de sociale gezondheidszorg', *De geneesheer en het recht* (Deventer, 1968), pp. 30–33.
49. QUAETHOVEN, P., op. cit., pp. 130–7, 233–8.
50. *Code des Assurances Sociales*, art. 308bis.
51. SCHEWE, D., and NORDHORN, K., op. cit.
52. National Agreement physicians-sickness funds of 14 January 1970, K., § 4.
53. 'De sociale Verzekeringswetten', *Ziekenfondswet* (Deventer, sd), pp. 620–1.
54. KAYSER, A., op. cit., p. 579.
55. Act of 9 August 1963, art. 35; DILLEMANS, R., 'De nieuwe wetgeving inzake ziekteverzekering', *Actuele problemen van sociaal recht* (Antwerp, 1966), pp. 168–9.
56. 'Normativa per l'erogazione dell'assistenza sanitaria da parte dei medici generici', *I problemi della sicurezza sociale*, **4** (Rome, 1966), 652.
57. SOZIALENQUETE-KOMMISSION, op. cit., p. 277.
58. *Ziekenfondswet* (Sickness Funds Act), art. 13 and Royal Decree, 4 January 1966, art. 3.
59. CHIAPPELLI, U., op. cit., pp. 45, 121–2.

# PART TWO

## MAJOR DIFFERENCES

# 5
# *Structure, organization, and area of application*

The systems of social health insurance in the original EEC countries are very similar. However, there are important points of difference. They relate to the structure of the systems, their organization and some aspects of their field of application.

### Structure
*Structure* in this context means the division of the systems into different forms of insurance and into independent schemes.

FORMS OF INSURANCE

The relative importance of voluntary and compulsory insurance varies from country to country.

In Belgium voluntary insurance has declined in importance and lately has been absorbed by compulsory insurance. The notion of *voluntary insurance* has been replaced here by *voluntary joining compulsory insurance* (1). Voluntary insurance only plays a significant complementary role for the self-employed whose insurance obligation only covers heavy risks. However it provides some extra benefits to almost all compulsorily insured.

In France only about 2 per cent of the people have to rely on voluntary insurance. These are the limited group of people who cannot be incorporated in a compulsory system by connection. However, voluntary insurance is still important in France as complementary insurance above the legal minima.

In contrast, voluntary insurance is still important in the Netherlands and in Germany. It caters for all self-employed and nonactive persons and in Germany voluntary insurance is applied to the former compulsorily insured people who have exceeded the wage limit.

The possibility of voluntary membership of social insurance also exists in Luxemburg, but it does not cover such a large part of the public as in the Netherlands and in Germany: it only concerns defined categories of people. Others are left to private insurance.

In Italy, voluntary insurance has only a limited role. It focuses specially on the protection of some marginal categories. Voluntary social insurance especially appears in the form of complementary benefits to the funds for independents.

INDEPENDENT SCHEMES

Not one of the countries has a national system of social health insurance, which would apply to everybody (2).

Insurance is most unified in Germany and Belgium. In Belgium the general scheme applies to all workers in the private and public sector including (but partially) the self-employed. Only seamen (about 3,500), and permanent railway personnel (about 50,000) still have a separate system. The system in Germany is also concentrated. There is one big legal system and only one special scheme for miners.

The Dutch situation is similar to that in Germany, but the number of different schemes is greater. The basis is a general insurance which protects the whole population against heavy risks. On top of this there is compulsory 'health funds insurance' for all wage-earners below a wage limit, and voluntary health insurance for all other people with an income below the same wage limit. There is special voluntary insurance for all aged people with low income.

Social health insurance in Luxemburg is also spread over a number of schemes. One scheme covers all blue-collar workers and another scheme applies to white-collar workers, together with the public servants. The Grand Duchy also has separate systems for merchants and craftsmen, and for farmers.

The French arrangement has a richer diversity of schemes. Officials and workmen of the state, the military, the permanent personnel of central government, the local authorities and the official institutions, seamen, miners, the staff of the state railway, of the Metro, and of the autonomous monopoly of public transport in Marseilles, the statutory personnel of electricity and gas enterprises (also the enterprises which are not nationalized), the personnel of the general water company, the *Banque de France,* the Bank of Algeria and Tunisia, the independent port of Bordeaux, the Paris Chamber of Commerce, of the independent national fund of social security for miners and of that for the clerks and employees of notaries all have their own regime, altogether fifteen different schemes (3). Special schemes, which are totally different from the social insurance for wage-earners, also exist for farmers and other self-employed.

A real abundance of special systems and schemes—which seem to be related to the Latin national character—exists in Italy. First of all, tuberculosis is insured totally separately, under the management of the INPS, which is in fact an institute for pensions. This institution also manages the medical care of the clergy and retired clergy.

A national system for all workers was organized during the Second World War, under the management of the INAM. However, after more than twenty-five years, there still exist three national funds (two for the employees of the airline companies and one for the personnel of newspaper companies) and about sixty-five industrial funds (especially energy industries) which legally should have been incorporated in the INAM (4).

The number of special systems which are not administrated by the INAM is impressive: three for seamen, one for workers in agriculture and forestry, another for the government officials, and others for local administration, public bodies, the railway, show-business artistes, journalists, buses, trolley-buses, and tramways, veterinary surgeons, and so on. For all these groups there are special health insurance schemes.

## Organization

Insurance is centralized if the responsibility for balancing income and expenditure is concentrated into one single national body per system. Conversely decentralization exists when this responsibility rests with regional or local bodies. In France and Italy within each health insurance scheme the responsibility clearly rests with one national institution; for each group of insured the financing is organized at the national level. France offers an apparent exception with the insurance of independent workers. Although some people believe the contrary, this is only apparent, because all financial operations of insurance agencies are compensated at the national level by one central fund, called *'Caisse centrale de secours mutuels agricoles'* for farmers and *'caisse nationale interprofessionnelle'* for non-agricultural self-employed (5).

Belgium and the Netherlands manage their health insurance through a multitude of private insurance funds, organized into national federations and confederations, sometimes on political, ideological, or even religious basis. But the true responsibility for the insurance lies in the hands of a central official body. In the Netherlands this is the *'Ziekenfondsraad'* (Sickness Funds Council); in Belgium it is the *'Rijksinstituut voor Ziekte—en Invaliditeitsverzekering'* (National Health and Disability Insurance Institute)—even if the contrary is generally said (6).

A very different situation exists in Germany and under German influence in Luxemburg. Here the health insurance funds have by law the privilege to establish their own premiums and benefits; they are also responsible for their financial balance. Given the large number of independent funds (about 2,000 in Germany) insurance can be said to be extremely decentralized. One must, however, bear in mind that the funds see their freedom limited by very strict legal rules concerning maximum premiums and minimum benefits. In fact most, if not all funds have reached the legal limit as far as premiums are concerned. This means that in fact the public authorities determine their policies—by the process of approval or disapproval (7).

One can conclude that in general financial control is spread over autonomous institutions in the systems which became compulsory a long time ago (especially Luxemburg [1901] and Germany [1884]), whereas management is totally centralized in the countries which have had more recent reforms (France [1928] and Italy [1927]). On the other hand, the countries with the oldest tradition in the field of mutual aid decentralize their executive organization (Belgium and the Netherlands), but centralize their financing.

## Field of application

PRIMARY FIELD OF APPLICATION

Classical social insurance in Western Europe is primarily directed to wage-earners in industrial and commercial firms, not only for social-economic but also for technical reasons. Originally, the idea was even narrower. Application was limited to certain categories of workers, who needed protection most: workmen in dangerous or unhealthy workshops and the lowest-paid groups. This was linked to the concept of assistance: these groups were automatically assimilated with the indigent. After the Second World War, and especially in the years 1950-60 insurance was extended to the self-employed, and afterwards even to different kinds of the non-active (8).

Today there are still remainders of the oldest concept of social insurance in some countries. This is true of Germany and the Netherlands. The field of compulsory workers' insurance is in both countries restricted by a wage-limit. The self-employed of both countries can only join the social insurance on a voluntary basis, if their income is lower than this wage-limit. Above this limit they have to take private insurance. But in the Netherlands the risk of heavy medical care expenditures is insured for the whole population, and in Germany farmers are brought under social insurance.

Some countries show a more modern approach to social insurance. This modern view came after the crisis period 1929-30 and found its strongest expression in the Beveridge Report. It holds (besides many other points) that risks such as the risk of medical expenses are common to everybody and have to be covered for everybody (9).

The mixing of these old and new opinions has resulted in a very unequal spreading of insurance protection in the six countries.

The strongest relative similarity comes in the sector of the *wage-earners in commerce and industry*. Roughly speaking, all the employed workers in the private sector in the European countries participate in compulsory health insurance including more or less marginal categories such as farmworkers, workmen in family firms, apprentices, etc. However, as noted above in the Netherlands and Germany, insurance obligation for workers is restricted by a wage limit. In Germany, the limit only concerns white-collar workers. Even in Bismarck's time there was no restriction for blue-collar workers (they all had very low wages). In the Netherlands, restriction concerns workmen as well but its practical importance is limited by the existence of general insurance for heavy medical risks.

The Netherlands is exceptional for a second reason. Retired ex-workers of the private sector belong in all countries to the compulsory insurance which covered them during their active career. The only exception is in the Netherlands, where retired people only enjoy voluntary insurance, although this may be a very advantageous insurance for aged people (depending on their income).

However, the differences in the field of application are more important for other social groups: government officials, self-employed, and non-actives.

For the *government officials* (personnel of the state, of the local authorities, and the public institutions) a clear distinction can be made between the countries with compulsory insurance for these persons and the countries without. In the Netherlands and in Germany the government officials are excluded. The German civil servants join private insurance, but the Dutch government itself established insurance bodies to meet the health costs of officials and their families.

In the four other States, government personnel, and those of public institutions are compulsorily insured for medical expenses. They are, in two countries, incorporated together with the wage earners in the general system of social insurance: in the scheme for white-collar workers in Luxemburg and in Belgium in the general scheme. The two remaining countries have created special systems for this group. France has a special system in the framework of the general regime for all officials. For them, provisions are guaranteed at least equal to these for other insured. Italy has separate systems for officials in central administration, local government, and all kinds of public institutions.

### TABLE 3
### Self-employed and compulsory insurance

|  | Belgium | Germany | France | Italy | Luxemburg | Netherlands |
|---|---|---|---|---|---|---|
| Artisans | x | — | X | x | X | x |
| Traders and manufacturers | x | — | X | x[1] | X | x |
| Professions | x | —[2] | X | X[3] | X | x |
| Farmers | x | X | X | X[4] | X | x |

Key. X = total protection; x = protection limited to heavy medical risks; — = not protected.

1. Only the traders, whose income is lower than 3 million lire, not the manufacturers.
2. Some self-employed workers are joined together with workers, for the purposes of social insurance: independents, teachers, musicians, educators, artists, midwives, nursemaids, and sick-nurses provided that they do not employ other people ('Reichsversicherungsordnung', § 166).
3. Separate systems for the different professions.
4. For the farmers in Italy who spend at least thirty working days per year in their business, but whose work is at least 50 per cent done by members of their family (according to certain estimation methods) (Article 4, Act, 22 November 1954, no. 136).

Protection of *self-employed* workers varies even more. This can be shown in Table 3.

The six countries fall into three groups: those where the self-employed have complete medical insurance (Italy, France, Luxemburg); those where they are only insured against heavy medical risks (Belgium and the Netherlands); and one country (Germany) where only farmers are protected.

Of course, some reservations are required here. Certain self-employed people in the German system join the workers' compulsory insurance and others can take voluntary insurance if their income is below the wage limit. Another condition, that they should not employ more than two persons, was abolished in 1970.

It is also useful to bear in mind that the concept *heavy medical risks* has a more limited meaning in the Netherlands than in Belgium (10).

Not all Italian self-employed people are included: manufacturers have only voluntary insurance, some agricultural occupations are excluded: this applies to very small as well as large industrialized farms.

With regard to *non-active persons*, again three groups of countries can be distinguished. The first is Belgium and France, where students, pensioners, and disabled persons (in France: only when the disablement has its origin in war circumstances) receive full insurance protection. The second group is Luxemburg and Germany, where only pensioners, and non-active persons who are dependent on a worker, are insured. And the third group is Italy and the Netherlands, where the entire population is covered for certain heavy risks. This rule was applied in 1967 in the Netherlands for care in specialized institutions and for long-term hospital care, and it was introduced as a voluntary insurance in Italy from 1 January 1975 on, for hospital care in the public hospitals.

SECONDARY FIELD OF APPLICATION

The beneficiaries, whose right to medical care is based on the insurance obligation of another person (the primarily insured or entitled) are different in the several countries. A good illustration are the general systems for wage-earners (11).

The worker's wife is always covered with him (as far as she does not have an autonomous right). The age limit for children considered as dependent for health insurance is varied: up to 14 years in Belgium (16 if he does not work), 16 years in France and Holland, 18 years in Italy, 19 years in Luxemburg for the blue-collar workers (18 for the other groups of insured), and without limitation in Germany if the child is supported mainly by the insured, and if the fund itself does not impose an age limit.

Age limitations are higher for children under a contract of apprenticeship: up to 18 years in France, 21 years in Italy, and without limitation in Belgium.

Age limitations are higher again for children who are in college: 20 years in France, 25 years in Luxemburg (reduced to 23 for children of self-employed and farmers) and Belgium, 26 years in Italy, 27 years in Holland, and without limitation in Germany if the student is supported mainly by the insured.

Special rules are made for invalid children who are unfit for work and therefore cannot support themselves. They are protected until they reach 20 years in France, 27 years in Holland, and without age limitation in the other countries.

Age limitation is only one example of the differences which exist between the national regulations. Some specify the relationship between the child and the family of the insured, or how far incomes are allowed before earning children are disqualified. The problem is similar with regard to other family members who may be covered as co-insured: parents, brothers and sisters, grandchildren, a concubine, somebody who is not a family member but supported, etc.

# 6
# *Financing*

In Part One we considered the general similarity of financing methods. However, there are differences. These can be grouped under three headings: the contributions of employers and workers in the general scheme for workers in private industry, the premiums of the self-employed and farmers and the State's contribution.

### Contribution by employers and workers in the general scheme for wage-earners

Generally the schemes are mainly financed by contributions of employers and workers. These are calculated as a percentage of the wage, with a certain maximum limit. Only in Italy is there no wage-ceiling for this premium.

The premium in some countries includes a portion for cash benefits during sickness, with or without long-term disability insurance. If this is calculated, the net premiums for health care benefits in Germany, France, Italy, and Luxemburg respectively would be: 7·4, 12·90, 12·91, and 4·90 per cent (12). This should be kept in mind. It does not, however, alter many of the following considerations.

Some disparities are apparent. The first is the unequal share between employers and workers: in Luxemburg the employer pays one-third of the premium, in Germany half, in Belgium and in the Netherlands something more than half, in France over three-quarters, and in Italy almost the whole premium (Table 4).

The Luxemburg worker could perhaps feel that he has a poor deal compared with his Italian colleague (and the reverse might be said for his employer) when he sees these figures. Harmonization would remove such effects and would not have much real impact

## TABLE 4
### Premium percentages and wage-ceilings in social health insurance (data for 1972)

|  | Belgium | Germany [1-5] | France [5] | Italy [1-3] | Luxemburg [1,5] | Netherlands [1-5] |
|---|---|---|---|---|---|---|
| Employer's premium | 3·75 | 4·20[2] | 12·45 | 14·46 | 2[6] | 6·10 |
| Worker's premium | 2·00 | 4·20[2] | 3·50 | 0·15 | 4[6] | 4·10 |
| Total premium | 5·75 | 8·40[2] | 15·95 | 14·61 | 6[6] | 10·20 |
| Monthly calculation ceiling | 24,550 BF | 1,575 DM | 1,830 FF[7] | — | 24,000 LF[8] | 1,322 fl.[9] |

1. Without long-term disability insurance.
2. Average between the various funds.
3. The percentages are slightly different for the banks, trading, and insurance enterprises.
4. Addition of the premiums for the Sickness Funds and for the General Insurance against Special Medical Care Costs.
5. Including sickness benefit.
6. For the national workers' fund. Other funds charge between 3·60 and 6·90 per cent.
7. Three per cent (1 per cent for the worker and 2 per cent for the employer) are calculated without wage-ceiling.
8. Exactly 800 LF per calendar-day. The ceilings for employees vary with the funds: employees also have minimum wages for premium calculation.
9. Ceiling for the Sickness Funds; the ceiling for the Special Medical Care Costs is 1,763 fl.

within single countries on wages and labour costs (13). This harmonization could perhaps evolve towards the abolition of the so-called worker's contribution so that it would simply be paid by the employer. This has already been realized in the Dutch General Insurance for Special Medical Care Costs and indeed in the Dutch system of general insurance.

This may not apply to the size of the premium as a whole. Two countries have a premium percentage lower than 6 per cent: Belgium and Luxemburg (in this latter country the premium is even lower for the white-collar workers and government officials); Germany has a premium of about 7 per cent; the Netherlands takes about 10 per cent; France and Italy reach the level of 12 or 13 per cent.

TABLE 5
Comparison of premium rates and average labour costs in industry (1971, in Belgian francs)

|  | Belgium | Germany | France | Italy | Luxemburg | Netherlands |
|---|---|---|---|---|---|---|
| Premium for Social health insurance (%)[1] | 5·75 | 7·00 | 12·30 | 12·91 | 4·90 | 9·30 |
| Total labour cost per hour in industry[2] | 109·17 | 112·92 | 105·47 | 91·55 | 116·59 | 114·53 |

1. For Germany, France, Italy, and Luxemburg: calculated from premium for health and disability insurance, on basis of expenditure for health and for disability benefits (Van Langendonck, J., *De Harmonisering van de Sociale Verzekering voor Gezondheidszorgen in de EEG* [Leuven, Rechtsfaculteit, 1971], pp. 233-4).
2. From: *Basic Statistics of the Community* (Luxemburg, EEC, 1972), table 140, pp. 180-1.

These are very significant differences, which naturally influence the gap between net and gross wages in the different countries. Their significance has to be more precisely examined with regard to the income level of the insured (the basis for getting premiums) and the level of benefits financed by this premium.

Table 5 gives an interesting correlation. If we rank the countries according to their premium percentage in a decreasing order, we then get the following series: Italy, France, the Netherlands, Germany, Belgium, Luxemburg. A similar ranking according to the hourly labour cost in industry gives the following: Luxemburg, the Netherlands, Germany, Belgium, France, Italy. The correlation is not total. It does, however, show that countries with higher wages get lower premiums and vice versa. Obviously with higher wages a smaller premium percentage is needed to cover a certain level of expenditure.

Another important point of comparison is the expenditure on medical care per insured person.

A strong correlation between the expenses per insured and the premium level can be seen: both countries with the highest expenses per insured have also the highest premium percentage (France and Italy), while the countries with the lowest premium percentage (Belgium and Luxemburg) are also similar in expenses

## TABLE 6
### Comparison of premium rates with cost of medical care per insured (figures for 1972)

|  | Belgium | Germany | France | Italy | Luxemburg | Netherlands |
|---|---|---|---|---|---|---|
| Premium for health care (%) | 5·75 | 7·00 | 12·30 | 12·91 | 4·90 | 9·30 |
| Annual expenses for medical care per insured (in BF) | 8,230 | 4,647 | 13,358 | 11,060 | 7,545 | 10,425 |

*Source:* Commission Administrative pour la Sécurité sociale des travailleurs migrants. *Annual Report 1972* (Brussels, EEC, sd); and Van Langendonck, J., op. cit. (see ref. 12).

per insured. Only Germany stands out with a remarkably low figure (Table 6).

More important for the system of social health insurance is the method used to fix the premium level. The picture shows both a degree of rigidity in fixing premiums, and some co-partnership in decision-making.

The premium percentage is fixed by law in Belgium. Article 7 of the Act of 27 June 1969 fixes the premiums for all sectors of social insurance. Two countries leave the minister of social affairs to fix the premium: this is the case in France and in the Netherlands. The premium percentage is, in two countries, fixed by the statutes of each fund: Luxemburg and Germany. In Italy the premium is in principle fixed by the funds; in practice it is done by the government and to a large extent by law (14).

However, it has to be noted that this premium does not necessarily have the same rigidity or flexibility merely because it is fixed by the same authority. The Dutch minister fixes every year the premium level in both systems of compulsory health insurance. But the French minister fixes the premium for an undetermined period, and the same practice is followed elsewhere.

It is clear that the premium determination is a typical government responsibility in four countries: Belgium, France, the Netherlands, and Italy. In the other countries, the insured in principle have control over the amount of the premium themselves. Special

## TABLE 7
### Premiums for social health insurance for the self-employed (situation in 1972)

|  | Occupational group | Premium arrangement |
|---|---|---|
| NETHERLANDS | Resident population[1] | 2% per year of the taxable revenue for maximum 21,150 fl. Full exemption or premium reduction scheme if income is below certain limits. |
| GERMANY | Farmers | Five to ten contribution classes (not yet in operation in 1972). |
| BELGIUM | All self-employed persons | 2% per year of taxable revenue for maximum 420,000 BF[5] and minimum 80,000 BF. |

| | | Annual income or pension (FF) | Annual premium (FF) |
|---|---|---|---|
| FRANCE | Self-employed (except farmers) | Below 5,000 | 400 |
| | | 5,000–7,000 | 450 |
| | | 7,000–9,000 | 640 |
| | | 9,000–11,000 | 800 |
| | | 11,000–13,000 | 970 |
| | | 13,000–15,000 | 1,100 |
| | | 15,000–17,000 | 1,250 |
| | | 17,000–20,000 | 1,320 |
| | | 20,000–25,000 | 1,380 |
| | | 25,000–30,000 | 1,490 |
| | | 30,000–35,000 | 1,600 |
| | | 35,000–40,000 | 1,700 |
| | | 40,000–45,000 | 1,820 |
| | | 45,000–50,000 | 1,930 |
| | | 50,000–60,000 | 2,040 |
| | | 60,000 and more | 2,200 |
| | Farmers[2] | Fixed annual premium each year decided by decree. | |
| | | Head of farm industry | 1,407 FF |
| | | Family member helping in the farm | 938 FF |
| | | Ditto aged 16–21 | 469 FF |
| | | Exemption arrangement according to the land registry income. | |

## Table 7 (cont.)

| | Occupational group | Premium arrangement |
|---|---|---|
| ITALY | Craftsmen[1] | Annual premium: 1,000 L per insured: complementary annual premium, fixed by the insurance company in function of the results.[3] |
| | Small traders[1] | Income below 1 million L per year: 1,500 L per insured and per year. Income between 1 and 1·5 million L per year: 3,000 L per insured and per year. Income higher than 1·5 million L per year: 3,500 L per insured per year. Plus complementary premium per year fixed by the insurance company in function of the results.[4] |
| | Farmers | Three kinds of premiums: 1. Premium per farm and per working day worked (minimum 50 days per industry and maximum 150 days per family member): fixed per province (between 3,057 and 13,858 L). 2. Premium per insured: 750 L per insured and per year. 3. Complementary premium, fixed each year by the insurance institutions in function of the results (between 1,000 and 11,000 L).[5] |

| | | Taxable income per year (LF) | Monthly premium (LF) |
|---|---|---|---|
| LUXEMBURG | Traders, craftsmen, and industrialists | Up to 76,500 | 198 |
| | | From 76,501 to 102,000 | 256 |
| | | From 102,001 to 170,000 | 323 |
| | | More than 170,000 | 396 |
| | Liberal professions | Premium of 3·9% on the revenue, over maximum 18,986 LF per month and minimum 9,493 LF per month.[6] | |

| | | Cultivated area (ha) | Monthly premium (LF) |
|---|---|---|---|
| | Farmers | Minimum premium | 224 |
| | | 0 – 10 | 269 |
| | | 10·01–20 | 314 |
| | | 20·01–30 | 359 |
| | | 30·01–50 | 403 |
| | | More than 50 | 448[6] |

attention is paid to this by German and Luxemburg authors who emphasize the representation of the insured people and the election of the boards of funds. It is doubtful if true democratic representation of the fund members is achieved at all, since the elections generally are not held. And the control over the premiums is kept between narrow legal limits anyhow (15).

## Premiums for self-employed people and farmers

Not very much can be said in this respect of Germany and the Netherlands.

Of all self-employed only the farmers are included in the field of application of compulsory health insurance in Germany and this is still very recent. Because all the inhabitants of the Netherlands are insured against heavy medical risks, independent workers and farmers are at least insured for these heavy risks; the ordinary sickness funds insurance does not apply to them. Most self-employed persons in Germany and the Netherlands turn to voluntary social insurance if their income is below the wage limit.

The form of the premium for the self-employed varies. It is a percentage of the taxable income in Belgium, and in the Dutch national insurance for special medical costs. In the other countries it is calculated at a flat rate, according to a scale which takes income into account.

The level of these premiums is particularly varied (Table 7).

It appears that the method of premium calculation is very different in different countries. It is a percentage of the income in the Netherlands and in Luxemburg (only for the professions).

---

NOTES TO TABLE 7

1. Only for heavy risks.
2. Incomplete protection; no benefits in case of accident, unless for a child or a retired person.
3. The complementary premium varies per province.
4. The complementary premium varies per province.
5. The ultimate result is that a contribution varies from 16,782 L in Sicilia and 16,639 L in Emilia (and even 23,961 in Regio Emilia) to 5,993 L in Valle d'Aosta, 5,969 L in Potenza, and 5,520 L in Bolzano. The average is 12,555 L in 1973 (Federazione Nazionale Casse Mutue di Malattia per i Coltivatori Diretti, *Bilancio Consuntivo, 1973* [Rome, 1974], p. 90).
6. Indexed figures.

# Financing

Elsewhere it is an annual amount at a flat rate. Belgium recently changed from the latter to the former.

The calculation method diverges greatly: general percentage with exemption for lower income in Belgium and for the Netherlands; uniform premiums for Italian farmers and craftsmen; three premium classes for the Italian traders, four classes for the French farmers and Luxemburg traders, craftsmen, and industrialists; six for the Luxemburg farmers; and up to ten or twelve for the French non-agricultural self-employed and for the German farmers.

The difference in the amount of the several premium arrangements is more important. The French premium for self-employed non-farmers (2,200 FF per year) is the highest (measured by its maximum). French farmers take the second place with an annual maximum premium of 1,407 FF. The Luxemburg professions come in the third place with more than 8,800 LF. After adding an average of the complementary premiums to the maximum legal premium, Italian traders come in the fourth place about level with the Luxemburg traders. The sixth is the maximum premium for the Dutch Special Medical Cost Insurance Law, followed closely by the Luxemburg farmers and the Belgian self-employed.

The maximum premiums for the Italian craftsmen and farmers are clearly the lowest, even after adding the complementary premiums.

We have already noted that a number of these systems do not cover all costs, but only guarantee so-called heavy medical risks. This notion means different things in different countries: its content is narrow in the Netherlands where it affects care in specialized institutions; and hospitalization after the 365th day. The concept is broader in the Italian systems for traders and craftsmen where it applies to all hospitalization, specialist care, and maternity care. The Belgian concept is broader still, where heavy medical risks include complete care of mental disease, cancer, tuberculosis, polio, and congenital malformations and defects (the so-called *social diseases*), complete maternity care, hospitalization and drugs during hospitalization, major surgery, and a number of specialist treatments. In a way the Italian system for farmers too offers a limited set of benefits, even if it covers the small risks: pharmaceutical products are not provided here.

If the systems are classified by the size of benefits they offer, then all the Luxemburg systems, the French system for self-employed and the German farmers are top of this list, immediately followed by the system for the French farmers for whom there are no benefits in the case of accidents except for children and the retired. Then come the Italian farmers, Belgian self-employed persons, Italian traders and craftsmen, and finally the Dutch self-employed persons, with the smallest set of benefits.

Premiums are, of course, not all of the same type. Special attention should be paid to the distinction made between individual and family premiums. Individual premiums are the rule in the Italian systems for self-employed persons. The same applies to the French system for independent farmers, but it exempts the spouse and children from paying contributions under certain conditions. In all the other systems, the premium is payable only by the active self-employed persons, who get the right to family cover.

## State contribution

The difference in state contribution in financing social security is considered by most authors as one of the strongest elements of disparity between the systems in the European countries. They distinguish two groups of countries: those with an important state intervention (Germany, Belgium, and Luxemburg) and those with a small state contribution (France, Italy, and the Netherlands).

The figures in Table 8 date from 1965. Changes have occurred since. The state contribution in the Belgium system, which was already very high, has increased. It can be valued now at 41 per cent. Germany, France, and Luxemburg stuck to their principle that health insurance should not be financed by the state but by the premiums from the insured persons and their employers. A 1970 report asserts that the state contribution even decreased in the German social health insurance until it reached 1·9 per cent (16). However, recent legislation in Germany on hospitals and on health insurance for farmers will result in an increase of the government subsidies.

## TABLE 8
Sources of revenue for health and maternity insurance (percentage) (figures for 1965)

|            | Insured | Employer | State | Other |
|------------|---------|----------|-------|-------|
| Germany    | 57·1    | 37·8     | 2·7   | 2·4   |
| Belgium    | 34·9    | 26·0     | 38·2  | 0·9   |
| France     | 27·8    | 65·3     | 5·8   | 1·1   |
| Italy      | 7·5     | 68·8     | 17·3  | 6·4   |
| Luxemburg  | 62·0    | 29·3     | 4·3   | 4·4   |
| Netherlands| 47·6    | 48·7     | 3·3   | 0·4   |

*Source:* Commission of the EEC, *Indicateurs de securité sociale* (Brussels, 1969) (doc. V/5363/69.N), 38, table 15.

The French Regulations of 21 August 1967 have even accentuated the financial responsibility of the social insurance institutions: they have to break into their reserves and perhaps increase certain premiums, if they are not sufficient to cover the expenses; they can never call for state contributions. However, within very strict limits, the French government gives subsidies to defined groups, which are not able to finance their own health insurance.

In this way, a subsidy of 2,400,000 FF is granted every year for the health insurance of students; social benefits for independent farmers are partially financed, amongst others, by certain taxes and levies, with a *budget annexe des prestations sociales agricoles* (annex budget of agricultural social benefits). The system for the self-employed receives a state subsidy equal to the minimum premium of those who get a free complementary pension, and the systems for seamen, miners, and war-invalids receive certain subsidies.

Luxemburg has a *Fonds national de solidarité* (national fund of solidarity), which offers a small grant of at most 15 per cent for health schemes for retired persons. In addition, a state contribution towards insurance for farmers enables them to get the same advantages as other insured persons. The Government also pays half of the administration costs of the sickness funds (except for industrial funds) and two-thirds of the expenses of medical inspection in the workmen's insurance. In all, this state contribution can be estimated at 6·64 per cent of the total expenses for health insurances (17). It will be considerably increased by the reform of 2 May 1974.

In the Netherlands, a certain increase in the state financing of social health insurance can be established. On the one side, part of the social insurance for elderly people is financed by a fund, sustained partly by the compulsory sickness funds insurance and partly by the Government; on the other side, an annual subsidy of 475 million fl. is spent on general insurance for heavy medical costs, this amount varies with the wages index. The premiums for certain groups (very low incomes and elderly people) of this general insurance are also supported by the Government. This brings the total government support in the Netherlands to about 20 per cent.

In Italy the Government has become more involved in financing social health insurance. A government subsidy of 3,000 L per insured had already been provided for the health insurance of farmers and self-employed persons. However, this was not sufficient and the Government had to pay large extra subsidies for health insurance schemes for self-employed persons as well as for wage-earners. These measures total about 15·6 per cent of the total expenses of Italian social health insurance. This has been increased recently in a considerable way by the special government subsidies to compensate the debts of the insurance institutions with the hospitals.

In brief, four situations appear in the European Community: the situation in Belgium, where the Government directly pays 40 per cent or more of social insurance for health care; the case of the Netherlands and Italy with 15–20 per cent income from the Treasury; France and Luxemburg, which maintain a low state contribution (about 5 per cent); and finally Germany where state intervention is trifling.

# 7
# *The services*

It was stated in the last chapter that the different systems of health insurance, with some exceptions, cover the same complete range of medical services. Medical care in all industrialized countries tends to be much the same. This does not mean that health insurance benefits in these systems are identical. There are big differences in the form of benefits, in relative prices and the conditions for receiving benefits.

## The form of the benefits

A group of experts made a study for the Commission of the European Economic Community of the systems of social security as a preliminary documentation for the European Conference on Social Security in December 1962. This study distinguishes two benefit forms: the 'organization insurance' and the 'reimbursement insurance' (*assurance-organisation* and *assurance-remboursement*). This definition is: the first insurance authorizes the insurance bodies to provide appropriate health care to protected persons by services in kind, in the real sense of this word: the insurance bodies can conclude agreements with physicians, dentists, pharmacists, etc., and administer care institutions. The other conception declines to interfere with the provision of care. It restricts its action to financial settlement with its members.

It is questionable whether this distinction is useful in practice. For the authors themselves admit that even the so-called *assurance-remboursement* exerts, in practice, much influence on the delivery of medical care (18).

The same distinction underlies that between *direct* and *indirect* supply of care.

The criteria for distinction between direct and indirect benefit are different between the authors: *Roemer*: dependence or independence of the care-suppliers with regard to the insurance (19); *Levi Sandri*: presence or absence of contracts (agreements) between the supplier and the insurance (20); *Chiappelli*: the provision of care by the insurance institution or by the insured himself (21); and *Carapezza*: payment by the insurance institution or by the insured (22).

*Dupeyroux* discerns three forms of medical care in social health insurance: *assurance-remboursement, médecine de caisse,* and *nationalisation de la médecine* (reimbursement-insurance, fund medicine, and nationalization of medicine [23]). The first form represents the traditional 'dialogue' between physician and patient. The care suppliers of the second form are paid directly by the insurance organizations. In the third form, the government is itself responsible for supplying medical care by establishing medical services and financing them.

What we are dealing with is in fact a distribution system of services and goods. Consequently, the essential questions are: how are these goods and services produced, distributed, and consumed? Is the free market economy respected or is the economic process centrally directed according to a plan? Or is there a middle form which contains a blending of both systems?

In terms of social insurance these questions can be translated as follows: are health services provided independently from the insurance or within the insurance, or independently but in a certain relationship to the insurance? This leads us to the three types of insurance benefit. If health care is provided independently the insurance only offers reimbursement according to its own tariffs. If health care is given in the framework of the insurance, the benefit consists of direct access to health services. If health care is provided independently but in a certain relationship to the insurance, the benefit will be a partial or total payment of the actual cost of care, according to the particular agreement.

Direct access to health care benefits is the usual benefit form in Germany. Only in the 'Ersatzkassen' are benefits supplied on a reimbursement basis for white-collar workers whose salaries exceed a certain limit. Otherwise medical care in the whole social health insurance is supplied in a direct form through the instrument of the associations of physicians. But allowances are provided by the funds for the supply of glasses, hearing-aids, dental prostheses, and other expensive appliances. Allowances are a certain percentage of the cost. Reimbursement is also applied in hospitals, where patients in private rooms pay their physician themselves and in general this system exists where the insured sees a doctor who is not authorized by his fund, without any medical necessity.

In the Netherlands, the sickness funds work in principle on the direct supply of medical care by the funds, without additional payment by the patient. There could only be an application of reimbursement in one case; where no agreement has been reached between a certain group of care suppliers and the association of sickness funds and the intervention of the minister (see below) had not produced agreement. In this case, the suppliers will fix their fee themselves and the funds pay only a part according to their own tariff.

Direct payment is also the most popular form in Italy. It is the usual method for the systems managed by the INAM. The only exceptions are prostheses and appliances where reimbursement is applied. Direct payment is the rule in the systems for craftsmen and traders, but the insured may choose the indirect benefit type. Only the systems for public servants normally have indirect benefits.

In Luxemburg, direct payment (in the form meant by the French term 'tiers payant') is legally obligatory for hospital costs. The agreements with the physicians also stipulate that direct payment can be applied at the discretion of the physician, if the income of the insured does not allow a reimbursement basis. This applies especially to surgery costs.

The direct method of payment is used in the same form by Belgian social health insurance in cases where care suppliers have concluded special arrangements containing such a clause. Almost all the pharmacists have, also most hospitals and paramedical co-operators, but very few physicians.

In France a direct method of payment on the German–Dutch–Italian model exists in the special system for miners. French schemes are, for the rest, entirely based on repayment of medical costs.

Full or partial repayment of the cost of care according to agreements, is the rule in Belgium, France, and Luxemburg. However, there are many exceptions in these three countries: most of them in Belgium, many in France, some in Luxemburg. These exceptions come about whenever for some reason the physician is not obliged to follow an official tariff.

Reimbursement is the easiest insurance method but it offers the smallest protection for the insured. It is the rule in private insurance, which has still some importance in a number of European countries. In social insurance it has been left aside as the main benefit form in all countries. The Belgian reform of 1963 was explicitly meant to change from this benefit form to a more modern form (24).

Still this minimal benefit form appears to a greater or lesser extent in all countries. The Belgian legislation provides for many cases where in practice the physicians can freely fix their fees and the insurance only gives the insured compensation according to its own tariffs. This is the case in the uncommitted regions, where 40 per cent of the suppliers (or 50 per cent of the family doctors and 50 per cent of the specialists) have rejected the agreement. In the 'committed' regions physicians freely fix their fees if they have personally rejected the agreement. This is even true for the committed physicians in those cases where the insured comes by appointment, if he has an income above 215,000 BF (16,000 BF added for each dependant), is admitted in a private hospital room or has other special requirements. The physicians can also notify in writing the days and the hours on which they apply the insurance tariffs. Altogether, the insured will only rarely receive from the insurance institution full reimbursement.

In France the situation is similar to that in Belgium. There is again a difference between committed and uncommitted physicians according to whether they have refused the agreement. Tariff excesses by the physicians are possible, as in Belgium. Doctors are free to fix their fees if the patient makes special requirements or if the doctor is particularly famous.

In Luxemburg there exists an analogous situation: the Luxemburg systems are in general oriented to the repayment of real medical costs, but the physician can ask for a supplement of his fee not covered by the insurance, when the insured has special requirements for personal convenience or opts for admission to a private hospital ward.

Reimbursement is explicitly applied in Italy under the name *assistenza indiretta* (indirect help or indirect benefits). This benefit form is the rule for the personnel of the public sector, but only for general medical care: there is free choice between direct and indirect benefit for hospital and special medical care. Reimbursement is also still used in the systems for workers in the private sector and for the self-employed where the direct benefit *(assistenza diretta)* applies, for the supply of prostheses, orthopaedic appliances, glasses, hearing-aids, and other appliances, and for thermal cures. In general all insurance members can choose between indirect and direct benefit. The majority prefer direct provision (25).

## The prices of medical services

The prices of medical services are in all countries in some way legally or conventionally fixed under social insurance. Official lists of fees for specific services are used even in countries which pay at a flat rate for GPs as specialist care never comes in the flat rate tariff.

It is not easy to compare the tariffs in the different countries. In the first place, the same country can have different tariff lists. This occurs mainly in Germany and in Luxemburg, where the individual sickness funds have power to conclude their own agreements with the suppliers of care. Again the value of the tariffs is not always the same.

The traditional *Gebührenordnung* in Germany, for instance, is only a model tariff of fees, to be observed for the division of the insurance money between the members of the association of fund-physicians, whereas the Belgian and French '*nomenclature*' directly fix the payments to the physicians. Further, the structure of the tariffs is different. Certain services, if they are supplied together

## TABLE 9
Comparison of prices of selected medical services in six countries (figures on 1 January 1971, in Swiss francs)

| Service | Belgium | Germany | France | Italy | Luxemburg | Netherlands |
|---|---|---|---|---|---|---|
| Consultation of GP | 8·93 | 4·44 | 13·25 | 4·84 | 12·14 | — |
| Home attendance by GP | 14·31 | 13·32 | 19·49 | 8·29 | 20·38 | — |
| Extraction grinder | 13·01 | 9·73 | 22·69 | — | 7·37 | 6·89 |
| Total tooth prosthesis (one jaw) | 233·91 | 421·94 | 321·43 | — | 303·55 | 167·92 |
| Normal confinement GP (pre- and post-natal care included) | 162·18 | 44·40 | 233·91 | — | 90·63 | 309·01 |
| Trepanation brain abscess by neurosurgeon | 224·63 | 88·79 | 486·53 | 1,244·16 | 558·11 | 143·00 |
| Intracardial surgery under hypothermy | 935·83 | 392·17 | 1,216·33 | 3,456·00 | 724·63 | 658·73 |
| Bilateral amygdalectomy on a child under 10 years | 62·36 | 59·19 | 81·09 | 86·40 | 85·43 | 43·12 |
| Anaesthesia by specialist for stereotaxia | 131·05 | 99·45 | 324·36 | — | 255·85 | 148·51 |
| Microscopic urine examination | 7·20 | 5·21 | 7·41 | 2·76 | 4·34 | — |
| Electrophorese | 29·92 | 20·72 | 41·32 | 15·24 | 21·68 | — |
| X-ray wrist (two negatives) | 23·94 | 22·20 | 15·67 | 17·28 | 7·81 | 9·88 |
| Electroencephalogram | 77·71 | 59·19 | 121·63 | 59·30 | 30·36 | 43·12 |
| Scintigraphy of the thyroid | 119·60 | 59·19 | 78·36 | 110·59 | 48·14 | — |

with some others, can be charged separately in some countries, not in other countries. The services can be mentioned under other names, which are not precisely comparable.

Table 9 is based on a study by the International Association of Mutual Funds (26). This study gives the situation in 1971. Certain characteristic medical services were selected, which are the least ambiguous in the different systems, to establish a comparison.

Clearly the prices of services are very uneven.

The price in the most expensive country equals often seven times and up to fourteen times the price in the cheapest country.

Prices in the most expensive country for the same type of service are usually 150–350 per cent above those in the cheapest country. These are extraordinary differences for countries which constitute a 'common market'.

The differences in price do not always follow the same direction. Italy, for instance, is the country with the most expensive surgery, but with the cheapest lab-tests and home attendance by GP. Germany is the cheapest country in many respects, but it has the most expensive dental prostheses.

France is the most expensive country for medical care: the price of no less than six of the fourteen selected items is the highest there. Belgium follows as the second. It is the most expensive in three cases, the second most expensive in four cases, and nowhere one of the two cheapest. The lowest prices for medical services are found in the Netherlands, Germany, and Italy. It is interesting to compare these results with the figures of the premium level, the cost per insured person, and the government contribution in the six EEC countries. France's high prices are clearly reflected in its high expenditure per insured (see Table 6); the same applies to Germany's low prices. But the question arises how Italy comes to rank so high on the list for expenditure per insured and for premium percentage, while it has such low prices, except for heavy surgery. There is also the question how Germany, with such low prices and low expenditure per insured, can offer its physicians satisfactory incomes (27).

## Conditions for obtaining benefits

The right to benefits is subject to conditions and limitations, which are not identical but similar in the six countries. Some conditions, sometimes very important ones, constitute remarkable differences.

QUALIFYING PERIOD AND MINIMUM PREMIUM
There is a clear distinction between two groups of countries: on the one hand Germany, the Netherlands, and Luxemburg, where

no qualifying period or minimum-premium payment is required for entitlement to benefits, and on the other hand Belgium, France, and some systems in Italy, where such conditions are required. It is worth examining the situation more closely.

No kind of qualifying period exists in the Netherlands, not even in the period between entry into insurance and registration in a health fund: a special text arranges the grant of benefits in this interval (28).

The German system distinguishes between legal insurance benefits (*Regelleistungen*) and the complementary benefits, granted by the funds in their articles of association (*Mehrleistungen*). The law, which prohibits the imposition of a qualifying period, only talks about *Regelleistungen,* not about *Mehrleistungen*. A qualifying period can be imposed (by the articles of association of the funds) for the latter benefits. The distinction has its importance, because *Mehrleistungen* include services such as convalescent care, rehabilitation of handicapped, and certain types of preventive care.

Another distinction has to be made for Germany: between the compulsorily insured and the voluntarily insured. The latter are mainly government officials, workers in family enterprises, small employers, and other self-employed people, whose income does not exceed the wage limit of compulsory insurance for employees. The articles of association of the health funds can prescribe for these voluntarily insured a qualifying period not to exceed six weeks. This has a certain importance because they constitute a substantial group in social health insurance: in 1969 they were 5,294,500 in number in a total of 29,843,750 social insured persons of 17·5 per cent (29).

The general system for workmen in the Grand Duchy of Luxemburg expressly stipulates that the benefits in case of illness start from the first day of illness. However, it should be mentioned that permission is given to the funds to provide in their articles of association for a qualifying period of six months for illnesses which already existed at the time of joining the fund, unless the insured was regularly insured with another fund before. Moreover, the articles of association can, just as in Germany, impose a qualifying period of six weeks for voluntarily insured persons and even a qualifying period of six months for complementary benefits. The same rules on qualifying periods are in force in the system for self-employed persons and for farmers, with an explicit reference to the system for workmen. No qualifying period at all occurs in the system for employees and officials, which also includes the liberal professions.

Qualifying periods are moderately used in the Italian systems, managed by the INAM. But in this field there are indeed big differences between the several systems.

No qualifying period is provided for the farmworkers, once they appear on the name-list of farmworkers. The workmen of industry and trade have a certain qualifying period, in the sense that their claim for benefits only starts after completion of a period of probation, provided by article 1096 of the Civil Code and the National Collective Agreement of 3 January 1939. This period of probation is generally thirty days for the white-collar workers in industry and trade, and for all workers of the banks, insurance companies, and similar institutions. The same applies to the staff of trade unions and political parties (30).

The situation is totally different for domestic staff. Two conditions are imposed: a qualifying period of six months from the beginning of employment and payment of at least twelve weekly premiums in the period of twenty-four weeks before the application for benefits. Also for fishermen there is a qualifying period of two months in which at least one monthly premium must have been paid (31).

It is remarkable that a qualifying period of three months is imposed for 'civilian' blind persons, whereas several categories (apprentices, ministers of religion, pensioners, dockers, orphans) can obtain services without any qualifying period (32).

No qualifying period is imposed in the Italian system for state officials (ENPAS), in the system for officials of local governments (INADEL), and public bodies (ENPDEP). Craftsmen though have only right to benefits from the ninetieth day after their registration in the insurance name-lists. The compulsorily insured traders are in the same situation. But not the self-employed farmers: they are entitled from the day of publication of the name-lists.

French rules on the qualifying period are stricter. In the general system for workers of the private sector, the right to benefits only comes about when the insured has worked 120 to 200 labour hours as a wage-earner in a period of one month or three months respectively before the date of the services. The three months (or one month) can be calculated either currently or from the beginning of the previous calendar trimester or the previous calendar month. Younger insured persons, under 25 years old, have another arrangement: they are entitled (and also their dependants) during the trimester when they became registered and also during the following trimester, if they can prove 60 labour hours as wage-earner before the day they received services.

The self-employed have to fulfil two conditions in their new system: a minimum period of insurance and the payment of sufficient premiums. The minimum insurance period is three months from the beginning of the insurance obligation, and ten months for maternity. Furthermore, the insured should prove that he paid all the premiums due before the date of application for benefits.

Independent farmers have the right to benefits from the day when they became subject to their health insurance legislation. Farmworkers however, have to fulfil more stringent conditions: they must have worked during two-thirds of the year before medical care was received and have paid in the same period at least two-thirds of the premiums due.

The Belgian regulations are the most restrictive. They are the same for all the systems. The insured has to fulfil three conditions at the same time to be entitled to benefits:

(*a*) He should have completed a qualifying period of six months with at least 120 work days or assimilated days (72 days for a female worker who supports her family) and paid premiums to a certain minimum amount.

(*b*) He should be insured for 120 days in the six months before the calendar trimester of his application for benefits (72 days for the female worker with dependants).

(*c*) He should have earned in the same period an income of 16,500 BF per trimester, on which he paid premiums (this income is lower if the insured is under 21 years old), or have paid supplementary premiums if his income is lower.

The differences are very striking: the requirements of qualifying period and minimum premiums are different between the different countries as well as within them: sometimes only a qualifying period is required, sometimes also a minimum premium payment or even the full payment of all the premiums due up to the date of service; some qualifying periods only concern the period from the beginning of the insurance obligation, other qualifying periods have to be fulfilled every time in the period before an application for benefits, etc.

PARTIAL PAYMENT BY PATIENTS

Where payment by patients towards the cost of service is concerned the six countries can be divided into three groups (33): those where in principle the insured does not pay at the time of service (the Netherlands, Germany), those where such payments are generally applied (France, Belgium), and those where systems with and without co-insurance coexist (Italy, Luxemburg) (34). The importance of the additional payment in relation to costs, the degree and the way of its application are also very different in the countries considered.

It has been claimed that the *German* insurance covers the cost of health care totally (35). Consequently, there should not exist any additional payment by the insured. This is only partially true. There is no additional payment for care, supplied by physicians and hospitals, provided that the patient does not have special requirements. However the insured has to pay 20 per cent of the price of drugs with a maximum of 2·50 DM per prescription; some categories of insured persons are exempt (such as pensioners, invalids with at least 50 per cent disablement, recipients of sickness allowances with work-absence of at least ten days, pregnancy or confinement). More important is the fact that the funds give only a subsidy of about one-third of the cost of expensive appliances, glasses, hearing-aids, dentures, and other prostheses. The payment by the insured is one-third, because in general pension insurance also pays one-third. Furthermore, the funds are allowed to fix a maximum amount for the supply of bandages and dressings and they sometimes do so (36).

The *Dutch* health funds pay practically the total cost of medical care for their insured. However, there are still some kinds of additional payment by the insured. First of all there is the important sector of dental care in the sickness funds insurance. The sickness funds do not intervene for tartar removal, and pulp treatment of irregularly checked patients and for examination before regular checking; the insured is charged according to age for fillings of irregularly checked patients. The insured always pays a certain part of the cost of tooth prostheses, usually more than 60 per cent of the price, and never less than 50 per cent. There are also additional payments for jaw-orthopaedic treatment; they vary from 10 fl. to 68 fl. per month of treatment.

There is a personal payment of 5 fl. per session for psychotherapy.

The insured who is admitted to a nursing home pays 50 per cent up to an amount of 21 fl. Transportation also requires additional payment: 1·80 fl. per ride (with ambulance or personal car) with a maximum of 10 fl. (5 fl. if public transport is used) per prolonged case of illness. No additional payment is due for transport from one institution to another. Finally, additional payment is due for appliances and aids. Some of them require a contribution of 10 per cent of total cost, for others the sickness fund pays a fixed amount and the insured pays the rest himself.

Sometimes the two systems are combined: the insured pays 10 per cent of the price up to a certain maximum and the total price above this maximum. The age of the insured is also taken into account for certain benefits, such as orthopaedic shoes, spectacle-frames, hearing-aids, etc.

An additional payment also exists under the General Insurance for Special Medical Care Costs. It concerns elderly people, who are entitled to a pension under the General Old-Age Pension Law and have been in an institution for more than 365 days. In this case, an amount of 331 fl. (for married people 375 fl.) each month is taken off their GOPL pension. Before this General Insurance came into being these old people usually handed over the biggest part of their pension to the institution and only kept a little pocket-money (37).

The *Luxemburg* health insurance for blue-collar workers in the private sector, regulated by the *Code des Assurances Sociales*, is very similar to the German *Reichsversicherungsordnung*. The regulations on additional payments are very similar to those under German social insurance. This applies especially to more expensive appliances for which the funds give only a subsidy calculated as a percentage of the costs (50–100 per cent) up to a maximum amount, so that the rest has to be paid by the patient. Teeth prosthesis only gets subsidy at a flat rate. The workmen pay according to the type of fund, 3 or 5 LF for consulting a physician, and 7 or 8 LF for a home attendance. The personal contribution in pharmaceutic expenses is 15 per cent; except for patients in hospitals. Some funds also charge 2·50 LF per kilometre of the travel expenses of the physician, and 25 per cent of the cost of hospitalization when the beneficiary is a pensioner without any dependent family (38).

However, the real effect of these additional payments can be very limited. The beneficiaries of health insurance for blue-collar workers are also subject to the pension insurance of Book III of the *Code des Assurances Sociales*. This pension insurance supplies medical care to its members, to prevent or treat a labour disablement, just like the German pension insurances. Care is supplied by the sickness fund which the patient joined. The text of Article 220 requires the pension funds to reimburse health care expenses for this purpose, if they exceed the benefits of the health insurance scheme. Little information is available as to the practical effect of this text.

Health insurance for employees, officials, self-employed persons, and farmers in Luxemburg is closer to the French–Belgian type, with built-in co-insurance as a percentage of costs (between 20 and 30 per cent). The actual percentages of additional payment are fixed by the articles of association of the sickness funds, without any legal limitation in the system for employees and officials which also includes the intellectual professions. It should not exceed 20 per cent of the legal tariff, for the self-employed craftsmen, traders, and employers. In addition, these groups have a flat rate co-insurance (deductible) related to the index of prices. The same regulation is in force for the farmers. Co-insurance varies for this group according to the amount and the kind of services. The legal maximum is not less than 50 per cent. The recent act of 2 May 1974 has extended the co-insurance system of these funds, with a general participation of 20 per cent of the cost and the possibility of a deductible, to the funds for blue-collar workers.

Italy has some systems which resemble the German system by offering complete cover and at the same time other systems which use the French system of reimbursement. The various schemes, administered by the INAM, confer complete insurance protection, without any additional payment by the patient. Some systems require a small additional payment for certain drugs: 100 to 200 L in the INAM, 4–9 per cent for the government officials. As in Germany only a fixed subsidy is paid by the insurance for prostheses, orthopaedic appliances, spectacles, hearing-aids, and appliances: the rest is to be paid by the insured. Where care is paid for indirectly the insurance pays a prefixed rate and the insured pays the difference between this rate and the actual fee, over which there is no control.

Cost-sharing by the insured in *Belgian* health insurance is fixed by the law: it amounts to 25 per cent of the agreement rates for ordinary medical care, for the cost of travelling by physicians and for hospital care. The rule does not have real application in hospital care because the hospital act provides for payment of 25 per cent of the day price in hospital by the government. Patients pay for drugs at a flat rate of 50 BF for proprietary drugs (25 BF for certain medicines which are used in large quantities or are used for certain diseases) and 25 BF for generic preparations.

Four groups of insured are privileged in this respect: the pensioners, the invalids, the widows, and orphans. No additional payment is due by these beneficiaries, if their annual income is below 75,000 BF per year, increased by 15,000 BF per dependant (figures related to the index of prices). Only drugs are not supplied free to these vulnerable groups, but the deterrent charge is reduced to 22 BF, and waived in the case of 'social diseases'. The granting conditions in Belgium are very strict for appliances and aids (for teeth prostheses a minimum age of 55 years, apart from exceptional cases).

All other medical services are paid by the insurance at 100 per cent of the agreement rates. However, the physicians have the right to exceed the agreed rates at their own discretion if the income of the insured is higher than 215,000 BF per year (increased by 16,000 BF per dependant), if the insured is admitted in a private room in hospital (and this without medical reasons) or if the patient has special requirements. This creates a major increase in the additional payments by patients. Besides, the physicians are only obliged by the agreements to follow the rates in certain places and hours, which must amount to at least twelve hours spread over three days or three-quarters of the activity in the consulting-room (for specialists: thirty hours, spread over four days), which is another limitation on the guarantees for the insured.

This is not the complete picture of payments by patients in the Belgian system. Indeed, the legal system only applies when at least 60 per cent of the physicians and other care suppliers are bound by an agreement. This figure is largely exceeded by pharmacists, hospitals, and paramedical practitioners, but only in 1970 were all regions of the country subject to agreement with physicians (39). Even so 20 per cent of the physicians refuse to collaborate. The insured who consults a physican not bound by agreement has to pay the difference between the insurance rates and the true fee himself.

The *French* legislation is in this respect similar to the Belgian but it is much more complicated by a variety of regulations for the various schemes. In the general system for wage-earners a general rule requires deterrent fees (fixed each year by decree) for all services. The amount is set at 30, 25, 20, or 10 per cent according to the type of care. It is 30 per cent for drugs, laboratory analyses, spectacles, hearing-aids, and prostheses; 25 per cent for physician's services (other than in institutions where it is 20 per cent); and 10 per cent for some special drugs (40).

Charges are not imposed on war invalids, victims of industrial accidents with two-thirds disablement, and invalidity pensioners. Exempt too are certain prolonged illnesses, such as diabetes, poliomyelitis, and cancer. There is also no co-insurance for expensive services which need hospitalization for at least thirty days (exemption from the thirty-first day) or which disable the insured patient for at least three months (from the fourth month).

These rules would only fully apply where all the care suppliers were bound to social insurance agreements. This is largely true for hospitals, but only partially for doctors. If patients go to one of the other physicians they have to pay the difference between the insurance tariff and the actual fees themselves.

Furthermore, the physicians under convention have in certain cases also the right to exceed the rates without any increase in the insurance payment. This is when the insured has special requirements without medical necessity, and when the physician is recorded on a list of very skilled physicians, which gives him the permanent right to exceed the fees.

Additional payments at the time of service are even greater in the system for self-employed. This group pay 50 per cent of medical fees outside an institution, 20 per cent in an institution, 20 per cent for the treatment of serious diseases which are recorded on a list, and 40 per cent for medicines and prostheses. The personal payment is limited to 15 per cent for serious diseases and 30 per cent for other services if supplied in the out-patient department of a care institution (41).

Clearly the six countries present a varied scene when it comes to payments by patients at the time of use.

# 8
# *Relations with suppliers*

The relations between the suppliers of care and the social insurance institutions are in all countries the result of long evolution characterized, especially for the physicians, by many serious conflicts. These conflicts have generated specific compromise solutions according to the special national situation of the time (42). It is therefore no wonder that the several European systems are so different in organizing the supply of medical care to the insured and regulating the medical professions in the framework of social insurance. There are strong divergencies in this field, and, what is more, the will to harmonize is very weak. The conflicts are still fresh in mind and compromises are clung to from fear that the difficulties may return.

## The operation of the agreement system

One of the points of similarity between the European systems of social health insurance consists of the fact that relations with the medical care suppliers are everywhere regulated by means of agreements. These agreements are concluded much in the same way. They are also similar in their institutional framework, in requiring governmental sanction, and in the main outlines of their contents. However, there are also serious differences. These occur especially in the legal status of the agreements. The questions here are: who is bound by the agreement? For how long? How is this effect sanctioned and supervised?

### ONE OR MORE LEVELS OF AGREEMENT

Disputes between physicians and social security concern the fundamental question of freedom. The solution of the conflicts always involves a basic agreement on a national level, covering the delivery of health care in all national systems. This is found in practically all the countries.

France was, until recently, the only country not having a national agreement text. But, added to the decree which regulated the relations with the care suppliers, there was a model of an agreement, the paragraphs of which were nearly all binding. There were also maximum tariffs, fixed by decree, which could not be exceeded in local agreements. These maximum tariffs in combination with the model agreement could be considered in fact as a national agreement, because they were the result of, sometimes difficult, negotiations between the physicians' unions and the government (43). Since the *convention nationale* of 28 October 1971 all doubts on the existence of a national agreement in France have been dismissed as far as physicians and kinesitherapists are concerned. For other suppliers of care the existing arrangement remains in operation.

Most countries have also agreements on a lower level apart from these national agreements. These are most of the time applicable in a certain region, and sometimes they are even individually concluded. In Italy and Luxemburg the local relations between the individual suppliers of medical care and the insurance institutions are directly regulated by national agreements. In France this is true only for physicians and kinesitherapists.

Until recently, Belgium had a double system of national arrangements and individual agreements for the physicians and dentists. A national arrangement was only applicable to those who signed an individual agreement under it, and this under the suspensive condition that a sufficient number of individual agreements should be signed per region. This system still exists for hospitals, pharmacists, and paramedical auxiliaries, for whom the 'arrangements' are called 'conventions'. But since the amendment of the law, the concluded arrangements are now, under the name *accords* directly applicable to the physicians and dentists except when they expressly refuse their collaboration and under the condition that not too many refusals are recorded.

The Netherlands have individual agreements between each sickness fund and each provider of care, besides the national agreements (model agreements). They are concluded under the special condition that every supplier of care who entered into an agreement with one sickness fund, if asked, has to conclude the same agreement with other funds in the same region, and each sickness fund should agree to contract with the care supplier who asks it, all this subject to reservations where there is serious objection (44).

Except for physicians, regional agreements can be concluded in France in the absence of a national agreement, according to an official agreement model and within the limits of maximum tariffs between the primary funds of the health insurance and the recognized unions of care suppliers on the level of the territory of a *Caisse primaire d'assurance maladie* (primary fund of health insurance), which is about the same as a *département*. France also has individual engagements beside these regional (collective) agreements. Every care supplier can personally sign an agreement, when no collective agreement has been reached on the national level or in his *département*. Then, he agrees with the terms of the model agreement on tariffs fixed by interministerial decree (45).

In Germany, the relations between the social health insurance and the physicians are mainly ruled by the regional agreements which have been concluded between the association of fund physicians and the several organizations of sickness funds on the level of the state (*Land*).

On a higher level there are national agreements which set the general principles of the physicians/health funds relation. Under the regional agreements one finds individual contracts, as a third level of agreements. Only those physicians who voluntarily contracted into the association of fund physicians are bound, according to the legal procedure of admission to funds' practice (46).

NATURE OF AGREEMENTS

The French national agreement or the regional agreements between the *Caisses primaires d'assurance maladie* and the recognized unions of physicians are real collective agreements, declared to be binding by the executive power: these agreements apply with both their compulsory and facultative clauses to all the members of the concerned professional group in the country or in the *département* or other territory for which the agreement has been concluded, once they have been sanctioned by the ministers concerned. Only in the case of the physicians and kinesitherapists is there a possibility of escape, by sending in a written refusal within one month of the conclusion of the agreement (47).

The new Belgian regulations for physicians and dentists (not for the other medical care suppliers) should be regarded as equivalent to the French system from the legal point of view: the national arrangement is a collective agreement, declared binding by the authorities, with a limited possibility for opting-out.

The Luxemburg agreements should also be considered as real collective agreements, declared to be binding by the authorities.

In Belgium as well as in France relations between the physicians and the health insurance are often supposed, erroneously, to be contractual (48). The rights and obligations of the concerned person are of a statutory nature. Once a collective agreement has been declared to be binding by the authorities, it derives its binding power from the law or royal decree, and not from the agreement, where the concerned were mostly not a party (49).

In all the other systems and countries of the EEC the regulation of relations between care suppliers and social health insurance lies less with public authorities and more with personal approval by the persons concerned. The rules are laid down in agreements which have a true contractual nature. These agreements can be collective or individual. Moreover, there is an intermediate form in practice: the collective agreement with individual joining.

Real collective agreements are concluded in Germany between the associations of fund physicians and the sickness funds about the total sums which the fund will pay to the association of fund physicians, and between the same associations of fund physicians and the associations of sickness funds on the level of the *Land* or *Bund* about the way to provide medical care and the calculation method of total compensation. These agreements directly and exclusively bind all the members of the subscribing associations.

The arrangements on the national level between the Italian health insurance (the INAM) and the different groups of medical care suppliers are in fact collective agreements even if they are issued as regulations. These collective arrangements only bind those who notify their acceptance by entering their name on a special list held by the provincial leagues of physicians, or by concluding a contract with the INAM for service as specialist in a dispensary or in a private clinic (50).

The Belgian national agreements with hospitals, pharmacists, and other paramedical practitioners are of the same nature. The agreement binds indeed only those institutions and practitioners, who have notified their adherence by signing individually.

From a legal point of view the Dutch agreements are not collective agreements, but individual contracts between a supplier of care and a sickness fund. Therefore, it was necessary to introduce a rule of non-discrimination in the conclusion of agreements, so that a certain physician cannot refuse to work for members of a certain sickness fund and conversely a sickness fund cannot refuse to contract with a certain physician who lives in the locality. In reality the contents of these individual contracts are fixed by national agreements between the associations of suppliers of care and the associations of health funds (51). The practitioners and the sickness funds can still conclude individual contracts which are variable, but they seem not to do this. All these agreements need to be sanctioned by the sickness funds council: however it is accepted that this sanction can be given once and forever for a national model agreement and for all the individual agreements based on this model (52).

EXTENT OF AGREEMENTS

Luxemburg has the broadest coverage. All engaged in medical practice in a region where a recognized association has signed an agreement, are bound by this agreement. And because they are always signed by the national associations of funds and care suppliers these agreements bind all the medical care suppliers throughout the Grand Duchy (53).

Italy comes near to this situation. The agreements are concluded on the national level, but are only applicable to the physicians who have their name on lists of mutual funds or who conclude a special contract with the INAM for work in a dispensary or as specialist under agreement. In 1971, 41,087 GPs were recorded on the lists. On top of that figure 1,222 public hospitals, 565 private hospitals, 832 dispensaries, 106 centres for ambulatory treatment, and 8,883 private medical clinics were bound to the INAM, either under direct management, or under an agreement in the framework of the national agreement (54). In 1968, 80,000 physicians (6,000 of them are pensioners) were registered in the *Ente nazionale di providenza ed assistenza dei medici* where all the practising physicians are compulsorily insured (55). Consequently, a very high percentage of physicians work under agreements.

The field of application of the agreements is also very broad in France, where all the physicians in the country are bound by the agreement which has been signed by their most representative associations, unless they expressly refuse their co-operation. After the adoption of the agreement system in 1966, 75 out of 90 *départements* came under agreement, and in the other *départements*, with the exception of Paris and Lyons, the number of individually bound physicians varied between 67 and 100 per cent. Since the 1971 reform, and especially since the signing of the 1972 '*avenant*' on tariffs, 96 per cent of the French physicians participate in social health insurance (56). It has, however, been feared that the possibility of opting-out would have resulted in a fewer number of physicians under agreement (57).

The collective agreements in Germany receive also very broad application. The national agreements and the regional agreements bind all the members of an association of funds physicians. How many physicians are members of these associations? Originally, this number was limited by law to 1 physician for every 1,350 registered insured persons; this figure has been gradually reduced to 600. This rule has been declared unconstitutional in 1960 by the constitutional court: henceforth, only criteria of competence are applied to decide the admission to or exclusion from fund practice. By this measure, the number of fund physicians in Germany grew from 36,800 at the end of 1959 to 42,100 (and 1,500 *part-time*) in 1960 (58). According to Coppini and Illuminati, Germany had in 1964 84,000 physicians, 45,650 of them were fund physicians (*full-time+part-time*) (59). However, it should be mentioned that this figure does not include the hospital physicians, who also work for the social insurance with the hospital to which they are attached. Germany has more than 30,000 hospital physicians and practically all the hospitals have a contract with the sickness funds (60). Consequently, the large majority of German physicians supply care under social health insurance.

In Belgium the arrangements bind everyone who does not notify his refusal to co-operate. However, it is as yet impossible to check how many Belgian physicians or dentists participate in fact. The old system, introduced by the law of 9 August 1963 (the so-called Leburton Act), is still in force for hospitals and paramedical auxiliaries. Under it national agreements bind only those who showed their willingness to co-operate by signing an individual engagement. It is known that practically all the hospitals, pharmacists, and paramedical auxiliaries have signed the agreements (61).

Theoretically, the Netherlands should have the smallest field of application of the agreements between the health funds and the co-operators: indeed, the agreements have only an individual effect. But the conclusion of the individual agreements has been considerably facilitated by the creation of national model agreements. A great number of physicians are bound to the health funds by agreements. For 1963 a figure of 53 per cent is given (62). The figures which appear in the reports of the sickness fund council are, however, totally different: they say that the very large majority of the Dutch physicians joined the system of agreements (63).

DURATION OF THE AGREEMENT

The duration of operation of the agreements between the suppliers of care and the insurance is one of the most striking points of difference between the regulations in the several European systems. First of all, a distinction must be made between the countries where agreements are concluded for a fixed period, and those where they are concluded for an undetermined time, with a termination procedure. The first group is the most important; it covers Belgium, France, Italy, and the Netherlands.

The agreements in Belgium with the hospitals and the paramedical auxiliaries expressly provide that they are only in force for a defined period. This period is in most cases one year, but tacit renewal is stipulated, if the agreement is not cancelled in good time. A longer time is provided in the agreements between the physicians or dentists and the health funds, but then without the possibility of tacit renewal. The French legislation expressly regulates the duration and termination of the agreements, by referring to the stipulations of the model agreement, with which the agreements have to comply. In this way, all the regional agreements are concluded for one year. They come to an end on 1 May of each year, but they are tacitly renewed if not cancelled in time. The national convention of 28 October 1971 with the physicians is valid until 1 May 1975, and can be explicitly renewed. The national convention of 29 May 1972 with the kinesitherapists has to be renewed on 19 June 1976. In Italy, national arrangements are concluded for a period longer than one year, but without tacit renewal. In the scheme for public servants this period is four years.

The general *Normative* issued by the INAM on the basis of arrangements with the suppliers of care do not specify duration.

The Dutch agreements are mostly concluded for an undefined period, with a termination possibility for both parties with notice. However, the part concerning the fees is each year renewed or at least each year adapted. All the agreements in Germany and in Luxemburg are concluded for an undefined period, with the possibility of termination for both parties. In Luxemburg, the law delegates its regulation to the agreements themselves.

In Germany the duration of the agreements between the associations of fund physicians and the sickness funds is also defined by the agreements themselves and not by the law. These agreements define the notice, but not the end of their validity.

### Remuneration

Differences in payment systems may be considered under three headings: differences in payment form, differences in the calculation of amounts, and differences in adjusting levels of pay to the cost of living.

PAYMENT FORM

'Payment form' means the criterion or criteria which determine the structure of payment. The structure of payment and its amount are not always fixed by the same procedure. The structure is often fixed by the law (for instance a fee schedule), whereas the fees themselves will be set by agreement.

Two main forms are usually distinguished: fee-per-item-of-service and payment at flat rate. Both are considered fundamentally opposite systems (64). Both can exist in a number of different variations: the fee-per-item-of-service can be freely fixed or can be governed by a previously accepted list of services; it can be calculated for groups of services of great or small extent or for each single technical service; it can be combined with other methods (65).

As far as *family doctors* are concerned, general fee-for-service remuneration is found in Belgium, France, and Luxemburg. In the Netherlands, the family doctors receive a fee per item of service in certain cases only: confinements, services to transients and casual residents or travellers; they are in general paid at a flat rate in the form of capitation fees, per person registered on their list.

Italy, in direct benefit schemes, also applies payment at a flat rate for family doctors. An option is left between the payment 'a notula', ie per attendance, 'doppio forfait' and 'quota a componenti variabili', ie capitation payment and 'sistema misto', ie capitation payment, except for attendance at the patient's home. In 1971 of 41,087 physicians, 14,094 chose the 'notula', 20,585 capitation payment, and 6,408 mixed systems (66). The choice is not made by the individual, but by the group of physicians of a locality. Payment per item of service is retained in systems offering indirect benefits, especially in the public servants' scheme.

Payment of physicians is the subject of a very special regulation in German social health insurance. It can be considered as a combination of a flat rate form and payment per item of service. This is achieved through the agency of the association of fund physicians, the *Kassenärtzliche Vereinigung*. It receives a fixed sum from the sickness fund as a collective payment for the work of all physicians and divides it between the physicians individually in relation to the number of services rendered.

This system was approved by the *Sozialenquête-Kommission*, which was asked by the Government in 1965 to study the situation of social insurance in Germany: 'The institution of the association of fund physicians has done much to resolve within a free market system the near insoluble problem of physicians' remuneration' (67).

The payment form for *specialists* is not uniform in the six countries. First of all, there are specialists *outside* the hospitals. Some countries pay their specialists predominantly by item of service. Such countries are of course Belgium, France, and Luxemburg. But also the Netherlands use this form: the agreement with specialists stipulates payment per item of service (even though less detailed than in the Belgian–French schedules).

Italy comes halfway between the two systems: in the schemes offering indirect benefits the specialists are paid per item of service according to a tariff of fees; the insurance institutions run a large network of dispensaries where specialists work at a fixed salary; but they also pay independent specialists a fee per service.

For non in-patient medicine in Germany the same rules apply to the specialists as to the family doctors: both are members of the *Kassenärtzliche Vereinigung* on equal terms and are consequently compensated in the same way.

The situation is, again, totally different for the specialists who work *in* hospitals (68). Most German and Italian hospital physicians are appointed to the staff and are paid a fixed salary. In the other countries, some are paid a salary, as in Germany and Italy, and some are paid in some other flat rate form by the hospital while others are, with or without the intermediary of the hospital, paid per item of service. The payment of a hospital specialist is also often a mixture of these compensation forms. The payment form is sometimes ambiguous: physicians may be paid by the hospital at a flat rate (salaried), while the hospital charges fees per item of service for their medical work.

The form for *pharmacists* is of course not the same. The profession is usually very similar to an independent retail business (69).

Consequently, the classic compensation form for the pharmacist is the profit margin on his sales. This classic form is preserved most clearly in Germany: the agreements with the insurance institutions only deal with the price of medicines (including increased prices for urgent dispensing at night or during the week-end).

The pharmacists in the other EEC countries tend to have fees. This is usually a payment per service: this is the case in Belgium, Luxemburg, and Italy, even if this fee has a different structure in the various countries. Only the Dutch pharmacists are paid at a flat rate. The Dutch pharmacists receive an annual fixed amount per person registered on their list, just like the GPs, besides specific payment per script dispensed including a sum for container and a (small) profit margin on the products.

Payments to hospitals are quite different. These institutions can be owned by the insurance fund or have concluded a contract with a fund. The former system is little used in Europe. In the second case, the hospital can agree with the insurance institution to apply several tariff forms, within the framework of the legislation or the regulations which control the hospital tariffs.

## CALCULATION OF PAYMENT

In Belgium and France, the fees of the *family doctors* are calculated on the basis of a schedule of medical services. This nomenclature fixes the relative value of all individual medical services. The values result from the multiplication of their coefficient with a certain amount of money, fixed by agreement. The services are not always paid separately: the consultation or home visit in France as well as in Belgium includes the usual examination and treatment, and the fee for a technical service may not be added.

Luxemburg has different calculation methods, according to the insurance scheme. In the general scheme for blue-collar workers, the system is like Belgium and France. But the schemes for employees and officials and for self-employed persons introduce a distinction according to the income of the insured: the fees are higher for the insured with higher income, the reimbursement by the fund remaining the same to all the insured. The physician is entirely free to fix his fees for the highest income class of the self-employed.

The Dutch GPs' capitation fee is fixed annually by agreement between the physicians and the health funds. Fees are weighted for the first 1,800 registered patients to promote an average practice size. Beside this annual capitation payment, the family doctor receives specific payments per service for the care of patients not registered on his list and for confinements, and he may charge travelling expenses if he has to cover more than 4 km to visit patients. On top of this, the funds pay per registered patient a certain sum (about 10 per cent of the capitation fee) directly to the physicians' pension fund (70).

In Italy, GPs have a choice between two compensation systems in schemes offering direct benefits. Under one system the doctor receives each year a certain amount per insured person registered on his list. These amounts vary according to the categories of the insured (farmers, other sectors, children under 6 years, and pensioners) and according to the type of municipality (below 100,000 inhabitants, between 100,000 and 500,000, and more than 500,000). Under the other system, the physician receives a fee per item of service. This is an amount at a flat rate per visit or per house attendance varying according to the type of municipality. It seems that physicians in cities prefer the payment per item of service, and that in the country capitation payment prevails. Both types of payment are increased with 'quote aggiuntive' according to the geographical spreading of patients (71). In the *assistenza indiretta,* the physician fixes his fee freely in the classic liberal way.

German physicians are paid differently because of the mediation of the association of fund physicians, the *Kassenärtzliche Vereinigungen*. The sickness fund pays a total amount to this association, which divides it between its members in ratio to their services. The total amount is calculated according to two opposite systems, called by the typical German names *Pauschalhonorierungsverfahren* (PHV) and *Einzelleistungshonorierungsverfahren* (EHV), dependent on the type of agreement concluded between the sickness fund and the association of fund physicians. In the first case, the total amount to be paid by the fund is calculated on the basis of objective factors, fixed by the law; the physicians send in their fee-bills, according to the official tariff; the total amount is compared with the sum paid by the fund (minus administrative expenses) and thus the payment quota of the fees is fixed (with some corrections). Consequently, the relative value of the services is stated in the official tariff, but the amount of the actual fee depends on the total amount paid by the fund. In the second case (EHV) the fees for medical services are directly negotiated with the *Krankenkasse*. The total amount payable by the fund is then calculated, proceeding from the sum of these fees.

*Specialists* outside hospital are paid in the same way as the family doctors in Belgium, France, Luxemburg, and Germany. However, their remuneration calculation in the Netherlands and in Italy has some special aspects.

The Dutch specialists are paid per item of service. The basis of payment, however, is the card by which the family doctor refers a patient to a specialist. This referral card has a certain value, fixed by agreement. It covers the price of a month of examination and treatment. When the specialist thinks proper to do so he writes a repeat card, which has the same duration but is worth less money; certain examinations or treatments are paid for separately.

Specialists in Italy usually provide their services in dispensaries of the INAM. They work there for a monthly salary, the amount of which is calculated according to the number of hours spent per week on duty and the type of municipality. Besides, independent specialists under agreement are compensated according to a fee-for-service tariff, whose detail and amounts are directly fixed by agreement between the associations of physicians and the insurance institution. The same applies to out-of-hours work of specialists in the dispensaries.

The payment of *hospital physicians* is made in too many different ways to be described here (72). The hospital often itself sets the criteria for paying its medical personnel, in other cases the medical staff of a hospital decide among themselves the division of fees. In still other cases the authorities set the wage-scales of medical staff in hospitals.

ADAPTATION OF REMUNERATION TO PRICE RISES

Variable procedures are used to adapt income levels to the effects of inflation.

The six countries fall into two groups: those which adjust health care prices automatically by linking to an index number, and those where a special or new agreement is negotiated. Belgium, Luxemburg, and Italy belong to the first group; the second group includes France, Germany, and the Netherlands.

The fees of the Belgian physicians are related to changes in the index number of consumer prices (formerly the retail-trade index number). The money-value of the key letters in the schedule are changed each year on 1 January and again increased by 5 per cent on 1 July if the index number has risen by 4·235 per cent between 1 December and 31 May.

The Luxemburg agreements provide index-linking of payment through a system in force for wage scales of all public officials. This means that all remunerations are raised each time the index number increases by 2·5 points on average over the last six months. The compensation of care suppliers in Italy is also adapted to the cost of living. It was impossible to deduce from our sources how it works.

France is one of the countries without any index linking or other automatic adjustment of fees. This situation originates in the short duration of the agreements. They originally expired every year on a fixed day. Under the new national agreement a review can be asked for every year before 31 March. This gives the parties ample opportunities to discuss adaptation of the fees.

Germany does not have automatic adaptations either, because the lump-sum payments between the funds and the associations of fund physicians are revised each year anyway. For these annual revisions in the framework of the PHV the law fixes some criteria to be followed. These criteria are: the demand for health care by the insured, the financial situation of the sickness fund, and the changes in incomes of the insured. In the case of the EHV the annual total payment by the fund is directly related to the tariff of medical fees. Here, the physicians can cancel at any moment the fee regulation and ask for a change, with notice of six months from the beginning of each calendar quarter.

The Dutch agreements also require a notice of six months (in some cases only one month). Furthermore, each agreement is revised annually at least with regard to the part concerning payments. In the meantime, an adaptation of the fees is only carried through if a very exceptional rise in prices and wages occurs.

### REFERENCES

1. ENGELS, J., *De evolutie van de verplichte ziekte- en invaliditeitsverzekering* (Brussels, 1970), p. 99.
2. See for Belgium, Germany, and the Netherlands: FULCHER, D., *Medical Care Systems* (Geneva, ILO, 1974), pp. 71–72, 101–2, 131–2.
3. REVOL, J., 'Régimes spéciaux de sécurité sociale', *Répertoire de droit social et du travail* (Paris, Dalloz, 1960), pp. 473–4.
4. CHIAPPELLI, U., op. cit., pp. 184–7.
5. LAROQUE, P., 'La Place de la mutualité dans la protection sociale en France', *La Mutualité Agricole, Droit Social* (no. spécial), **11** (1969), 19; CULAUD, H., and LAGRAVE, M., 'Analyse', *L'Assurance maladie des travailleurs non salariés des professions non agricoles, Droit Social* (no. spécial), **3** (1971), 138–9.
6. FULCHER, D., op. cit., pp. 135–6.
7. SOZIALENQUETE-KOMMISSION, *Soziale Sicherung in der Bundesrepublik Deutschland* (Stuttgart, sd).
8. DUPEYROUX, J. J., *Développement et tendances des régimes de sécurité sociale dans les pays membres des communautés européennes et de la Grande-Bretagne* (Luxemburg, ECSA, 1966), pp. 49–50, 170.
9. —— ibid., p. 81.
10. COMMISSION DE LA CE, *Rapport sur l'évolution de la situation sociale dans la communauté en 1968* (Brussels, EEC, 1969), no. 330, pp. 178–9.
11. COMMISSION OF THE EUROPEAN COMMUNITIES, *Comparative Tables of Social Security* (Brussels, EEC, 1970).
12. VAN LANGENDONCK, J., *De Harmonisering van de Sociale Verzekering voor Gezondheidszorgen in de EEG* (Leuven, 1971), pp. 233–4.
13. COPPINI, M. A., *Les Incidences économiques de la sécurité sociale* (Brussels, EEC), Doc. V/5483/68-F, pp. 96–97, 124.
14. CHIAPPELLI, U., op. cit., p. 159.
15. RIBAS, J. J., *La Politique sociale des communautès européennes* (Paris, 1969), p. 400.
16. JANTZ, K., and KAUPPER, H., German report, in EUROPEAN INSTITUTE OF SOCIAL SECURITY, *Yearbook 1970* (Leuven, 1970), p. 56.
17. AHLBOUN, H., 'Sickness insurance in the Grand Duchy of Luxemburg', *Health Services Financing* (London, BMA, 1970), p. 435.

18. DOUBLET, J., and DUPEYROUX, J. J., *Etude sur la physionomie actuelle de la sécurité sociale dans les pays de la C.E.E.* (Brussels, EEC, 1962), p. 88.
19. ROEMER, M. I., *L'Organisation des soins médicaux dans le cadre de la sécurité sociale* (Geneva, BIT, 1969), p. 33; in the same sense: DEJARDIN, J., 'L'Organisation des soins médicaux dans la sécurité sociale', *Revue internationale de sécurité sociale* (1968), pp. 378–82.
20. LEVI-SANDRI, L., *Istituzioni di Legislazione Sociale* (Milan, 1966), p. 287.
21. CHIAPPELLI, U., op. cit., p. 23.
22. CARAPEZZA, G., *Les Rapports entre les médecins et l'assurance contre les maladies dans la république italienne* (Brussels, 1965), pp. 7–8.
23. DUPEYROUX, J. J., *Sécurité sociale* (Paris, 1967), pp. 117, 122.
24. DILLEMANS, R., 'De nieuwe wetgeving inzake ziekeverzekering', in *Actuele problemen van sociaal recht* (Leuven, 1966), p. 158.
25. CARAPEZZA, G., op. cit., pp. 7–8.
26. ASSOCIATION INTERNATIONALE DE LA MUTUALITE, *Les Relations avec le corps médical* (Geneva, 30 July 1971), pp. 32, 36, 38, 40, 44, 46–49.
27. SOZIALENQUETE-KOMMISSION, op. cit., p. 226.
28. Royal Decree of 4 January 1966, art. 28, b. and Decision of the Sickness Funds Council *(Besluit Ziekenfondsraad)* of 21 December 1967, art. 2.
29. BUNDESMINISTER FÜR ARBEIT UND SOZIALORDNUNG, *Hauptergebnisse der Arbeits- und Sozialstatistik 1969* (Bonn, 1970), p. 103.
30. CHIAPPELLI, U., op. cit., p. 111.
31. FERRARI, G., and LAGONEGRO, G., *Le assicurazioni sociali* (Milan, 1971), pp. 604–5; INAM *(Il sistema assistenziale dell'INAM* [Rome, INAM, 1973], pp. 49–50) seems to say the contrary.
32. CHIAPPELLI, U., op. cit., pp. 110–11.
33. ASSOCIATION INTERNATIONALE DE LA MUTUALITE, op. cit., pp. 4–5; DOUBLET, J., and DUPEYROUX, J. J., op. cit., pp. 89–90; ANDRIESSEN, L., 'De driehoeken zijn niet congruent', *Ziekenfondsvragen* (1965), pp. 275–8.
34. The recent reform act of 2 May 1974 will bring Luxemburg into the second group, together with Belgium and France (art. 10 of the act). See: *Rapport concernant la réforme de l'assurance maladie des ouvriers*, Chambre des Députés, Session ordinaire 1972–3, no. 1653, pp. 11–14.
35. RANG, J. F., 'Het eigen risico in de ziekenfondsverzekering', *Tijdschrift voor Sociale Geneeskunde*, **19** (1966), 740.
36. SCHEWE, D., NORDHORN, K., and SCHENKE, K., *Survey of Social Security in the Federal Republic of Germany* (Bonn, Federal Ministry for Labour and Social Affairs, 1972), p. 134.
37. LEDEBOER, L. V., *Heden en verleden van de ziekenfondsverzekering en de verzekering van bijzondere ziektekosten* ('s Gravenhage, 1973), p. 41.

38. *L'Assurance maladie au Grand Duché de Luxembourg pendant l'exercice 1972* (Luxemburg, sd), pp. 44–47.
39. GOSSERIES, PH., 'La Collaboration des médecins et des praticiens de l'art dentaire à l'assurance maladie obligatoire', *Journal des Tribunaux du Travail*, 5 (1970), 49–50.
40. In the *départments Haut-Rhin, Bas-Rhin*, and *Moselle* (close to Germany) the patient pays only 10 per cent on drugs and on physicians' services and nothing for all care in hospital (UCANSS, *Guide de la sécurité sociale*, p. 49).
41. CULAUD, H., and LAGRAVE, M., op. cit., p. 144.
42. LYNCH, M. J., and RAPHAEL, S. S., *Medicine and the State* (Springfield [Ill.], Ch. Thomas, 1963), 880 pp.; COPPINI, M. A., and ILLUMINATI, F., 'Les Relations entre les institutions de sécurité sociale et le corps médical', *Revue Internationale de sécurité sociale* (Geneva), 2 (1968), 216.
43. BARJOT, A., 'Les Relations entre les organismes de sécurité sociale et le corps médical en France', *Revue Française du Travail*, 1 (1965), 16.
44. VELDKAMP, G. M. J., 'De plaats van de geneesheer in de wettelijke struktuur van de sociale gezondheidszorg', *De geneesheer en het recht* (Deventer, 1968), p. 29.
45. 'La Convention nationale entre la sécurité sociale et le corps médical', *Droit Social* (no. spécial), 9–10 (1971), 596–7.
46. WANNAGAT, G., *Lehrbuch des Sozialversicherungsrechts* (Tübingen, 1965), part 7, pp. 132–3.
47. UCANSS, *Guide de la sécurité sociale*, p. 363.
48. GOSSERIES, PH. P., 'La Collaboration des médecins et des praticiens de l'art dentaire à l'assurance-maladie obligatoire', *Journal des Tribunaux du Travail*, 5 (1970), 45; BARJOT, A., op. cit., p. 14; DUPEYROUX, J. J., 'La Sécurité sociale et les médecins', *Recueil Dalloz*, 31 (1960), 185.
49. BLANPAIN, R., *De collectieve overeenkomst in de bedrijfstak naar Belgisch recht* (Leuven, 1961), pp. 173–6.
50. *Il sistema assistenziale dell'INAM*, pp. 15–18.
51. LEDEBOER, L. V., op. cit., pp. 36–37.
52. MANNOURY, J., *Hoofdtakken van de sociale verzekering* (Alphen a.d. Rijn, 1967), p. 130.
53. KAYSER, A., op. cit., p. 579.
54. INAM, *Bilancio Consuntivo dell'Esercizio 1971* (Rome, INAM, sd), pp. 189, 203, 216.
55. CHIAPPELLI, U., op. cit., pp. 603, 609.
56. DUPEYROUX, J. J., *Sécurité sociale* (5th edn), p. 367.
57. 'La Convention nationale entre la sécurité sociale et le corps médical', *Droit Social* (no. spécial), 9–10 (1971), 574.

58. LYNCH, M. J., and RAPHAEL, S. S., op. cit., p. 60.
59. COPPINI, M. A., and ILLUMINATI, F., op. cit., p. 270, table 1.
60. FULCHER, D., *Medical Care Systems* (Geneva, BIT, 1974), pp. 74–75.
61. RIZIV, *Algemeen Verslag*, 4° deel, (Brussels, RIZIV, 1971), pp. 12–17.
62. COPPINI, M. A., and ILLUMINATI, F., op. cit., p. 271.
63. ZIEKENFONDSRAAD, *Jaarverslag 1972*, p. 181.
64. ROEMER, M. I., *L'Organisation des soins médicaux dans le cadre de la sécurité sociale* (Geneva, BIT, 1969), pp. 35–38; RIBETTES-TILHET, J., op. cit., p. 640; HOGARTH, J., *The Payment of the General Practitioner* (Oxford, 1963), p. 525; GLASER, W. A., *Paying the Doctor* (Baltimore, London, 1970), p. 25.
65. BURNS, E., *Social Security and Public Policy* (New York, 1963), pp. 139–42.
66. INAM, *Bilancio Consuntivo 1971* (Rome, INAM, sd), p. 189.
67. SOZIALENQUETE-KOMMISSION, op. cit., p. 223.
68. QUAETHOVEN, P., op. cit., pp. 408–10.
69. ROEMER, M. I., op. cit., p. 16.
70. LEDEBOER, L. V., op. cit., pp. 46–48.
71. *Il sistema assistenziale dell'INAM*, 17; FRY, J., and FARNDALE, A. J., *International Medical Care* (Oxford, Lancaster, 1972), p. 48.
72. QUAETHOVEN, P., op. cit., pp. 408–10.

# PART THREE

# CONVERGING AND DIVERGING PATHS

# 9
# Evolution of social insurance as an institution

## The future of the insurance principle

Only at the end of the nineteenth century can one start to speak of real social insurance. At that time the public authorities began supporting the mutual sickness funds by providing them with a legal status and by granting some subsidies (1). Only in the Netherlands did the mutual funds continue to exist until as late as the Second World War without any intervention from the state (2).

In Germany and Luxemburg the period of state-supported voluntary insurance was very short or even nonexistent because of the very early introduction of compulsory insurance. In the Netherlands too health insurance went immediately from private insurance without government intervention to a compulsory insurance; but this occurred at a very much later stage, at a time when most countries had experienced compulsory insurance for some years. In Italy the transition from voluntary to compulsory insurance was made in a very different way. Compulsory insurance was not imposed by the government for the whole of the employed working class, but in every branch of industry the trade unions joined with the employers in collective agreements which among other things organized compulsory health insurance (3).

In Belgium and France the voluntary health insurance funds received government subsidies from the beginning of the twentieth century on. The great success of the mutual funds movement in these countries certainly delayed the introduction of compulsory insurance considerably. But the depression period of the 1930s and the Second World War brought about such large movements towards social security that the introduction of compulsory health insurance could not be postponed any longer. After the Second World War in all of the six countries the situation was reached that the majority of the population was protected against the cost of health care by compulsory insurance.

Much similarity in the nature of health insurance had existed earlier in the nineteenth century, with all countries resting on the private sickness funds. During the first half of the twentieth century the evolution developed at a very different pace in the various countries. First in Germany and Luxemburg, afterwards in Italy, then in the Netherlands and finally in France and Belgium, the voluntary insurance principle was abandoned in favour of compulsory insurance for all workers.

A second period of similarity lasted about twenty years: from 1945 until 1965. In recent years however new divergent evolutions have occurred. In France and Belgium recent legislative measures have extended the field of application to practically the entire population, including non-employed persons. At the same time in the Netherlands a general insurance for special health care costs has been introduced, which protects the entire population against a few of the heaviest health care costs, such as long-term hospital stay and care in special institutions. These developments break with one of the elements which belong to the very nature of the compulsory insurance system, the link between the contribution of the worker, based upon his salary or his occupational income, and the entitlement to insurance benefits (4). The evolution goes even further in Italy, where the introduction of a national health service is being prepared in the framework of national social and economic planning (5). In other countries as well supporters of the idea of a national health insurance are frequently found (6).

Three different positions can be taken on future developments. One can believe that the future development will return towards voluntary insurance schemes. One can also believe that the system of national compulsory insurance will be maintained, and one can be in favour of an evolution towards a national health service.

Some people will ask a more fundamental question: will social health insurance be needed at all? Will not the general wealth have risen so high that people can care for themselves by way of private insurance? Nobody can seriously pretend that at this moment social insurance is not necessary for the majority of the population of the rich industrialized countries to finance health care. It appears that the rapid development of medical science and techniques increases both the number and the cost of diagnostic and curative devices. The rate of increase goes on every year. So one may conclude that in the future, whatever the level of income of the population may be, not more and very probably fewer persons will be able to pay for their own medical expenses either out of pocket or by private insurance (7). So the question is merely whether the *social* insurance will be voluntary or compulsory or if there will be a national health service.

In some industrialized countries voluntary health insurance has prevailed. Indeed some economists advocate a general return to the principles of voluntary insurance in order to solve the problems of financing health care (8). It should be pointed out, however, that every type of voluntary scheme has to deal with the problems of selection and of opting out. By selection the insurance organization tries to avoid the bad risks, such as the elderly, handicapped, and so on. So voluntary insurance tends to exclude those people who need coverage most. Opting out means that the best risks, such as young people in good health, stay out of insurance because they fail to see the need for it. Thus the voluntary insurance schemes are biased towards a limited field of application and high premiums, which can only be paid by richer people. The whole system tends to benefit only those who need cover least. Even if the government decides to grant subsidies to the voluntary insurance fund in order to maintain the premiums at a reasonable level, this system cannot be really satisfactory. The financial situation of the various sickness funds will always be different, and common financing policy by government will result in a varied level of protection for various groups of the population (9).

The obvious answer to this situation is compulsory insurance. By making membership of the insurance funds compulsory the government eliminates the effects of selection and opting out mechanisms. In all the countries under review voluntary insurance was abandoned for compulsory insurance. But compulsory health insurance also has its problems. On the one hand it does not achieve complete equality between all citizens either because the level of protection is not the same for all social groups or by the fact that charges are not divided according to capacity to pay, or by both. On the other hand, the explosion in medical care costs lays a very heavy strain on the insurance system. The compulsory health insurance systems face very serious financial problems unless they can succeed in setting up meaningful controls over the supply of medical services (10).

These are precisely the two most distinctive characteristics of a national health service: the extension of protection to all inhabitants of the country in an equal spirit and direct government responsibility for the supply of medical care (11). It could therefore be argued that the creation of national health services in the different countries is the next step in the evolution which formerly led to compulsory health insurance. Developments in Belgium and France, in the Netherlands, and in Italy seem to point in this direction.

Are we to conclude that the future of health insurance systems in Europe lies in the creation of national health services? Not necessarily. If we look at the evolution of social security as a whole, it is generally believed that the future situation will be of a mixed nature (12). There will be a basic general minimum protection for the whole of the population. In addition to this basic system large occupational schemes of income maintenance will be created for all workers. On top of this structure will come additional schemes of a private nature. The provision of health care is generally regarded as a basic need. Most authors expect that, as part of the basic protection of the population, a unified and generalized national health care financing system will be provided, which may or may not carry the name of national health service.

A national health service would certainly provide for an appropriate structure to tackle the problems of health care and its financing. But within the framework of compulsory insurance too these problems may be attacked. The French, Belgian, and Dutch examples show that compulsory health insurance can be extended to protect the entire population. Also in all countries at this moment solutions are sought for the problem of rationalization of medical care within the structure of health insurance (13). Of course such a health insurance system will have to change its aspect so as to resemble very closely a national health service: it will have to cover all inhabitants equally and to allocate costs according to ability to pay, and it will have to assume responsibility for the rational supply of medical care in order to control the evolution of medical care costs. Whether such a system receives the name of national health service or not is immaterial.

So far we are dealing with basic protection for the population. It is not very likely that only this basic protection will subsist in the future. The general orientation of development in social security points elsewhere (14). It may be expected that, in addition to this basic protection, large compulsory or voluntary occupational systems for certain social groups will give the members a higher level of cover and that on top of this structure private provision, either by firms or by commercial insurance companies will give more complete protection.

## Field of application

Initially the health insurance systems in Europe were of the classical Bismarckian type. That is, they were intended for wage-earners, as is clearly indicated by their financing, which includes employers' and employees' contributions. One may object that the Belgian, French, and Italian legislation on compulsory health insurance was based on a wider perspective, inspired by Roosevelt's ideas (15). They were intended to give protection to the entire population. But in reality these systems did not go so far. They remained, at least temporarily, limited in their field of application to wage-earners only.

Originally most systems did not even include all wage-earners. The field of application was limited by a wage limit which was at first very low. Only Italy and Belgium provided exceptions to this. In France a low wage limit was abolished in 1945 and this example was followed by Luxemburg in 1951. In the Netherlands and Germany, where the wage limit has remained in operation, the level has been raised several times. Recently the German wage limit, which applies only to white-collar workers has been made dynamic in that it has been linked to the general level of wages. Apart from this it may be said that in Europe all wage-earners are protected by compulsory insurance against most medical care costs.

In the period after the Second World War came the extension movement towards self-employed workers. Formerly, self-employed workers had shown very little inclination to enter the social security system, which was considered to be something for wage-earners. From the 1950s one may observe that this attitude changed. More and more the self-employed workers expressed their desire for social protection in the same way as wage-earners. The progressive extension of social security to the self-employed is considered by most writers as the most remarkable convergent trend in the evolution of the European social security systems (16).

Italy is the only country which already had official compulsory health insurance funds for self-employed workers before the Second World War. It underwent also the most rapid changes after the war, although it still does not provide compulsory insurance for large employers. France, Belgium, and Luxemburg followed in the period between 1957 and 1966. In 1967 in the Netherlands general insurance was established to protect the entire population, and also of course self-employed workers, against the most heavy medical risks. And most recently Germany has created a compulsory system for self-employed farmers.

This evolution points evidently towards a future situation in which all employed and self-employed workers will be protected for health care costs. Meanwhile, a new development has taken place: the extension of protection to non-employed persons.

The first of this group to receive benefits were, of course, those persons no longer employed: old-age pensioners who had been compulsorily insured during their active life. And in the group of pensioners it was the formerly employed who were the first to be protected. Insurance could be extended to retired self-employed workers only after the inclusion of self-employed workers themselves.

Certain countries have protected their retired workers much later than others. It happened during the Second World War or immediately afterwards in Germany, France, and Belgium. In Italy it had to wait until 1955. The health insurance system for elderly in the Netherlands is not a compulsory one and the German health insurance for retired employed workers is not compulsory for all of them. It is typical that in these countries, where the right to protection against medical care costs is most closely linked to occupation, the retired workers are not yet under compulsory insurance and that in Italy, where for other reasons the link between work and health insurance is historically very strong (17), extension to the retired came later than elsewhere.

For the same reasons European systems have been slow in including other groups of non-active persons, such as students, handicapped people, unemployed, etc. Students were only insured in their own right in France in 1949 and in Belgium in 1969. In the other European countries students are not yet considered to be entitled to health care insurance in their own right. Belgium was the first country to recognize handicapped persons and civilian invalids as beneficiaries of compulsory insurance. In most countries these persons are dependent on national assistance.

In recent years developments in a number of countries have been such that the field of application of their compulsory health insurance systems includes practically the entire population. If one includes those who are entitled to join the health insurance system voluntarily this is true for Luxemburg, France, and Belgium. To a certain extent it is true for the Netherlands where all inhabitants are protected against the heaviest medical care costs and Italy certainly is heading this way, with a projected national health service in the near future. This evolution leads to the conclusion that a convergent trend is observed towards generalization of the field of application.

The figures in Table 10 generally confirm the trend towards 100 per cent inclusion. Only in the Netherlands over the last twenty years the number of beneficiaries of sickness funds insurance as a percentage of the population has not increased: but here one should bear in mind that the Netherlands really protects 100 per cent of its population through the general insurance scheme for special medical care costs. Yet, this special system only offers

TABLE 10
Trend in total number of beneficiaries of
health care insurance as a percentage of the total population

|  | Belgium | Germany | France | Italy | Luxemburg | Netherlands |
|---|---|---|---|---|---|---|
| 1955[1] | 67·4 | 84·0 | 64·2 | 60·0 | 73·8 | 75·9 |
| 1960[2] | 73·1 | 85·1 | 66·3 | 78·3 | 83·2 | 75·4 |
| 1965[3] | 90·6 | 87·3 | 88·0 | 85·2 | 98·1 | 74·1 |
| 1970[4] | 99·0 | 90·0 | 98·0 | 91·0 | 99·0 | 76·0 |

1. From: EEC-Commission, *Rapport sur la situation sociale dans la Communauté en 1959* (Brussels, 1960), table 7, 334–5.
2. Ibid., *1965* (Brussels, 1966), table 8, 255.
3. Ibid., *1968* (Brussels, 1969), table 1, 297.
4. Ibid., *1973* (Brussels, 1974), table VII, 242–3.

protection against the heaviest risks so that it appears to be marginal compared with sickness funds insurance. In Italy a recent act has already offered voluntary insurance for free hospital care to the entire population in the public hospitals (18).

In reality the two countries with essentially divergent trends are Germany and the Netherlands, because of the limitation of the field of application for wage-earners by a wage limit and because of the exclusion of most self-employed workers and non-active groups. From the above it is clear that in these countries we cannot expect insurance to be extended to self-employed workers or to non-employed people if the wage limit for employed workers remains. This does not seem likely to happen soon. In Germany, where the salary limit only applies to the white-collar workers, recent discussions on its abolition have not been successful (19). The only result has been that the salary limit has been linked to the general wage level, so that at least the number of beneficiaries will no longer be reduced by increases in the level of salaries. It seems probable that this system will be maintained for a number of years. In the Netherlands also there seems to be little hope that the wage limit will be removed in the near future, as the medical profession and the insurance industry are even strongly opposed to any change in the limit beyond normal adjustment to the cost of living (20). Moreover, the existence of the general insurance for special medical care costs reduces the urge for an extension of sickness funds insurance. Nevertheless the actual government prepares legislation to introduce general health insurance for the entire population; it has committed itself to realization of this plan in the near future (21).

What should be the conclusion for the future? If one looks at the development from a wider angle, it appears that the divergent evolution in Germany and the Netherlands cannot be maintained. The progress of social security has permitted us to clarify certain ideas. Some social insurance systems aim at guaranteeing their income to workers in the case of illness, accident, old age, or unemployment, other social insurance systems intend to protect all citizens against certain heavy charges which may be a threat to their economic security, such as children and medical care costs. The latter type of insurance should be organized for the population at large and not for employed workers alone. The protection systems for family allowances and medical costs have been linked with labour at a time when the employed workers were considered to coincide with the economically weak, and would not be able to bear these charges themselves. Nowadays this has completely changed. Employed workers are not the poorest members of the community, and moreover medical care costs have risen so high that even the richest citizens cannot always meet them (22). In so far as a link between labour, and especially low-paid labour, and health insurance still exists, this may be expected to disappear in the long term.

If this is true we may conclude that the national health service systems (Great Britain, Italy) or the general insurance systems (Netherlands) will be the systems of the future. If the entire population has to be insured, it does not make sense to organize separate insurance systems. So we may believe that the recent tendency to add to existing systems for various social groups a residual system for all people not already in one of these schemes, will not last long. This is the more true as this elaborate technique brings about difficult problems with regard to the members of the family of the workers. All the different problems and the various solutions on the qualification of a head of a family and of dependent persons cease to be relevant when all inhabitants are insured as inhabitants.

## Organization

UNIFICATION OR DIVERSIFICATION OF INSURANCE

If one considers the history of social health insurance in continental Europe one notes a convergence in the evolution towards the creation in all countries of an ever-increasing number of special statutory health insurance regimes. This seems to contradict the conclusions above.

At the beginning of this development every country had only one statutory health insurance regime for wage-earners in industry and commerce with less than a certain wage. This formal unity of insurance in fact hid great diversity in the funds which were largely autonomous. Legally however, there was one system only. But the extension of the field of application to new social groups regularly led to the creation of special systems, if it was felt that the problems of these groups were of such a nature, that they could only with difficulty be included in the general plan.

This extension first concerned special groups of wage-earners. These were usually workers employed in agriculture. Within the framework of the general system Germany created in 1914 a special health insurance organization for agricultural workers, with its own funds. In France, the *'mutualité sociale agricole'* has been in existence since the beginning of this century, and it has always remained completely outside the social security structure for other workers. Coal-miners also frequently have their own systems. The German *'Knappschaftskrankenkassen'* existed already before Bismarck's legislation; from 1883 on they became part of the general system but with their own institutional structure; in 1894 they received their own legal basis and became again independent of the general system. Again with seamen: in France health insurance for seamen was organized on a proper legal basis by a *'caisse des invalides de la marine'*, founded under Louis XIV. In Germany a special *'Seekrankenkasse'* works within the general framework, but with distinct organizational rules. In Belgium health insurance for seamen is organized as *'Hulp-en Voorzorgskas'* for seamen and is completely independent. Italy also has special funds for seamen, which are even separate for those of the Mediterranean, the Tyrrenean, and the Adriatic Seas.

The result of this evolution is that now for special groups of wage-earners in various countries special independent regimes exist. Only in the Netherlands is there no special regime for a particular group of wage-earners. In Belgium this is limited only to seamen and railway personnel. In Germany it applies only to the coal-miners, the seamen being in fact integrated into the general system. Luxemburg has a special scheme for white-collar workers, which they share with the civil servants. But France has a large number of special schemes for various industries and public enterprises. Italy has an immense number of special schemes for all types of special groups.

Most of the special schemes for wage-earners were created before the Second World War and a few of them are very old, being created in the middle of the nineteenth century or even earlier. The Luxemburg health insurance system for white-collar workers and civil servants, which lifted the white-collar workers out of the general scheme for wage-earners, is the only case we know of a special system for wage-earners, created after the Second World War.

The extension of compulsory health insurance to self-employed workers is a much more recent phenomenon. Thus the special schemes for self-employed workers are much younger than those for wage-earners. Only in Italy were a few of the special funds for the self-employed created before the Second World War. This is true for the funds of physicians (1937), midwives (1937), pharmacists (1926), notaries (1919), painters and sculptors (1936), musicians (1936), and also in a certain sense for authors whose fund was created in 1948 as an offshoot from a fund that existed before the war.

From 1951 on one sees the creation of an impressive series of special schemes for the self-employed: in 1952 for Italian lawyers, in 1954 for Italian farmers, in 1955 for Italian draftsmen, in 1956 for Italian craftsmen, in 1957 for the self-employed in Luxemburg except for professions, in 1958 for Italian veterinary surgeons and architects, in 1960 for Italian merchants, in 1961 for French self-employed farmers, in 1962 for Luxemburg farmers, in 1963 for Italian commercial advisors, in 1964 for professions in Luxemburg, in 1965 for self-employed workers in Belgium, in 1966 for self-employed workers in France, and in 1972 for farmers in Germany.

If a conclusion is to be drawn from this evolution it is a negative one. There appears to be no tendency in the European health insurance systems to reduce the number of special schemes. Apart from the integration of the civil servants into the Belgian general scheme for wage-earners (1964), which is in fact only an extension of the general scheme and not really an incorporation of a special scheme (which civil servants never had), we cannot point out any single example of a merger of two health insurance regimes in one country in Europe in the last hundred years.

It must be noted that plans to that effect have always existed. But the funds have stoutly defended their independence. The most comprehensive attempt at unification was the 1943 legislation in Italy which tried to create one central health insurance institution instead of the existing multiplicity of funds. But even within this central institution a large number of autonomous schemes were retained and outside it a large number of special systems remained in existence or were even newly created (23). The Italian government is now trying to create a national health service, starting with an attempt to merge all existing funds into one; it is not possible at present to predict if this attempt is going to be more successful. We may conclude that, although there has always been concern to rationalize health insurance by unifying the different special schemes, such plans have never seen any practical effect so far. A tendency towards diversification has always prevailed.

On this point Dupeyroux says that the conflict of interests shifted inside social insurance, where the particularism of social groups shows itself in the creation and the preservation of special schemes (24).

The continued existence of such special schemes is defended on serious grounds, based especially on the economic problems or the demographic situation facing certain social groups. Yet it is a remarkable fact that there is no one single group common to all countries for whom a special regime has been created. In the wage-earners' group special schemes are found largely for agricultural workers, for coal-miners, and for seamen, but in the Netherlands and in Germany seamen are under the general scheme; in Italy, Belgium, and the Netherlands coal-miners are under the general scheme; and in all countries except France the same applies to agricultural workers. As far as self-employed workers are concerned in the countries where they have health insurance protection, no uniformity in the special systems is found either. In Italy, France, Germany, and Luxemburg there is special provision for farmers, in Luxemburg and Italy for the professions, and in Italy for merchants and craftsmen, but in the other countries and especially in Belgium and the Netherlands there is found nothing of this kind. Even the self-employed as a whole cannot be regarded as a special risk group to be separated from the health insurance for wage-earners. In Belgium independent workers are included in the general scheme; even though their protection is limited they have essentially the same financing system. And in the Netherlands and Germany self-employed workers whose income is lower than the wage limits for the compulsory insurance of the wage-earners can voluntarily join the sickness funds for wage-earners. So finally, it appears impossible to maintain that any special social group has necessarily to be separated from the general scheme.

Everybody knows that there is a strong argument against diversification of special schemes. A large number of special schemes increases administration costs and reduces the chances for a rational policy in the health insurance field. Moreover, a large number of special funds reduces the average number of members per fund and this makes it more difficult for every fund to cover risks in a well-balanced way. A final reason why special funds should be rejected is that they create barriers between different social groups, making it more difficult to move from one group to another. This may hinder social and professional mobility, which is one of the primary objectives of the EEC (25).

One may hope that in the future reason will prevail over particularist attitudes. Some indications justify such a hope. One may observe that the creation of new systems for wage-earners stopped before the Second World War, and that since 1966 only two new special schemes for self-employed workers have been established. It is improbable that special schemes for non-active groups will ever be created, because of the impossible problems of finance. For these groups the extension of compulsory health insurance comes by integration into the general scheme for wage-earners although this sometimes has to occur in a rather artificial way. If our comments on the generalization of the field of application are true, and if also developments in financing follow the course we expect, then in future it would make even less sense to have particular regimes for various social groups. Therefore, we believe that the historical tendency to increase the number of special schemes will be reversed, and that at the same time a tendency towards unification of the national systems will appear.

CENTRALIZATION AND DECENTRALIZATION

Centralization or decentralization is not the same as unification or diversification. A country can have a diversity of centralized regimes or a unified decentralized system. Centralization is understood here as the concentration of financial and administrative responsibility in a central institution per statutory health insurance system. The insurance is considered to be decentralized if this responsibility is carried by several autonomous funds, the national institutions playing the role of co-ordinator only.

In all countries compulsory legal health insurance sprang from voluntary health insurance systems administered by mutual aid funds, called in the northern countries 'sickness funds' and in the southern countries 'mutual funds'. This coincided with a situation of maximum decentralization. Each fund was completely autonomous in its decisions and in its management. At a later stage, when the funds received official recognition, unions of funds were created. But these mainly served to defend the interests of their members at a higher political level and took no part in the administration of the insurance as such.

The introduction of compulsory insurance has in all countries given a strong impulse towards centralization. Its effect has been very different according to the strong or weak financial position of the local organizations. Nowhere has compulsory insurance been centralized completely at the outset, not even in the new systems created after 1945 which were very strongly influenced by the Beveridge doctrine. The ancient Bismarck legislation in Germany and Luxemburg did not affect the responsibility of the existing sickness funds and it created new types of funds, also active at the local level. More centralization is found in the French 1928-30 legislation, which established official insurance institutions besides the existing mutual funds. These official institutions were created on a regional level, generally one per department. They had their own responsibility for insurance, in the same way as the private mutual funds.

The Dutch in 1941 did not go so far. They maintained the existing variety of sickness funds. If they offered sufficient guarantee they were officially recognized and granted the title of '*Algemeen Ziekenfonds*'. Here the option was exercised in favour of decentralization, against the central organization which was favoured by the German occupiers (26).

The end of the Second World War led to a number of reforms towards centralization. In France the ordinance of 1945 excluded mutual funds and gave the administration of social insurance to official institutions alone. These had already been reformed in 1935 by a limited centralization, consisting of the creation of regional guarantee and clearing institutions which would carry a real part of the insurance responsibility. In Belgium at the same time compulsory health insurance was introduced within the framework of a comprehensive social security system. This also meant an important step towards centralization. A national institution was created to administer health insurance. This institution was intended to control and regulate insurance without bearing direct responsibility, except for a limited number of insured persons, not members of private insurance organizations (27). The mutual funds remained in operation. The administration of compulsory insurance, however, was not entrusted to local mutual funds but to the five existing national confederations of mutual funds.

In more recent times a still stronger tendency towards centralization has been shown in various countries. Firstly there was the creation of the Dutch Sickness Funds Council on 1 January 1949. This council was to replace the commissioner charged with control of sickness funds but, although not the intention of its creation, this council has such powers that in fact people are insured with the council rather than with their sickness fund (28). In the French system for wage-earners a reform of August 1967 withdrew all financial autonomy from the local 'Caisse Primaire' and entrusted the insurance to the 'Caisse Nationale de l'Assurance Maladie'. About the same time, on 1 January 1968, in the Netherlands the general insurance for special medical care costs was created. This insurance is completely centralized, all expenditure being concentrated in one fund, the 'General Fund for Heavy Medical Risks'. Private organizations and even commercial insurers may co-operate in the administration of this general insurance, yet there is no splitting of the insurance risk or responsibility (29).

A further tendency to centralization is shown in the Italian proposal for a national health service. Also in France and Germany there is a current in favour of more centralization of insurance responsibility. In the Netherlands, as has been noted, the government has announced a proposal for a general insurance for health care costs. The membership of Great Britain in the Common Market may well influence the development of ideas in this direction.

PUBLIC OR PRIVATE ADMINISTRATION

The problem of public or private administration of the health insurance system is not identical with that of centralization or decentralization discussed above. It is possible to have decentralized public institutions (for instance the 'Caisses primaires' in France) as well as centralized private organizations (the confederations of mutual funds in Belgium).

Obviously the tendency to centralization has some connections with the tendency to enlarge the role of public institutions in insurance. In the first period, before the public authorities dealt in any way with health insurance, the insurance organizations, sickness funds, and mutual funds, were at the same time private and decentralized. The intervention of the state has gradually led to both centralization and a growing influence of public institutions.

The earliest public institutions in the field of health insurance in Italy are found from 1926 on, with the establishing of the 'Legge sindacale' which made it a duty of the trade unions to integrate mutual aid in the case of sickness in collective agreements. The sickness insurance institutions, created by collective agreement, received recognition as public institutions (30). They conserved this public nature also after the 1943 reform. Before the Second World War the German '*Krankenkassen*' including the '*Ersatzkassen*' whose membership is voluntary, were recognized as public institutions by a law on the organization of social insurance of 5 July 1934.

The French legislation of 1928–30 which introduced compulsory health insurance, modified to a large extent the way of operation of the private mutual funds and it created new public institutions with equal responsibility, but it obviously did not want to place insurance responsibility solely in the hands of public institutions. It is said of the 1945 reform that it was inspired by the same intention to conserve private insurance organization (31). Consequently the 'Caisses primaires' would have to be considered as private institutions endowed with a public service. This theory seems very doubtful though. Everything in the legal position of the 'Caisses primaires' seems to indicate that they are and have been from the beginning public institutions (32). The situation seems to be very different in the French regime for independent farmers, called AMEXA. Here private organizations, even commercial firms, manage the insurance. The more recent system for non-agricultural self-employed workers in France is also conceived in this privately managed sense. But in both cases the ultimate insurance responsibility is carried by official institutions (33).

In Belgium and in the Netherlands the private nature of the mutual funds is not at issue. But this does not mean that insurance in these countries is completely independent. The Belgian mutual funds, or at least their national confederations are undoubtedly of a private nature but a growing part of the insurance responsibility is withdrawn from them and held directly by the public authorities. The Dutch sickness funds are more independent as they are responsible for their own financial balance. But this has become largely theoretical. Responsibility is in fact nil for compulsory insurance, very limited in the special scheme for elderly people, and limited also in voluntary insurance. The effect is that insurance is in fact managed by the sickness funds council and not by the sickness funds (34).

Over-all this evolution displays a convergent trend towards public administration of social health insurance in Europe.

# 10
# *Evolution of financing*

A number of technical factors in the health insurance systems give rise neither to convergence nor to divergence, because they seem not to evolve at all. An example of this is found in the way of fixing the contribution level. In most countries since the introduction of compulsory insurance the fixing of contributions has not changed over the years. The same may be said of other aspects of the contribution system. The premiums are ascertained and recovered in the same way, by the same organization, according to the same procedures, in all countries since compulsory insurance began. And yet the problems grow.

### Growing financial strain

All health insurance systems face difficulty in maintaining a financial balance because of the continual increase in the cost of medical care. This increase is not limited to one particular system of health insurance. It appears to be an international phenomenon which gives the social insurance systems of all countries the same problems (35).

The general increase of expenditure for health care under social security can be seen from Table 11.

One should bear in mind that the number of inhabitants of the countries concerned and the number of beneficiaries of health insurance have both been growing. The number of beneficiaries has increased much more quickly than the number of inhabitants. Therefore it seems more appropriate to calculate the expenditure per insured person (see Table 12).

From these figures it is obvious not only that the need for finance for social health insurance is constantly increasing but also follows convergent lines. The very marked backwardness of Italy

TABLE 11
Evolution of over-all expenditure for health care under social security, 1962–70

|      | Belgium (BF million) | Germany (DM million) | France (FF million) | Italy (L billion) | Luxemburg (LF million) | Netherlands (fl. million) |
|------|----------------------|----------------------|---------------------|-------------------|------------------------|---------------------------|
| 1962 | 9·929                | 8·730                | 9·451               | 0·6284            | 0·484                  | 0·919                     |
| 1968 | 27·818               | 17·505               | 21·529              | 1·7527            | 1·026                  | 3·035                     |
| 1969 | 32·260               | 19·728               | 26·796              | 2·0137            | 1·134                  | 3·655                     |
| 1970 | 36·526               | 21·969               | 31·570              | 2·3013            | 1·266                  | 4·390                     |

*Source:* Statistical office of the European Communities, *Yearbook of Social Statistics 1972* (Luxemburg, 1972), VII/5, pp. 318–23.

TABLE 12
Evolution of expenditure on health care by social insurance, per insured person (1962–70) in US $

|                    |      | Belgium | Germany | France | Italy | Luxemburg | Netherlands |
|--------------------|------|---------|---------|--------|-------|-----------|-------------|
| General practitioner | 1962 | 11·01   | 11·20   | 7·60   | 6·78  | 9·57      | 6·67        |
|                    | 1964 | 12·79   | 12·60   | 9·90   | 10·92 | 10·72     | 8·30        |
|                    | 1966 | 23·72   | 17·05   | 11·91  | 14·50 | 14·06     | 10·43       |
|                    | 1968 | 16·55   | 19·45   | 15·86  | 16·55 | 16·25     | 14·49       |
|                    | 1970 | 36·38   | 25·25   | 18·21  | 22·10 | 19·77     | —           |
| Hospital care      | 1962 | 7·98    | 9·65    | 20·99  | 7·20  | 3·94[1]   | 6·67        |
|                    | 1964 | 6·79    | 11·29   | 23·12  | 11·69 | 4·54[1]   | 8·30        |
|                    | 1966 | 11·69   | 14·66   | 27·61  | 16·77 | 5·83[1]   | 10·43       |
|                    | 1968 | 14·00   | 18·75   | 36·08  | 22·48 | 7·96[1]   | 14·49       |
|                    | 1970 | 18·43   | 27·02   | 47·32  | 35·54 | 10·96[1]  | —           |
| Pharmaceutical care | 1962 | 7·98    | 6·68    | 10·23  | 8·65  | 12·65     | 3·72        |
|                    | 1964 | 8·70    | 7·64    | 12·12  | 12·06 | 13·89     | 5·15        |
|                    | 1966 | 12·21   | 10·59   | 15·87  | 16·28 | 16·75     | 6·97        |
|                    | 1968 | 14·80   | 14·00   | 23·69  | 19·57 | 21·22     | 9·30        |
|                    | 1970 | 19·68   | 19·01   | 27·50  | 21·74 | 26·98     | —           |

1. Without surgery, medical care, or drugs.
*Source:* Illuminati, F., 'Le coût de la santé', *Revue Internationale de Sécurité Sociale*, 4 (Geneva, 1972), 410–11.

in 1962 was for the most part corrected by 1970. The same goes for the Netherlands, but there the increase was less rapid.

It may be expected that such a tendency in the cost of health care will also bring the systems of finance closer to each other. The distribution of charges to the different social groups will have to coincide more with their true capacity to pay. By the operation of the Common Market the existing differences in paying capacity in the various countries are bound to be ironed out (36). So the part of each group in financing is bound to be levelled. This development will be strongly supported by the ever-recurring financial difficulties of the health insurance systems. Each country will have to provide structural solutions sooner or later. The chances are that these solutions will be sought in a context of harmonization.

INCREASE IN CONTRIBUTION RATES

For most countries separate figures for health insurance contributions are not available, because these contributions are integrated into a larger social insurance contribution covering health care and sickness benefits as well. But comparison of the development of these premiums may well give a reliable guide to the development of the health insurance contributions, especially as the sickness benefits sector is of decreasing importance in all countries.

The trend towards increases in premiums is evident from Table 13. Only in one case does one see a decrease in the contribution rate: Germany, 1970. But this decrease has a specific cause. By the law on the continued payment of wages of 27 July 1969, from 1 January 1970 the employer is obliged to continue paying wages during the first six weeks of illness. This caused a very marked decrease in expenditure for sickness benefits. The contribution for health care has not decreased at all (37). An apparent exception to the general trend is found in Luxemburg where the contribution rate has remained unchanged for twenty years. But a recent reform in Luxemburg has made it possible to increase the financial resources devoted to health insurance (38).

The increase in contribution rates is related to a simultaneous increase in the wage limits.

## TABLE 13
Level of contributions for compulsory health and sickness benefits insurance, general regime, 1950–70
(as a percentage of wages)

|  | Belgium | Germany | France | Italy | Luxemburg | Netherlands |
|---|---|---|---|---|---|---|
| 1950[2] | 6·0 | 6·0[3] | 9·0[1] | 5·53[4] | 6·0[3] | 3·8[5] |
| 1955[2] | 7·0 | 6·0[3] | 9·0[1] | 6·53[4] | 6·0[3] | 4·0[5] |
| 1960[6] | 7·0 | 7·8[3] | 11·0[1] | 9·83 | 6·0 | 4·9[5] |
| 1965[7] | 8·55 | 9·87 | 11·5[1] | 12·03 | 6·0 | 5·8[5] |
| 1970[8] | 8·65 | 8·0 | 15·0 | 14·61 | 6·0 | 8·7[5] |

1. Calculated from the premium for the *assurances sociales* on a 9/16 basis according to: Association Internationale de la Sécurité Sociale, *Développement et tendances de la sécurité sociale: France* (Geneva, 1959), p. 53.
2. From: AISS, *Développement et tendances de la sécurité sociale: Belgique*, Part I, 97, *Allemagne*, 80, *France*, 52–53, *Luxemburg*, 20, *Pays-Bas*, Part II, 60, and *Italie*, 101.
3. Average figure for the German *Ortskrankenkassen* and the Luxemburg employers' and regional funds.
4. Only for workers in industry.
5. Only for medical care, not for sickness benefit.
6. From: EEC-Commission, *Rapport sur la situation sociale dans la Communauté en 1960* (Brussels, 1961), table 34, 339.
7. From: ibid., *1965* (Brussels, 1966), table 20, 268–9.
8. From: ibid., *1969* (Brussels, 1970), table 12, 238–9.

Here one should not jump to the conclusion that the wage-limits are being constantly increased. In fact their evolution reflects primarily the depreciation of money and the increase in the general wage-level (39) (Table 14). But the trend is towards abolition of the limits: Germany has 'dynamized' them by linking them to the general wage-level (40), Luxemburg has done the same (41), and Belgium is in the act of abolishing them (42).

FORM OF THE PREMIUM
The first compulsory health insurance system in France (1928 and 1930) raised contributions on a lump sum basis, the insured being divided into five income brackets. This was the last appearance of the lump sum basis contribution system in the employed workers' social insurance in Europe. From 1945 on all remaining elements of flat-rate contribution systems were abolished. The Dutch compulsory sickness insurance of 1941 calculated the contributions as a percentage of wages up to a certain limit, with-

TABLE 14
Wage limits for calculation of contributions,
general scheme for employed workers, 1945–70

|      | Belgium[1] | Germany[2] | France[3] | Italy[4] | Luxemburg[5] | Netherlands[6] |
|------|-----------|------------|-----------|----------|--------------|----------------|
| 1945 | 3,000     | 3,600      | 1,200     | —        |              |                |
| 1950 | 4,000     | 4,500      | 2,640     | —        |              |                |
| 1955 | 6,000     | 6,000      | 5,280     | —        | 270          | 19             |
| 1960 | 8,000     | 7,920      | 6,600     | —        | 320          | 22             |
| 1965 | 12,375    | 10,800     | 12,960    | —        | 420          | 30             |
| 1970 | 16,725    | 14,400     | 18,000[7] | —        | 520          | 40[8]          |

1. Per month in BF.
2. Per year, in DM. From: 1945–65: Schewe, D., and Nordhorn, K., *Uebersicht über die soziale Sicherung in Deutschland* (Bonn, 1967), 18.
3. Per month in NF.   4. No limits.
5. Per day in LF. No data on the period before 1955.
6. Per day in fl. No data on the period before 1955.
7. For a part (3 per cent) without limitation.
8. 56·3 fl. per day for the general insurance for special medical care costs, or 17,450 fl. per year.

*Source:* 1945–55: Association Internationale de la Sécurité Sociale, *Développement et tendances de la sécurité sociale, Belgique,* Part I, 96–97, *France,* 52, *Luxemburg,* 20, and *Pays-Bas,* Part II, 59. 1960–70: EEC-Commission, *Reports on the social situation in the Community* (yearly).

out any distinction according to groups, classes, or income brackets. The same system was introduced in the Belgian compulsory insurance from 1 January 1945 onwards: the French reform of 1935 had already adopted the same contribution system, and this was consolidated in the 1945 reform.

This evolution seems to repeat itself, with a certain shift in time, in the case of the self-employed workers. The compulsory health insurance programmes for self-employed persons in Italy again used the idea of flat-rate premiums. This occurred in the old funds for physicians, midwives, notaries, sculptors, etc., which preserved the old form and way of operation after the 1943 reform act. New systems for self-employed workers which were introduced in Italy in the 1950s used the flat-rate premiums system much less. Only some of them still have simple flat-rate contributions. This is true in the schemes for pharmacists, lawyers, architects, authors, and dramatic authors. A set of newer schemes have introduced a mixed system based upon yearly lump sum premiums for insured persons, complemented by a contribution based upon the capacity to pay, the volume of business, the cultivated acreage, etc. This arrangement was first introduced in 1954 for farmers and afterwards in 1956 and 1958 for craftsmen and the veterinarians. It may be important to observe that only a few years later, when compulsory health insurance was extended to the small merchants, the contributions were calculated according to income. In this system a technique was used that had its origins in the system for wage-earners: the calculation of premiums per income bracket.

If one studies the gradual introduction of compulsory health insurance for self-employed workers in France, Luxemburg, and Belgium one comes to the same conclusion. They follow the same pattern of development as earlier existed for the wage-earners. One finds the French compulsory health insurance for self-employed farmers (1960-1) still mainly founded on the principle of flat-rate contributions. These are fixed annually by decree. Yet this system does not maintain the principle so strictly as did the earlier Italian systems. It takes into account the income of the insured by conceding deductions for farmers whose income, calculated according to certain indicators, remains under certain minima. The same thing can be said of the extension of health insurance to self-employed workers in Belgium in 1965. Under this system financing was by flat-rate contributions, but this system was modified by a reduction in contributions for the self-employed whose income remained under certain limits. The somewhat older Luxemburg systems for self-employed workers (Act of 29 July 1957) and for farmers (Act of 13 March 1962) went a step further. Both are financed by way of contributions calculated according to the income of the insured. For the calculation they use income brackets. It is stipulated that the maximum contribution may not exceed the minimum contribution by more than 100 per cent.

The French system for all self-employed workers outside the agricultural sector, which was enacted in 1966, but only took effect in 1969 after rather serious political troubles, uses the same contribution method as Luxemburg: fixed premiums, linked to a scale of income brackets. And the more recent German health insurance for farmers has also taken this way of fixing contributions.

The financing system of the general insurance for special medical care costs in the Netherlands is very different. It extended protection for long-term medical care to the entire population, including the self-employed. Here financing is through a fixed percentage of income, calculated according to income tax returns but with an upper limit. This is the same as for the other general insurance systems in the Netherlands. The more recent reform of the French system for the self-employed has conserved more or less lump sum rates of contribution. But this is not the case in the 1970 reform of the Belgian system for self-employed workers. Contributions of the self-employed are now calculated as a percentage of the income, up to certain income limits, as was already the case for old age pensions and family allowances. One may conclude that this type of contribution calculation indicates a converging trend in all European social health insurance systems.

## Evolution towards national solidarity

The essential question in financing social insurance concerns the degree of solidarity which is to be realized. An important aspect of this is the financial risk of the insurance: is it going to be spread over the whole of the population, or will it be divided by region or by social-occupational groups? We will show here that the health insurance systems in Western Europe have gone from situations of limited solidarity to national solidarity.

In the initial situation of voluntary health insurance, the systems in Europe knew only limited solidarity because of the financial autonomy of all funds. The funds organized solidarity only between their own members, mostly at the local level without regard for the occupation of their members. But at the time (in the second half of the ninteenth century), when trade unions started to intervene in health insurance, the sickness funds imitated them by directing their action towards specific occupational groups (43). This meant an important extension of their field of action, and by the same operation, a meaningful solidification. In a sense local divisions were replaced by occupational divisions, which were much broader. In certain countries this evolution was stimulated by specific circumstances, leading to a stronger grip by the trade unions on the mutual funds. This was the case with the 'Le Chapelier' Act of the French Revolution, which forbade the creation and operation of trade unions, thus forcing workers to create mutual funds in such a way that they could also protect their professional interests (44). In Italy another piece of legislation had a similar effect: the 'Legge Sindacale', enacted by the Fascist government in 1926, made it compulsory for trade unions to arrange for health insurance in their collective agreements with employers. In this way a very strong link between trade unions and mutual sickness funds was achieved.

The introduction of compulsory insurance made quite a change in this situation, and more so when this introduction occurred at a later date. In Germany and Luxemburg, where compulsory insurance was introduced first, the regional and occupational limitations of solidarity in financing remained in existence, although they were somewhat broader than they were before.

This situation has maintained itself until the present day: one still finds in both countries independent sickness funds whose field of action is limited to people of a certain region or of a certain firm or occupation (45).

Thirty years later the introduction of compulsory insurance in France (1928–30) put an end largely to regional autonomy in social health insurance by creating national organizations which from 1935 on carried out an inter-regional clearing of the funds. So the first experience of national solidarity in financing health insurance saw the light; yet the French systems maintain a far-reaching occupational division in the spreading of risks, by conserving and even creating special regimes for various occupational groups. The more recent legislation of compulsory health insurance in the Netherlands and Belgium (1941–4) established national financial solidarity for the largest population group, wage-earners or those wage-earners under a certain wage limit in the Netherlands. Yet here also a division in solidarity was conserved through the fact that outside this general regime specific regimes for certain groups and also voluntary insurance with its own financial responsibility were maintained or created.

Other more recent reforms and new acts on compulsory health insurance indicate that further moves are being made on the way to complete national financial solidarity. It may be pointed out that the gradual extension of the field of application of the general regime in Belgium has absorbed the voluntary insurance systems so that practically a complete national solidarity is reached (46). The Dutch general insurance for special medical care costs has gone in the same direction by the creation, at least in a certain section of health care, of national solidarity in financing. The Italian plan for the gradual creation of a national health service also points in the same direction.

## The future model of financing

The most important questions about the future financing of all types of social insurance are problems of assessment. For instance: which part of the cost might be financed out of government subsidies and which part out of the contributions of the insured people?

It appears in the analysis made above that in exactly these essential points of the European systems of social health insurance no clear tendency in evolution can be shown. In a number of elements there has been hardly any change at all. The only distinct lines of evolution are the relative increase in the part of the government in financing in certain countries, such as Belgium, the Netherlands, and Italy (see Table 8), and the relative increase in the part of the employer in the insurance contribution in Belgium, France, and Italy. This tendency is not counterbalanced by a contrary tendency in other countries, but one must note that in the other countries a contrary attitude has prevailed without change for a very long time: very limited government participation in financing in Germany, France, and Luxemburg and at least half of the contribution for the worker himself in Luxemburg and Germany.

It is hard to draw any firm conclusion but ideas and structures are changing. The way of financing the social insurance systems in Europe, which has been inherited from the past, is now being questioned in all branches. This is especially the result of recurrent deficits which occur in certain branches and of course more particularly in the health insurance branch. A fundamental reform is needed in this field (47).

Comparative study of financing systems in social security as a whole, of which health insurance is only a part, gives very little indication as to the way to be followed. Certain countries give major state subsidies, in other countries these are very limited. Also within each national social security system one finds the same differences with regard to the various regimes. Generally government subsidies are very small in the general scheme for wage-earners, much more important in the special schemes, such as those for agricultural workers, coal-miners, seamen, and the self-employed. Even within one regime the government subsidy is variable; for instance in Belgium it is very limited for family allowances, also rather small in the pension branch, but it is very important in health and disability insurance. And in Germany the health insurance branch receives practically no government subsidies while family allowances are completely charged to the nation. So hardly any line can be drawn from such a comparison.

A certain orientation may be found in what Dupeyroux calls the clarification of ideas, which has resulted from the long experience with social security in European countries. This clarification of ideas means among other things, that a distinction is drawn between the risks which bear a relation to the occupation of the insured worker and those which do not (48). In other words the risks against which only the occupied workers should be protected and those against which the entire population should be protected. This distinction leads to certain consequences in the field of financing. Financing out of general taxation is more appropriate for the latter type of risks and financing out of contributions by employers and employees is more appropriate for the occupational risks.

One must also consider that contributions calculated upon wages can certainly not provide the necessary finance for a health insurance system. Nobody can doubt that the cost of health care in all countries increases much quicker than wages, and will continue to do so (49). Moreover, the tendency to extend insurance to the entire population brings into the social insurance system certain social groups, which do not earn wages or another type of income on which the contribution could be based. This gives to a system based on wage calculated contributions the choice either to fix flat rate (and necessarily unjust) premiums for these special groups or to give them health care at the expense of the contributions of the normal wage-earners, and their employers.

On the other hand it must be observed that a type of financing completely out of general taxation, such as is usually the case in a national health service, and advocated by a number of authors, may also fail in the long run. Such a type of financing has to deal with the tension between quickly rising costs and the unwillingness of the taxpayers to pay more taxes (50). This problem has been studied repeatedly in relation to the 'underfinancing' of the British National Health Service (51).

My personal preference is for the method of financing which was introduced by the Dutch system of general insurances, as a real innovation in European social insurance. Here the contribution is calculated upon all taxable income of all inhabitants in the country, on the basis of a fixed percentage. (Although I would prefer to see a progressive percentage.) The lowest income groups pay no contributions. The establishment and recovery of these contributions is entrusted to the Income Tax Administration but it is handled separately from the income tax. This system makes sure that the charges of health care are divided among all the possible beneficiaries of the system in relation to their ability to pay. The inclusion of income from all sources in the calculation of the contribution makes it more flexible than a contribution based on wages alone. Besides that, the contributions are supplemented by a government subsidy, which is calculated as a lump sum, fluctuating according to the evolution of welfare (related to the wage index). These government subsidies represent the part of public health policy which is realized by means of health insurance and which would otherwise be at the charge of the Minister of Public Health or of the National Assistance Agencies.

A negative element in the Dutch financing system is the existence of an income limit for calculation of the contribution. This creates a danger of inverse redistribution of income, because higher income groups pay relatively less for their health care and make at least the same and probably a better use of the services that are financed by it (52). Another criticism concerns the lack of dynamics in this system. The over-all revenue of the health insurance under such a financial arrangement will increase with the increase of each personal income, but this increase will probably lag behind the increase in medical care costs. So government subsidies must be expected to increase in the years to come.

The Dutch system has at least the merit of abolishing the distinction between the employees' and the employers' part in the contribution. This distinction is bound to disappear in the future. It should be considered as a historically developed device, based upon the structure of industrial labour and for that reason inappropriate for a general risk which has to be financed on a national basis. Workers have a tendency to consider the employers' contribution as some type of supplementary finance paid by the employer on top of wages. But there is reason to doubt very seriously the reality of such a consideration. At closer scrutiny it will be clear that the workers' and the employers' contribution in fact are one and the same, and that the whole of it has to be considered as a deduction from the employees' wages (53). Once the fictitious nature of the distinction is recognized it will certainly not be maintained, especially as it is the cause of complications in the administrative work of the insurance agencies and of individual firms.

The main characteristics of the Dutch system, which we believe will become general in all systems of financing are the uniform method of calculation of the contributions for all persons concerned and the clear definition of government responsibility in financing health insurance. Both are consistent with the convergent trends which have been asserted in the preceding sections of this chapter and are also logical in themselves and fully acceptable in the over-all evolution of social security with the European countries.

# 11
# Evolution of insurance benefits

There appears to be a general consensus that a spontaneous convergence occurs in the EEC as far as social insurance benefits are concerned. Some people consider this to be a result of the increasing wealth and the closer contacts within the Common Market. The well-known European expert and former Dutch Minister for Social Affairs, Dr G. M. J. Veldkamp, has supported the view that the harmonization of social insurance systems is promoted by the action of the Common Market itself (54). This spontaneous harmonization concerns mainly the level of benefits as compared with the national income and the amount of benefits per head of population. It is considered to be much less visible in the matter of conditions for admission to benefits, which remain very different among the various countries.

### The type of benefits

We have already shown that the six countries fall into two groups: those which mainly give direct provision of benefits (Germany, the Netherlands, and Italy) and those which mainly provide reimbursement of medical expenses (Belgium, France, and Luxemburg). Is there a tendency towards a coming together of both groups or is the gap still widening? This question can only be answered from a study of the historical evolution of these various systems.

As far as the first group is concerned the evolution has been far from spectacular. It appears that these countries have inherited their system of direct provision of benefits from the earliest health insurance funds. In Germany it may be said that health care has been provided *in natura,* since social health insurance first began (55).

In the Netherlands, although the benefits of the sickness funds in the period before the introduction of compulsory insurance (1941) were markedly varied, they had one point in common: direct provision of services. The various suppliers of care were paid directly by the funds for the provision of care, without any financial intervention by the insured (56).

The situation in both countries is still largely unchanged. Modifications in the type of benefits have only occurred in very minor respects. Time and again there are disputes over the reimbursement system, but in Germany and the Netherlands no significant change has occurred so far as the type of benefit is concerned.

In Italy in the early period of health insurance two types of benefit were used jointly: direct provision of services, such as in Germany and the Netherlands, was used mainly for the lower income classes, and indirect benefits, in the form of a payment to the members in the case of medical expenses, were given to the more wealthy groups of the population. This duality in the benefit-type still exists, but in a somewhat different way. Both types of benefit have been made available to all groups of the population, by conceding to all insured people the right to choose. This change in fact induced a shift from indirect benefits towards the direct provision of care, as most insured persons chose direct provision (57). Rules were made to enable an insured person who had opted for indirect provision to change his mind when he needed very expensive services, such as hospital care. If the plans for a national health service are carried out in their present form, this will mean that the system has evolved towards general direct provision of care.

For the second group of countries the situation is different.

In France and Belgium the mutual funds originally paid a certain sum to their members when they used medical services, and fixed this sum according to a tariff established for their own use, unrelated to actual fees or prices. The fees were still fixed by the physicians themselves in the way which was described by the French as the '*entente directe*' (direct agreement) between the physician and the patient.

Gradually these countries shifted towards reimbursement on

the basis of fees and prices actually paid by the patient. This was the type of benefit sought by French and Belgian compulsory insurance at the time of their creation, in France in 1930 and in Belgium in 1945 (58).

It was, however, achieved only much later. In France the system of agreements with physicians remained inoperative for a long time, until it received a more practical form by the Reform of 1960. In the years after 1960 it reached a point at which it could claim to some extent that real reimbursement of fees took place. In Belgium, until 1963 in fact there existed the old situation where the insurance only paid certain sums to its members according to its own tariff, entirely independent of the physicians' fees. It was the express aim of the Reform Act of 9 August 1963 to put an end to this situation by concluding a sufficient number of agreements with physicians on the fees to be charged to insured patients. But it was not until November 1970, as a result of a number of successive reforms, that, in the whole country, sufficient physicians and dentists had joined the agreement system and made their fees known to the insurance.

In Luxemburg evolution went the other way around. The 1901 system was oriented towards the German model, which it followed until after the Second World War. At that time the influence of Germany in Luxemburg was replaced by that of Belgium and France. Consequently the health insurance benefits were reorganized according to the French and Belgian model: reimbursement of fees and prices paid by the insured. This principle was enacted in 1957 and still dominates the Luxemburg system, with a few exceptions for the lower-paid groups and more expensive types of care. It has not been altered by the 1974 reform.

These comments apply to the care given by physicians. The situation is different with pharmaceutical products and hospital care. In these sectors direct provision of services without intervention by the insured, or with very limited payment by the insured at the time of service, is much older in these countries. The physicians have always been suspicious of such a relationship with insurance. In Belgium, as well as in France, from the earliest periods of the agreement system between health insurance and the suppliers of care this system provided for pharmacists and hospitals to agree on direct payment by the sickness funds. They have always made extensive use of this possibility, even if this was never general and took a certain time to be established (59).

Nowadays direct payment is practically general for the pharmacists in Belgium and is largely applied by the hospitals in that country. In France the system is compulsory for the public hospitals and is also very common in the private hospitals. In the case of pharmaceuticals in France there was much suspicion for a long time, not as one might expect from the French pharmacists, but from the French government. It feared that direct payment would lead to a big increase in pharmaceutical consumption. But now the tendency is to provide for direct payment of pharmacists in regional agreements which cover an ever larger part of the country (60).

In Luxemburg too direct payment for services is much more common for drugs and hospital care than for care by physicians. For drugs the sickness funds in the scheme for blue-collar workers pay direct, but in the other schemes the insured has first to pay the pharmacist. Direct payment of hospitals is applied by all sickness funds in all schemes, according to a legal rule, maintained after the recent reform.

One may conclude from the foregoing that the division between the two groups of countries, one with direct and the other with indirect provision of services, cannot be drawn so sharply as might appear at first sight. In the countries of the first group the benefits are sometimes given in the form of a simple lump sum payment to the insured patient. At the same time in the second group in a large and increasing number of cases direct payment is made to suppliers.

In Italy direct payment for care by the insurance organizations has been more and more widely spread and is almost general. In Belgium and France it is progressing. Even physicians have started using the 'third party' formula. In France direct provision of care (already) applies to the important group of specialists in hospitals. In Belgium legislation provides for particular individual agreements by which physicians and other providers of care can arrange for direct payment of their fees by the insurance organizations.

In conclusion it may be said that the tendency is towards the abolition of the reimbursement system in favour of direct payment by the insurance, at least for the part of it that is not paid by the patient himself. In countries where direct financing was already the rule in the early days of social insurance, the situation has remained unchanged in this respect, while countries where originally the reimbursement system prevailed have shifted gradually towards the direct payment system. So this latter system appears as the type of benefit system for the future.

An evolution in this sense would correspond with more than one trend which can be ascertained. In the first place one can point out that the ever-increasing costs of medical care will make it more difficult for the patient to pay in advance. So patients will exert more and more pressure on the insurance to provide for direct payment. One may observe that the direct financing system is most widely spread in those branches of health care where cost increase has been greatest: hospital care and drugs.

A second trend in this respect is the stronger connection between health insurance and public health policy. Health insurance is nowadays seen by most governments no longer as a neutral device but as an important instrument for public health policy. So the policymakers are no longer concerned only with the sound financial basis of the insurance institutions but also with the impact of the system on the health status of the insured population. In this respect it is feared that payment in advance by the patient will hinder some people in their access to medical care. In particular it is felt that preventive care through early consultation with the physician is discouraged when financial barriers exist between the patient and the physician.

A third argument is the general consideration of rationalization in health insurance, which is common to all fields of social administration. Rationalizing means among other things the avoidance of unnecessary detours in money flows. Advance payment by the insured patient who receives reimbursement afterwards is an unnecessary step in the financing system. It makes the flow of funds longer and more difficult to control, it creates administration costs, and leads to greater possibilities of abuse.

Finally, the changing attitude of the medical profession towards social security should be noted. Originally the physicians took the same attitude to insurance fund patients as to the poor (61). They had to be treated for ethical reasons at a lower fee or even completely free. As the tiny health insurance funds of the nineteenth century grew stronger and especially when they became compulsory for certain groups the physicians saw them as a threat to their profession (62). They created militant organizations directed against the extension of social health insurance. But now this extension has gone so far in a number of countries that social health insurance covers practically all the population. This has exerted much influence upon relations with the medical profession. Physicians no longer want to have as little as possible to do with health insurance, but they appear to be willing to co-operate in a constructive way with their inevitable partner (63). Refusal by the physicians of direct payment by the health insurance institutions was a reaction of distrust towards health insurance. They feared they would be dependent upon the insurance institution if they received their money from them. One may expect that the improvement of relationship between the medical profession and the health insurance institutions will eventually eliminate this distrust and that at the same time direct payment by the insurance funds will be more easily accepted by the medical profession.

But if we believe that in the future direct provision of care will be general in European health insurance this does not mean that all health insurance systems will provide benefits in exactly the same way. Direct provision of care as a type of insurance benefit is not uniform, it may exist in varying ways. The essential element of it is that not the insured patient but the scheme pays for care, the patient paying only part of the cost not covered by insurance (64). But to provide for this type of payment the relationship between insurance and supplier may be of a varied nature. The insurance organizations may run their own health care institutions or they may conclude special arrangements with existing institutions; physicians may be employed with certain institutions or even directly by a sickness insurance fund. Within these contracts or legal provisions, all sorts of variations are possible. So a generalized direct provision of care does not mean uniformity in insurance benefits.

One should also bear in mind that the direct type of benefit in health insurance will probably not be the only benefit type in the future. Never in the history of social insurance in Europe has a situation occurred in which only one type of benefit was given. One can hardly imagine a situation where all physicians and suppliers of health care in a given country will have imposed upon them one exclusive method of remuneration. This will certainly be impossible with such a rigid type of payment as the direct payment by the insurance organization. It seems much more likely that the large sector of directly financed social health care will always find at its side a kind of residual private sector. This will be composed in part by physicians and other providers of care who want to keep themselves completely out of the system of social health insurance. But it will also include suppliers of care working under social health insurance who will have the opportunity to treat private patients within certain limits. They already possess this right in all countries included in our review.

It is difficult to foresee precisely the future of this residual private sector. Probably there will be even less uniformity in this sector than in the socially financed sector. The only element which seems to be certain is the payment of fees per item of service by the patients themselves. This will distinguish the private sector from the socially financed sector in a more precise way than it does today. It does not matter if these fees are fixed freely by the physician himself or if they are agreed upon in advance, if they are reimbursed partly or completely by some insurance agency; it is the system of payment which will be distinctive. But it seems likely that not much effort will be made to establish a system of agreement tariffs for the private sector.

Given the difficulties inherent in the creation of agreements on tariffs of fees, it seems more probable that the fees will be left to be fixed by the physician himself. It also seems most likely that the health insurance system will not play any part in the financing of the expenses of their members when they choose the private sector, because they have full opportunity to receive free care under the insurance. In a few countries, such as in Belgium and France, the medical profession, the trade unions, and other organizations will oppose this on the principle of non-discrimination, according to which insurance members should receive the same benefits, whatever provider of care they choose. But it will hardly be possible to maintain this position seeing the financial situation of the insurance and the need for rationalization in the distribution of care. And a consequent application of this principle would result in a uniformization of all medical fees, and in a complete prohibition of private practice.

A possible solution could be found by adopting the Italian system whereby each year and also at every hospitalization the insured can choose between direct provision of care through the network of services of the health insurance schemes or have complete free choice of provider including the private sector with lump sum reimbursement. This seems an attractive device, combining both individual freedom of the insured patient and the possibility for the insurance to organize the supply of health care in a rational way. Yet in reality this would only mean a more complicated method of exerting the right of option which already exists and will exist for the future. The patient has, in fact, and will have, an option between calling the insurance doctor and going to the insurance hospital or paying himself for treatment as a private patient.

### Extent of insurance protection

We noted earlier that in the six countries the range of benefits 'in kind' under health insurance practically coincides with the range of known and accepted medical care techniques. Generally items which are used domestically or which can be considered nutritive are excluded as are the types of care given by persons who are not licensed according to the national legislation on medical practice (65). So the range of benefits seems to leave little room for extension.

Yet a few developments in this field may be observed. In the first place one should point out that in the origins of social health insurance a full range of benefits was not always offered to the insured. In Germany, for instance, under the Bismarckian legislation, not all types of appliances were financed by the insurance: only if their price remained under a certain limit. Under the Italian systems for wage-earners originally drugs were limited to the products prepared by the pharmacist himself and proprietary drugs were only admitted if they could not be produced by the pharmacists; also out-patient specialist care could not be given in all parts of the country. These limitations have been eliminated over the years.

Certain specifications have been added to the enumeration of benefits. This gave the insured entitlement to such benefits as reimbursement of transport costs, health cures, and care in nursing homes, which had previously been considered as unnecessary or even luxurious.

In the second place one should pay attention to the distinction between obligatory and optional benefits. In Germany the distinction existed from the very beginning of compulsory insurance, and was known as 'Regelleistungen' and 'Mehrleistungen'. The distinction has not disappeared as yet. In Belgium compulsory insurance has always been supplemented by a complementary voluntary insurance, which provides, among other things, for transport of the sick, which is not one of the statutory insurance benefits. The more recent French and Italian systems for self-employed workers also have included this distinction. The individual funds are invited to supplement the legally obligatory minimum benefits by broader optional benefits, which they may finance out of voluntary contribution supplements.

It may be expected that services which were for a long time provided by way of additional voluntary benefits will be integrated into the obligatory benefits sooner or later. Historical examples of such an evolution are found in the prolonging of the length of hospital care in the Netherlands, to seventy days per year, then to one year per case (66), and finally to an indefinite period, and also the measures in the British occupation zone in Germany where a number of 'Mehrleistungen' have been promoted to the rank of 'Regelleistung' (67).

A recent evolution, however, seems to go in a very different direction. The systems for self-employed workers which were created in Europe after 1950 have limited the range of benefits to the so-called heavy medical risks, the more expensive types of health services. The first example was the Italian Act of 1956, which limited the right to medical care for craftsmen to hospital, maternity, and specialist care. The same formula was taken over by the Act of 1960, on health insurance for the small traders. The extension in Belgium of health and disability insurance to the self-employed also was limited to hospital care, drugs in hospital, surgery, and treatment for social diseases. Shortly afterwards the Act of 1966, on health and maternity insurance for agricultural self-employed in France, also limited entitlement to hospital care, care for chronic illnesses, very expensive services, and the care of children and the elderly. Shortly afterwards in the Netherlands the General Insurance for Special Medical Care Costs of 1967 guaranteed to all inhabitants, including the self-employed, treatment in nursing homes and special institutions for handicapped and mentally ill and treatment from the 366th day on in hospitals, sanatoriums, and psychiatric institutions.

The question arises whether this is the beginning of a divergent trend towards a situation in which the systems for the self-employed will be limited to heavy medical care costs. Some even believe that this development will lead to a situation where all health insurance will limit itself to the heavy medical care costs, excluding the so-called minor risks. These would have to be paid for by the insured themselves, either out of pocket or by some private insurance (68).

History gives a certain indication to the contrary. Certain tendencies which enlarge the range of benefits are observed, but no examples can be shown of a limitation of benefits. In Belgium the range of benefits in favour of self-employed workers was considerably extended from 1965 to 1970. The Dutch general insurance for special medical care has also extended the range of its benefits; the legislation permits still further extension and this is provided for in the government plan. Also in France, by the Act of 1970, the protection of non-agricultural self-employed workers

## Evolution of insurance benefits

has been considerably improved by the integration of minor risks into the legal range of benefits. These examples seem to indicate that the systems for the self-employed have gone through the same over-all evolution as the system for the wage-earners. With an important lag in time they are both engaged in a convergent trend towards ever fuller protection.

Yet some believe that in the future health insurance for all social groups will be limited to the more expensive medical care costs. They contend that increasing costs of insurance will meet refusal by contribution payers and taxpayers to pay more money so that a limitation of benefits becomes inevitable. They also hold that people's wealth has generally become high enough to enable the insured to pay for cheaper types of health care themselves. This would at the same time make financial resources available for improvements in certain fields where there is still a severe shortage (69).

It is not very likely that these predictions will ever come about. In the first place it should be pointed out that systems where only heavy medical risks were covered have always created complementary voluntary insurance programmes for minor risks, and these show the tendency to be integrated into the obligatory benefits scheme. It must also be recognized that the tendency towards the improvement and extension of insurance benefits is a general feature of social insurance of all types and kinds. The insured person considers benefits as vested rights; every limitation of benefits would be considered as an intolerable social regression.

Moreover distinction between minor and heavy risks in medical care is dubious. One and the same health service may be a minor or heavy risk according to circumstances. Of course, expensive surgery will always be a heavy risk, but the simple consultation of the family physician may go far beyond the level of the small risk, for instance when it has to be repeated frequently. All attempts to draw clear lines between minor and heavy risks have until now failed (70). The tendency to improve benefits will prevail in future; the distinction between minor and heavy risks is bound to disappear.

It seems likely that in future further extension in the range of benefits will include prevention (71). Until now a rather sharp distinction has always been drawn between preventive and curative care. Prevention is generally considered part of the public health policy of the government, financed out of taxation and administered by government agencies. On the other hand, curative care is considered a matter of free medical practice. This situation gives rise to severe problems of co-ordination of services.

The evolution of social health insurance systems in Western Europe shows that, especially in recent years, an effort has been made to integrate preventive care into the obligatory benefits of compulsory insurance. The development is a very recent one. It was only after the Second World War that one saw the first steps towards integration of care. The new Luxemburg systems for civil servants and white-collar workers, the self-employed and farmers (1951, 1957, and 1962) include, as part of their obligatory benefits, the early detection of illnesses. The Belgian Health Insurance Act of 1963 includes preventive care as an insurance benefit under the obligatory benefits. In Italy from 1965 on certain vaccinations are considered to be benefits under compulsory health insurance. In Germany the law on protection of maternity has included preventive measures as obligatory benefits and, by an Act of 1970, children under 4 years are entitled to regular medical examinations; and women over the age of 30 and men over 45 are entitled to anti-cancer preventive examinations once a year.

The health insurance institutions have also been active by way of collective preventive measures. In Germany and in the Netherlands the associations of sickness funds pay certain sums to help to finance the school health services and other public health measures. This type of activity has been best developed in France, where the investment in public health services is considered to be an integral part of the activity of the health insurance organizations; it is known under the name *action sanitaire et sociale* (72).

There are several reasons for suggesting that in future preventive care will be more important to social health insurance. The public increasingly are aware of the value of preventive care. As knowledge about the possibility of early detection of illnesses is spread more pressure will be exerted upon health insurance institutions to include such services in their range of benefits. They may find it hard to resist this demand. Another argument can be found in the difficulty of co-ordinating preventive and curative medicine. These problems will always exist, as long as their organization and financing are separate. For a number of specific services it is not always easy to distinguish preventive from curative care. The activities of most physicians and health institutions combine in fact both types of care. It would be much less complicated to organize and pay for both in the same way.

THE DURATION OF BENEFIT

At the beginning of social health insurance in Europe the funds were financially very limited, so protection could only be offered to the insured within very sharply defined limits. Certainly the funds could not promise benefits for an indefinite period. The older compulsory insurance systems clearly illustrate the effects of this. The German compulsory health insurance of 1884 offered protection against medical costs for only six to ten weeks. The French legislation of 1930 set the duration of medical care under insurance to six months after the first assessment by the physician. In Italy during the period of Fascism (which Italian authors always call the period of the trade union mutual funds) the general limitation of insurance protection to 180 days per year was as valid as it is today, but was limited to 20 days per year in the case of hospital care.

The more recent compulsory systems of the Netherlands (1941) and Belgium (1945) had only a partial time limit or no time limits at all. In the Netherlands protection was limited to 42 days per year for hospital care but not for other services. In Belgium the limitation in duration of insurance protection was excluded from the very beginning. Insurance protection for indefinite periods was a cardinal feature of the 'project of agreement for social solidarity' between employers and employees during the war and which was the basis of the development of Belgian social security (73).

The elimination of time limits in the European systems was steadily promoted and gradually realized. By 1935 in France the six-month period was calculated in a more flexible way. In 1943 in Germany all limitations in duration for out-patient health care were abolished, only for hospital care was a limitation maintained. France introduced in 1945 a special regulation for the chronically ill, who would receive insurance benefits for three years. In 1955 France finally abolished all limitations on duration and in the Netherlands in the same year the period of hospital care for the insured was extended to 70 days per year. In Italy in 1959, the time limit was abolished for specific diseases of the elderly and the period for hospital care extended to 180 days per year. In 1961 Germany changed the limit for hospital care to 78 weeks per three years. The Netherlands changed the time limit for hospital care to 365 days per case of illness. On 1 January 1968 general insurance for special medical care costs was introduced in the Netherlands, guaranteeing free hospital care after the expiration of 365 days and without any time limit. And since 1 October 1973 the limit has been removed in Germany.

All these facts make it easy to conclude that there exists a strong tendency towards the abolition of all limitations in the duration of benefits. Moreover, a time limit is not in accordance with the fundamental objectives of health insurance. If health insurance is designed to provide the insured with health care when needed most, then it should be primarily concerned with long-term illnesses and the chronically ill. The abolition of time limits for benefits was one of the points of general agreement at the Brussels Conference on social security in 1962 (74). If this aim has not been fully realized until now, this is simply because of financial implications, but these cannot indefinitely prevent its realization.

## Conditions for admission to benefits

PARTIAL PAYMENT BY THE INSURED

As we have seen, payments by the insured either through deterrent charges or co-insurance fees, vary within the European systems. In each the present situation is only one point in a long evolution. A study of this evolution may throw light upon the significance of the actual differences, and upon the future situation which may be expected to occur.

It is striking that at the time of the introduction of compulsory insurance in each of the six countries the situation was roughly the same as today where payments by patients were concerned. In Germany the compulsory health insurance as early as 1884 provided free care by physicians, and hospitals, in the same way as this is done now, with only a few minor changes. The same may be said of the Netherlands. Before the introduction of compulsory insurance in 1941, free medical care had already been provided directly by the sickness fund physicians, by the pharmacists and the hospitals, in practically the same manner as at present. In France in 1930 when compulsory insurance began, the general rule was that 80 per cent of the fees would be reimbursed according to the insurance tariffs. Until 1967 this rule still applied. In the present system the part paid by the insured differs according to the type of service, varying from 10 to 30 per cent of the costs, but the average reimbursement is still 80 per cent.

Belgium began in 1945 with a personal payment by the insured of 25 per cent for ambulatory medical care, and this still applies. And in the various systems which were created in the 1920s in Italy were found two different situations. In some systems, direct provision of care prevailed, with free treatment. In other systems the care was provided indirectly, the funds paying lump sum benefits to their members who incurred medical costs. This situation is similar in its general outline to the present situation, but the duality has now been shifted from outside to inside the systems, by giving a right of choice to the insured.

Yet the impression that nothing has changed would be false. Important developments have occurred during the life of the compulsory systems and very often this problem has been an important political issue. Obviously these developments have taken place largely in France and Belgium, the two countries where participation by the insured in meeting costs is most pronounced.

In France the first change in the general rule of 20 per cent as far as medical care is concerned was made in 1945 in favour of the chronically ill. These patients were freed from all cost-sharing. From 1958 on, the government imposed a number of measures to secure the financial balance of the insurance. The most important of these was a limitation of the reimbursement tariff for medical care to certain fixed maxima. A serious gap developed between real fees and the total reimbursement. This government policy was not always successful. A decree limiting reimbursement for physiotherapy and radiology to 160 FF per case had to be repealed.

The well-known reform of May 1960 was taken primarily to eliminate this gap between reimbursement tariff and actual fees (75), by making agreements with the medical professions on tariffs of fees which would constitute the basis for reimbursement. The principle of 20 per cent from the patient was maintained. The 1967 reform resulted in an increase to 30 per cent. But shortly afterwards, as a result of the so-called agreement of Grenelle after the 'événements' of May 1968, it was reduced again to 25 per cent (76). The decrees of February 1969 finally extended the cases of exemption considerably.

The most important fluctuations have occurred with drugs. In 1930 a 'ticket modérateur' of 15 per cent was payable on all drugs. This was increased in 1935 to 20 per cent on the first 25 FF and 40 per cent of the rest. In 1938 the system was changed again. Four groups of products were distinguished: the insured paid 20 per cent for the irreplaceable products; for drugs which cost the same as if prepared by the pharmacist himself he paid 20 per cent over the first 20 FF and 40 per cent over the remainder. The patient had to pay 60 per cent of the price if the drug was 20 per cent dearer than if prepared by the pharmacist, and with products commercially advertised he paid 90 per cent of the price himself. This system was simplified in 1943. For the last group reimbursement was abolished altogether and for the first two groups it was made uniform at 20 per cent. In 1945 they returned to the simple system of the early days and the 'ticket modérateur' for drugs was fixed again at 20 per cent for all products. But in 1959 the system returned to a complicated form. The patient had to pay 10 per cent for irreplaceable products, 20 per cent for preparations by the pharmacist, and 30 per cent for all other agreed products.

The evolution was similar in Belgium. In the beginning reimbursement was generally 75 per cent of the agreed tariffs for general medical care and 100 per cent for specialists' care. But the part paid by the insured was in reality much larger because of the gap between the actual fees and the insurance tariffs. This led to regular increases of insurance tariffs during 1946 and 1948 until the insurance got into financial difficulties. Reimbursement for dental care was drastically limited and for specialist care was limited to certain maxima. From 1952 on attempts were made to conclude tariff agreements with the physicians, but without success (77).

In the meantime, charges for drugs fluctuated as in France. In 1945 it was decided that generally the insured would pay 25 per cent of the average price of preparations by the pharmacists in the preceding year. For commercial drugs the insured would pay 50 per cent up to a maximum of 20 BF per product. By 1947 commercial drugs were divided into three groups. For the irreplaceable products the insured would pay only 4 BF. For recognized products the rule of 50 per cent with a maximum reimbursement of 20 BF was maintained and for other products nothing would be paid by the insurance. The 'ticket modérateur' for irreplaceable products was gradually increased to 6·27 BF. In 1957 the insurance reimbursement was calculated differently. It would be fixed at 75 per cent of the official price of all recognized commercial drugs and so it was to remain until the 1963 reform.

The new act of August 1963 introduced an important reform. Reimbursement was maintained at the rate of 75 per cent of the agreed tariffs for general medical care and at 100 per cent for specialist care, but exemption from charges for all types of care was given to widows, invalids, old age pensioners, and orphans whose income did not exceed certain limits. Prime Minister Lefèvre said one of the primary objectives of the reform was to ensure complete protection against medical care costs for these special groups (78). But this objective was not fully reached because these priority groups still have to pay a significant part of the cost of commercial drugs except in the case of 'social diseases'.

For all other insured persons the reform of 1963 established a system of participation which is in line with the 1945 system. A flat rate participation is supposed to represent about 25 per cent of the average costs of pharmaceutical products. It was fixed at 12 BF per prescription for preparations by the pharmacist and at 22 BF for commercial drugs. In 1966 this changed again. The insurance has in principle to pay only 10 per cent of the cost of drugs but the insured's share may not exceed 20 BF for products prepared by the pharmacists, and 50 BF for other drugs. This latter figure was reduced to 25 BF for the chronically ill. The inefficient 10 per cent rule was abandoned after a short time and only the flat rate payment by the insured remained.

At one time the question of co-insurance was an important political issue. In March 1966, the government led by Prime Minister Pierre Harmel was forced to resign, at least apparently, because it could not find a satisfactory solution to the problem of seven clinics which charged lower fees to avoid payment by the insured (79). In the controversy over this issue a proposal was made to charge an admission fee for hospital care of 30 BF, a proposal which reminds one of the so-called '*Tientje van Veldkamp*' in the Netherlands, and which suffered the same fate: both were rejected (80).

In Germany cost-sharing has been the topic of much discussion, but in a different context. In 1930 an emergency decree was enacted, because of the difficult financial situation facing compulsory health insurance, caused by the general economic depression. A 'Krankenscheingebühr' and an 'Arzneikostenanteil' were introduced. This meant that the insured had to pay a certain sum to obtain from his sickness fund the document *Krankenschein* necessary to prove his entitlement to free care and also that he had to pay a certain sum for drugs. In July 1956 both types of payment were abolished, but discussion on the advisability of payment by the insured went on (81). In 1962 a bill was proposed to introduce payment of 1–3 DM per delivery of drugs, of 3 DM per day in hospital and of 25 per cent of the cost of glasses and appliances. This bill was rejected (82), but a few years later a payment of 0·5 DM per prescription was introduced. In 1967 this was increased to 1 DM, again for economic reasons. And from 1 January 1970 cost-sharing of drugs was introduced in a way which is very similar to the Belgian and French type of 'ticket modérateur'. It amounts to 20 per cent of the cost of drugs up to a maximum of 2·50 DM; certain groups of insured, such as invalids, pensioners, children, and in general those who do not receive a salary being exempt.

From these French, German, and Belgian examples we can see that the evolution of cost-sharing does not follow a specific direction. Sometimes it is increased and at other times it is diminished or abolished altogether. Sometimes it is determined at a flat rate and at other times it is calculated as a percentage of the costs. In fact, it seems to vary most according to the financial needs of the system and according to the whim of legislators and insurance organizations. A good example of fantasy is given by the reform in Germany, which created a kind of inverse 'ticket modérateur': the insured who did not make use of his right to medical care (except for dental care) during a given quarter of a year, and who had not had any drugs was reimbursed by his sickness fund a sum of 10 DM up to a maximum of 30 DM per year. This no-claim bonus proved to be inefficient to limit the number of claims; it was soon abandoned (83).

It should be pointed out that in such countries as Italy, the Netherlands, and Luxemburg there are very few changes in the regulations on cost-sharing over very long periods, and these countries certainly were not spared the general increase in medical care costs. For Italy one can only say that at the time of the reform of 1959, in the system of direct provision of care some sort of co-insurance was introduced as far as drugs are concerned. This reform established an official list of drugs which had to be delivered free of cost. Only half the cost of products not on the list was paid by the insurance. But the list of recognized products seems to be so large that such an occurrence would seem very rare and practically hypothetical. In the Netherlands a few changes in personal payments by the insured for dental care and for appliances should be mentioned. In 1951-2 for instance the extra payment for dental care was increased but at the same time the prices of appliances were moderated. In Luxemburg, no mention is found in the legislation for a long time of any change in personal payments by the insured for medical care. This has been left largely to the funds individually to decide. There have certainly been some decisions by the funds to increase or decrease the insured's contribution, notably to abolish it for the blue-collar workers. But the recent reform of 2 May 1974 has extended the principle of a personal payment to all medical fees outside hospital and to some pharmaceutical products and has introduced the possibility of a deductible per month (84).

Theoreticians of social insurance have of course been concerned with the problem. A number of them consider this to be an appropriate solution to the problems of health insurance, either because it would limit the over-consumption of medical care or because it would help to solve the problem of financial deficits. A large section of the report of the 'Sozialenquête-Kommission', charged by the German government with a comprehensive inquiry into the problems of social security in Germany, is taken up by an investigation into cost-sharing. On the recommendations of the report the 20 per cent personal payment up to a maximum of 2·50 DM for drugs and the reimbursement of 10 DM per quarter for non-use of medical care were introduced. The commission's proposals went much further: they included the payment by the insured for all types of care except for the most expensive (85). In the Netherlands too the government has sought advice on the future of health insurance and more particularly on the question of whether a personal contribution by the insured was advisable. The question was put to three official advisory bodies, the Social Economic Council, the Sickness Funds Council, and the Central Council for Public Health. Unlike the German experts these three bodies rejected cost-sharing (86).

Thus it appears that not only in practice but also in opinion the evolution has shown divergent trends. In all countries one will find supporters and adversaries of charges on patients. One finds, for example, a remarkable difference in the attitude of the medical profession who in certain countries are very strongly in favour of co-insurance because they expect important savings for the system and a limitation in over-consumption especially with regard to medicine, and in other countries they are much less in favour of such proposals (87).

QUALIFYING PERIODS

While conditions for admission to benefits have shown very little variation throughout the evolution of the systems, this cannot be said of the waiting period for entitlement. On this point the differences between the national systems are important and more changes have taken place.

In France under the original legislation of 1930 entitlement to benefits depended upon the insured having paid premiums for at least sixty days in the quarter preceding the one in which he asked for benefits. This severe rule was considerably eased in 1935. From that time on it was sufficient that the insured had worked as an employee at any time in that period. This was later explained as having worked for at least sixty hours in that period. Only for maternity benefits has a supplementary condition been adjoined: the insured had to be registered with the insurance at least ten months before the delivery. These rules remained unchanged for a long time, but in 1968 the conditions were made much more severe. Now the insured who wishes to claim health care benefits must prove that in the three months preceding his claim he has worked at least 200 hours as an employee or else 120 hours in the last month before his claim.

Even stricter are the conditions in the recent health insurance system for the non-agricultural self-employed. These must fulfil two conditions at the same time. On the one hand they must have registered for at least three months with the social insurance and on the other they must have paid all the premiums due from the time of registration until the time of their claim.

Belgium had a similar evolution. At the start of compulsory insurance in 1945 the only condition for entitlement was that the insured had paid a minimum value over the month preceding the claim. In 1949 a waiting period was established of three months for the under 25s and six months for older persons. During these waiting periods they had to work 70 and 140 days respectively. The requirement of a minimum value of contributions was maintained but soon the working periods required were reduced to 60 and 120 days respectively. These conditions were confirmed by royal decree in 1955.

With the 1963 reform these rules were changed. The special rules for insured persons under 25 were abolished and for the calculation of the 120 working days those who work a five-day week system may increase their number of working days by 20 per cent. The minimum value of contribution vouchers is no longer calculated by a minimum premium value, but as a minimum wage upon which contributions have to be paid. Finally in 1967 new regulations were issued to take into account the special situation of the female worker who has to work part-time because she has her husband and her children to provide for. For such a worker the minimum number of working days required in the waiting period is reduced to 72.

In Germany in 1911, insurance benefits in the case of pregnancy were only paid out if the insured had at least ten months of insurance in the two years previous to the date of delivery, and at least six months in the last year. At that time a waiting period existed also for other benefits; its duration was fixed by each fund individually. But this rule was abolished in 1945, and only the waiting period for maternity care was maintained until abolished in 1945. Now Germany no longer has a waiting period.

The same applies to the Netherlands. Here already in 1941 the insured received their benefits without any waiting time. Only in the voluntary insurance and in the complementary voluntary insurance could the sickness funds impose waiting periods. These are different from one fund to another and from one type of service to another.

In Italy the question of waiting periods varies with social groups. The situation differs from one system to another and sometimes they are even different within the same system. These differences stem partly from the Fascist era when all systems were created by collective labour agreements in each industry. These systems did not provide for waiting periods as such, but they would only give entitlement to benefits to those workers who were fully integrated in the industry, this meant those who had completed a test period. Such a test period usually lasted one week for manual workers and one month for white-collar workers. The 1943 reforms left this unchanged. And with the creation of new systems for newly insured groups the same practice was followed. For domestic servants, who received compulsory insurance in 1952, a real waiting period was introduced. These people only received entitlement to benefits if they had worked for at least six months and their employer had paid a minimum of twelve weekly premiums in the twenty-four weeks preceding the claim. Shortly afterwards the compulsory systems for craftsmen (1956) and for small merchants (1960) continued in the same way. The insured had to complete a waiting period of ninety days after addition of their name to the registration lists for the insurance before they would receive entitlement to benefits.

Looking back one notices no general lines of convergence. In certain countries, such as the Netherlands, and Germany, the waiting periods which existed in earlier days have now almost completely disappeared. But in other countries such as France and Italy especially in recent decades there have been new impositions or increases in waiting periods, especially where systems for the self-employed are concerned. This gives no clear indication as to the future development of waiting periods.

But the change which has taken place in ideas may give a clue. It can be stated that social health insurance, together with other branches of social security, moves away from the principles of private insurance and turns into a system of social welfare administration, as an integral part of public social policy. As a result of this development waiting periods and minimum premiums for entitlement to benefits may be regarded as remnants of private insurance techniques which do not make sense any more in a compulsory system and are bound to disappear with time (88).

A shift in the concepts of social security from the principle of causality to the principle of finality is apparent. Under the first principle, benefits were paid because the insured had fulfilled certain conditions which were the cause of his entitlement to benefits; under the second they are paid because the insured has a need for these benefits, and this need is the basis of the entire system (89). In this respect, waiting periods and minimum premiums as conditions for benefits are remainders of a concept of social security which is increasingly abandoned by the systems in practice. They will have to disappear along with all other conditions for entitlement to benefits which are not consistent with the aims of social insurance themselves.

# 12
# *Evolution of relations to suppliers*

From the description of the situation in the various health insurance systems the conclusion could be drawn that the relations with the medical profession and other providers of care are managed in a very different way. This is the result of a long evolution characterized by pressure group politics, resulting in strongly marked national features which make comparisons with similar developments in other countries hardly possible.

Yet one cannot conclude at once that the evolution is mainly divergent. If one leaves aside short-term incidents, convergent trends can be seen on several aspects over longer periods. Moreover it is possible that in the long run in all countries the relations with the providers of care have developed in the same sense, and that the differences which are now ascertained are merely different phases in a similar evolution.

In this chapter we will concentrate on the most important elements. First, the general principles which have to rule the relations between suppliers of medical care and health insurance. For example free choice of physician and freedom of therapy for the physician; second the systems of agreement and generally the legal basis of the relations between suppliers and health insurance; and third the ways of paying for medical work done by various persons and institutions for the socially insured patient.

### The principles

The problems created by the right to choose the supplier of care and the therapeutic autonomy of the physician are related to each other. Both belong to the field of health economics. They are problems of limited means and unlimited needs. Therefore, they are also problems of efficacy. They give rise to the inevitable question as to whether it is more efficient for a social health insurance system to pay for the services of all suppliers of care in the community or to organize its own health services. The same question may be raised about clinical autonomy. Does it (better) serve the aims of social health insurance to guarantee complete free choice of tests and treatments or to limit the number of services and/or the range of admitted products and devices? These are difficult questions. It is remarkable that in the debates on health insurance policy all parties, the public authorities as well as the insurance agencies and medical professions, proclaim themselves very strongly attached to the principles of free choice and of therapeutic autonomy. The practical conclusions of the different parties are, however, not at all the same.

FREE CHOICE OF SUPPLIER . . .

Free choice of provider is a typical example of those fundamental freedoms which were most valued in the liberal ideology of the nineteenth and early twentieth century. Free choice of physician by the patient was still one of the four principles which made up the 'Charte médicale' in France in 1927 (90). In other countries too and not only in Europe, this principle is very highly valued (91).

Before the development in the nineteenth century of the large movement towards mutual insurance against medical care costs, freedom of choice was in fact, for the vast majority of the population, an illusion. Their freedom of choice was limited to the social services for the poor and to the physicians and institutions which they could expect with sufficient certainty to charge little or no fees. There can be no doubt that through the development of health insurance real free choice of the patient has increased to an enormous extent.

Looking at Europe it appears that from the beginning of social health insurance change has taken opposite directions in two groups of countries. There are countries where the medieval structures of the corporations remained in existence. These are countries which escaped the influence of the French Revolution (92). Here the developing health insurance funds took over the structure of the old corporative funds which had usually registered their members with a certain physician who had in turn agreed to give them all the care which was necessary. This physician was paid a small sum of money every week by each member; this is of course a prefiguration of the capitation system (93). Free choice of physician was not an important issue, provided the members received satisfactory care. On the other hand there are the countries where the French 'Le Chapelier' Act was enforced. The Act abolished all corporations and forbade, for the future, all associations of workers on a professional basis. So the old corporative structures were completely wiped out (94). Health insurance developed in these countries in the form of so-called 'mutual funds' which were organized by workers mainly to provide a minimum income to sick members. Generally the mutual aid funds also paid their sick members a certain sum towards medical care. But these funds did not conclude special agreements with any given physician; and so they did not offend the rules of the traditional practice of medicine (95).

In these early days, that is in the nineteenth century, neither of these systems seemed to be of any concern to the medical profession. The members of health insurance funds were too few in number and the finances of the funds too small (96). In the countries with direct provision of care by a fund physician, fund practice only constituted a very limited (and badly paid) part of the whole of the physician's work; the physician found financial compensation in his private practice. In the countries with indirect provision of care the payments from the mutual funds were so small that their members were considered by physicians simply as poor persons who had to be treated at lower fees if they were not cared for without charge.

Problems were posed when about half the potential patients for the average doctor were members of the funds. This situation was reached in most countries at some time between the two world wars. In the countries with direct provision of care the problem was posed in two ways. In the first place the question rose whether the sickness fund had to contract with all physicians and providers of care who were active in the community or if it could appoint its own physicians who would be available full time. The latter system was the original type of fund practice in Germany, against which from 1900 there was violent reaction by the physicians' associations (97). One generation later the same conflict is found in the Netherlands, where one particular health insurance fund had created its own medical organization. The Royal Society for the Advancement of Medicine strongly opposed this but the conflict lasted for ten years (98). There still remain a few examples of such an organization of health services in the Netherlands, but generally speaking one can say that the conflict was resolved on the basis of free choice of supplier for members of the funds.

On the other hand in these countries there was conflict between physicians and health insurance funds over the free admission of physicians to fund practice. It was, of course, again in Germany that a conflict situation on this point was reached first. In 1892 the health insurance funds had authority to fix the number of insured members who would justify a full-time physician. From 1900 on the physicians started organizing action against this rule. Such action was already successful by 1913 when the Berlin Agreement stated that the funds would accept one physician for 1,350 insured members and one for 1,000 insured members where the workers' family members were also insured, and also that the admission of physicians to practice would be through an admission committee, comprising equal representatives of physicians and funds. In 1931 these conditions were more clearly specified and the extent of fund practice was reduced to 600 insured members. Finally in 1960 the 'Federal Constitutional Court' declared unconstitutional the limitation of a fund practice and so recognized the free right of admission to fund practice for all physicians (99).

A similar conflict took place in the Netherlands over the so-called morality clause required by the Catholic Health Insurance Funds in their contracts with physicians in the 1930s. This clause stated that the funds would refuse services of physicians if there was any danger of a violation of the Roman Catholic ethical principles. The solution to this problem came in the health insurance funds decree of 1941 which said that each fund had to conclude an agreement with every physician, dentist, pharmacist, or midwife who applied. The funds can only refuse to do so for reasons to be decided by the commissioner in charge of the supervision of health insurance funds (the commissioner is now replaced by the sickness funds council) (100). These regulations were superseded by the new health insurance act.

A similar dispute arose at a later stage in the Italian systems. For a long time a number of funds had used the *numerus clausus* formula in their relations with the physicians. This seems to have been accepted by the medical profession, until 1949, when a violent conflict opposed medical profession and health insurance organizations on this issue. The conflict lasted until 1955, when an agreement was reached in which it was stated that all physicians would have the right to act as physicians working for the funds if they wished to do so (101).

In those countries with indirect provision of care the problem of free choice of provider of care was unheard of for a long time. It only emerged when the insurance started trying to arrange with suppliers for tariff agreements to assure their members true reimbursement of the fees paid. The problem of free choice was then posed in these terms: would the insured be forced to call only on the physicians and institutions who would conclude an agreement with the insurance? This is known in most cases as the problem of non-discrimination (102).

In France the first serious attempt to establish tariffs of fees to be binding for the physicians was found in the proposals of Minister Gazier in 1956. These proposals were violently attacked by physicians, particularly because they were considered to be contrary to the principle of free choice of doctor because no reimbursement would be given by funds if the agreement tariffs were not respected.

The proposal was rejected but in 1960 another minister did achieve a system of agreements with binding tariffs for physicians. The decree of 1960 provided for a smaller reimbursement to the patient if care had been given by a physician who had remained outside the agreement system. This also was considered by the physicians as a violation of the principle of free choice (103). Yet throughout the subsequent reforms this rule has been maintained.

Shortly afterwards, the same kind of problem was found in Belgium. The Reform Act of 1963 provided for a transition period in which a reduced tariff would be used as the basis of the patient's reimbursement where care was given by a physician who had not signed the agreement. But in the same year this rule was eased to some extent; reimbursements for care by physicians outside the agreement system would be 75 per cent of the fees under the agreement tariffs. This was a method of putting pressure on the insurance members to use the services of physicians who signed the agreement. At the time it seemed innocent enough to the legislator; yet it appeared to the physicians as an insuperable obstacle for co-operation to the application of the Reform Act. They went so far as to hold a national strike which ended with an agreement on 25 June 1964. One of the first and main points of this agreement was the abolition of discrimination in reimbursements.

Can the evolution described above be considered as convergent or divergent? From the legal viewpoint the difference between the two groups of countries is as great now as it was at the time of the introduction of compulsory insurance. In the first group of countries (Italy, the Netherlands, and Germany) free choice of provider is in principle limited to that group who conclude an agreement with the fund of which the patient is a member. In the second group of countries (Belgium, France, and Luxemburg) the insured are free to call on the provider of their choice (in France the rate of reimbursement may be lower).

In these matters it is important to consider the social and economic significance of the rules. It has already been remarked that the free choice of provider was mainly theoretical in the period before health insurance, as was the case with so many other of those liberties which were proclaimed in the nineteenth century. The development of health insurance has in itself increased the free choice of provider of care.

This effect seems to have been produced to a similar extent both in the systems of direct and indirect benefit. In the first case the legal limitation of freedom of choice has little significance for the insured patient because practically all the providers of care (in the Netherlands) or the large majority of them (in Germany and Italy) have concluded agreements with the local sickness funds so that one can consider the free choice of patient as sufficiently guaranteed (104). And in the second group of countries freedom of choice is not so universal as may legally appear. In fact there may be more discrimination in these countries through differences in rates and price between providers of care (105).

So it may be concluded that the evolution in the various systems has moved towards a greater freedom of choice for the patient. At present apart from a few special schemes, all systems of health insurance in Europe proclaim free choice as one of their basic principles, and this freedom of choice is largely realized in practice.

We believe that the systems in each of the countries concerned will have a tendency to go further in this direction, as such freedom appears to be valued fairly highly by the insured. But this endeavour will not be directed towards a purification of the legal concept of freedom of choice, but to attainment of real free choice in a given social and economic context. Formal legal free choice no longer needs to be pursued. It exists in all countries as completely as it did in the nineteenth century. Every citizen is free to go at any time to any physician, dentist, pharmacist, hospital, or other supplier of care who has the time, capacity, and willingness to give him care. In none of the countries concerned does health insurance have any power of regulation over the medical profession or the organization of health care, even if it exerts influence upon it (106). In all those countries of the original European Community physicians and other providers of care in principle enjoy the professional position which was theirs by tradition. If they partially or completely abandon this position to organize their work in a different way, this is done voluntarily.

### ...AND RATIONALIZATION OF SUPPLY

If health insurance in future has no longer to deal with freedom of choice in the formal sense it is clear that it will try to extend freedom of choice in reality. The future action of health insurance systems in Europe will be directed towards removal of the barriers which exist between patient and suppliers of care. Such action has already been successful in one area. It can now be said that health insurance has abolished practically all financial barriers. This is not absolutely true with regard to all providers of care—such a goal could only be attained by nationalization of medicine—but the number of physicians and other suppliers taking part in health insurance is sufficiently large to allow one to speak of freedom of choice for the insured (107). But other barriers have received much less attention. One of these is the distance to be travelled by the patient and the time lost in order to receive health care, in emergency as well as in ordinary cases. Another important barrier is the skill-gap, which can be translated into the question of the guaranteed quality of care. How can the patient know that the physician is sufficiently trained, that his equipment is adequate and up to date, and his ancillary and nursing staff adequate to enable him to provide good medical care?

The answer is found in one word: rationalization. Rationalization is first of all desirable in the territorial spread of health manpower, and health institutions of all types. This should normally be the responsibility of the minister of public health, who may issue binding rules for planning health institutions and manpower distribution. In practice health insurance has often tried to influence the distribution of health services by its agreements with suppliers; without success, apparently (108).

Rationalization is also desirable in co-ordination of activities. Incompetent shopping around by a patient among specialists and health institutions is especially a source of waste. It should be replaced throughout the network of health services by competent streaming of patients, in which the general practitioner should play a central role.

To some extent this has already been achieved in a number of countries and in others steps have been taken in this direction. An example is in the Belgian Act of 1971 which permits the government to set rules for health insurance to promote co-operation among GPs and with specialists for better organization.

And rationalization is no less desirable in the organization of medical practice itself. Group structure should replace solo practice which has prevailed until now (109). This would give the physician more opportunity for study and continued education, it would permit more efficient investment in equipment and create more opportunities for adequate nursing and ancillary staff. In this field health insurance can play an important role.

The tendency towards better realization of free choice of supplier will result in future in more rationalization and organization. This will be based upon a rational spreading of health institutions and manpower, from the teaching hospital to local health centres, GPs, and allied health personnel. All these institutions and persons will maintain very close relations with health insurance, which will be their primary source of income. Inappropriate placing of patients in the network of health services will be avoided and good co-ordination between the services will provide for efficient care and at the lowest cost. This will probably mean a return towards health institutions run by the insurance institutions and towards physicians working under a special contract with health insurance funds, both devices which have been attacked violently in the past, precisely because of the principle of free choice.

CLINICAL FREEDOM AND CONTROL
Therapeutical autonomy is a functional freedom closely related to the professional skill of the supplier and his legally protected monopoly. This fundamental principle denies to any other person or institution the right to interfere with the decision of the supplier of care on examination and treatment (110). This basic principle is explicitly guaranteed to the physician under all systems.

With early developments of health insurance in the nineteenth century formal therapeutic autonomy was fully respected. The physicians in those days had only a limited choice of techniques anyway. In the expenditure of the funds health care had only a limited role, so there appeared to be little reason to restrict the free choice of the practitioner in medical techniques to be used. It may be typical that in the first years of the German compulsory system (from 1884 on) physicians in their protests and declarations of principle paid no attention to the problem of therapeutic autonomy, yet one generation later the French physicians in their

'Charte médicale' called therapeutic autonomy one of the basic principles to govern the relations between the medical profession and health insurance institutions. The difference between both situations was that medical techniques had seen tremendous advance and that health insurance funds had begun to feel the heavy burden of ever-increasing costs. If the funds were to continue, a limit on expenditure was necessary. The funds could only finance health care which was really necessary. This was the begining of control on medical practice and medical prescriptions.

**Medical services.** Control on medical services could be established in two ways. First one could create special control departments in the health insurance funds, which would employ their own medical officers. Or control could be developed mutually between physicians themselves. The latter type of control developed spontaneously in systems where agreements with insurance funds provide for a lump sum payment from the fund, to be divided by the physicians according to their own standards (111). In Germany such a regulation was made official by the agreement of July 1931 concluded between the physicians' associations and the government. By this agreement it was the responsibility of the Association of Physicians of the Funds to create special control committees of elected members, to prevent abuses of the system. Physicians who tried to exaggerate the number of their services and prescriptions (they are known as 'Funds Lions') were to be invited by this committee to justify their high provision. If their services were deemed unnecessarily high their fees would be reduced. This arrangement still applies.

In Belgium and France there were originally no collective relations between physicians and sickness funds, which could give rise to a type of mutual control. So it was health insurance which took the initiative by creating medical control departments, with medical control officials to detect abuse, and judicial means to penalize it. From the beginning these medical control departments had a double task. They had to control abuses by physicians and they had to control the insured who falsely claimed incapacity for work. Their legal position was also ambiguous. The medical control officers had to be independent from the insurance organizations, but they had to be paid by them as they worked in their interest. The result has been that the rules relating to their legal position have been frequently changed (112).

In all cases where the physicians were paid a salary or a capitation fee as is the case in the Netherlands and for a large part in Italy, medical examination and treatment as such give rise to few or no abuses which could oblige the fund to create some type of medical control. In these systems there are found neither in the law nor in the regulations specific rules to prevent excessive medical services.

**Prescription.** Even under types of remuneration which make it unnecessary for funds to control the number of examinations and treatments carried out by the physician, there always has to be control of their prescriptions. Moreover, expenditure for hospital care, drugs, and other health products has increased at a much faster rate than for physicians' services. The problems of control of expenditure for drugs and hospital care especially call for attention as the escalation threatens to unbalance the funds' accounts.

In this field the same two types of control have developed. In the Netherlands the physicians working for some funds spontaneously fixed a certain amount of prescriptions per patient on the list, which had normally not to be exceeded; if the physician went beyond this figure he had to justify himself, or his fees would be reduced by the amount of the excess. It is interesting to note that this type of control came into existence in a voluntary way in the period before the introduction of compulsory insurance; but it was abolished soon afterwards (113). In the German (compulsory) health insurance a similar type of control on prescriptions was developed fairly early. It was made official in the agreement of July 1931, mentioned above, and on this occasion was added to the competence of the associations of funds' physicians. The system is still in effect today.

In the countries with indirect benefits (France, Belgium, and Luxemburg) no type of mutual control was developed. Instead the insurance organizations gradually established control departments with their own medical staff.

Special attention should be paid to developments in control of drug expenses. Shortly before the Second World War and especially in the post-war period the increase in expenditure on drugs was so heavy, that strong measures had to be taken to limit this. In various countries special commissions were set up to study the problem. France was the first to fix in its general scheme a list of reimbursable drugs. At the same time a rather high personal payment was asked of the patient. This varied according to the therapeutic value of the products. It was changed frequently.

Belgium began its compulsory health insurance system in 1945 with a system of personal payments by the insured for drugs but it soon added a second control measure: a list of reimbursable products. In its original conception this list was remarkable. The first part of the list contained those products considered as irreplaceable, the second list mentioned those which were not paid for by the insurance at all, and for all other products, considered to be normally reimbursable but not irreplaceable products, a special list was established.

At about the same period in the Netherlands much the same took place. In 1950 a primary list of drugs to be used under health insurance was drawn up. Early in 1952 the official list was established; it was of course frequently changed and increased afterwards. This list was divided into three groups, one of the products which would be delivered to a certain quantity without any special measure, one group of products which would only be delivered after special authorization by the fund, and one group which would not be delivered by the funds at all. No personal payment is demanded. The same can be said in Italy, both of the systems of direct and indirect benefits. In 1949 a list ('*Prontuario*') of drugs containing all products which could be received free from the health insurance funds, was established by the INAM. This list contains a certain group of products for which special authorization by the fund is necessary. Its use is being extended to all funds. No personal payment can be asked from the patient.

One may conclude that with respect to pharmaceutical products in the period after the Second World War all countries except one (Germany) have established a list of products to be used by the insurance funds. This was seen in all countries as a method of controlling the increase in expenditure. One must keep in mind, however, that the actual importance of these lists as a limitation of the freedom of prescription of the physicians may be different from one country to another. For the remainder the countries have reacted in differing ways to the difficulties of the pharmaceutical market. One country has maintained the ancient form of mutual control (Germany), two countries require for the most expensive products special authorization by the funds (the Netherlands and Italy), and four countries require personal payment by the patient (Belgium, France, Germany, and Luxemburg).

The problem of the control of expenditure in the hospital sector is no less important but developments here have been sparse and we will deal with it very briefly.

In none of the countries has the supply of hospital care been limited by a list of recognized hospitals. In the early days of health insurance the insured had a free choice of hospital, and he still has. One may probably object that, for instance, in the Netherlands this free choice is limited to the hospitals which have concluded an agreement with the sickness fund of which the insured is a member. This limitation however, is without any practical importance because very few actual agreements are signed; all hospitals consider themselves to be under contract with the sickness funds in their area (114).

In all countries, at some period of their development, admission to hospital at the expense of the sickness fund has become conditional on the previous permission of the fund, except in emergency. This was already so in Germany from the beginning of compulsory insurance in 1883 and in Luxemburg from 1902. Attempts to limit the right to free admission to hospital in other ways, such as introducing extra payments by the insured at the time of admission, failed whenever they were proposed.

Very little evolution can be shown in the position of the European systems in respect of the supply of prostheses and appliances. From the beginning the various systems have required the previous permission of the fund for the financing of prostheses and expensive appliances and also from the beginning the patient has had to pay part of the cost himself. This position has remained unchanged until now and there is no evidence that a change will occur in the near future.

**The future.** Clinical freedom is of course recognized in all countries. It is in fact the logical result of the legal monopoly over the practice of medicine given to competent persons: no other person or institution can impose restrictions on a physician as far as diagnosis and treatment are concerned. He who interferes with diagnosis or treatment is liable to prosecution. On the other hand sickness funds and social insurance institutions are dependent on the decisions of individual physicians as to the techniques they are going to use and the drugs, specialist care, and hospital care they are going to prescribe. Any increase in these prescriptions and in the use of techniques is an immediate threat to the financial balance of the funds.

This is the main problem which will have to be solved in the future. The development of the various health insurance systems in Europe shows that it is not possible to maintain the existing organization of the supply of medical services without control. Two types of control have developed: collective control by physicians of each other and special control services under authority of the funds. In both cases control is exercised exclusively by physicians. No laymen interfere with the practice of medicine. The principle that other physicians are entitled to issue general rules for the supply of medical services and control their application is no longer contested (115).

Our review does not suggest a tendency towards generalization of either type of control. Should we then conclude that countries with mutual control will keep this type and countries with control departments will not change either? This is uncertain as in both groups there is much dissatisfaction with the efficacy of medical control. Certain developments indicate that both types are considered complementary and will be combined in future. On the one hand the role of the control officer of the medical control department is changing; he becomes a medical adviser, who essentially gives the GP or the specialist a second opinion on the case; he may also advise the insured of the necessity to consult a certain type of physician or institution and he may indicate preventive services (116). On the other hand the role of the mutual control bodies is being influenced by the phenomenon of medical audit, and mutual evaluation of medical care, especially in hospitals. The recent PSRO legislation in the USA will probably exert a positive influence upon this evolution. This development may be seen in line with the closer integration of social health insurance into public health policy. It seems probable that in all countries in the future medical advisers will assist physicians and other practitioners and that all institutions will have their own medical audits. Control of abuse will then shift into the background with more emphasis put on quality control.

It appears that the problem of cost control raises quite different issues in the field of drugs, hospital care, and the supply of prostheses and expensive appliances. The problem of drugs especially should be seen in the context of the larger question of the pharmaceutical industry. The extraordinary increase in expenditure in drugs is related to the organization of the market, its research, licences, price policy, advertising, and the extreme number of products. Social insurance in Europe has already exerted some influence on this market (117). The future of health insurance in this field will depend on the organization of the industry; this will have to be undertaken, at the European level, in close relation with the system of health insurance.

As far as physicians' prescriptions are concerned most countries provide, and will provide in future, a limited list of recognized drugs. In most countries the patient has also to pay part of the cost himself and this is likely to continue in future. For financing hospital care and prostheses and expensive appliances in all countries previous permission of the fund is required, and no change in this position can be expected. The most serious limitations exist for the prescription of prostheses and appliances, where, apart from the permission of the funds, personal payment and a list of recognized products are imposed; this too seems likely to remain.

## Payment of suppliers

This is a vast subject and we shall have to limit ourselves to the payment of physicians.

It is important to note that the systems of remuneration by health insurance funds before the introduction of compulsory insurance were already varied. In Germany the early voluntary funds supplied medical care free to their members through contracts with physicians who were paid directly by the funds. The calculation of the payment differed greatly between funds.

The 1883 legislation brought no change to this situation; the Act contained no provision concerning the relation between physicians and the funds. Yet the organization and the unification of the sickness funds as a consequence of the legislation brought some uniformity in payment through two basic types: the fee-for-service and capitation payment (118).

In this period strong reaction arose in the medical profession. The physicians created the *'Verband der Aerzte Deutschlands'*, also known by the name of its founder, *'Hartmann Bund'*. The aims of this movement included collective agreements with the funds and payment per item of service on the basis of agreed tariffs (119).

It was only many years later that these aims came to fruition, by way of the agreement of July 1931. The agreement did not formally change the system of individual contracts between sickness funds and physicians, but it created Associations of Funds' Physicians which would negotiate with the funds on collective agreements from which the contents of individual contracts would derive. It may seem that this agreement abandoned completely the principle of fee-for-service payment. Indeed, it provides that payment for medical care will be in a general lump sum by the funds to the association. The amount is negotiated between the association and the fund on the basis of a yearly fixed sum per insured. But remember that this lump payment is then divided by the association between its members, according to freely fixed rules. Thus the physicians were paid per item of service.

Later developments, and especially the Act of 1955, abolished individual contracts with the physicians. The physician now has legal relations only with his association and not with the funds.

There has, however, been an important change in the actual method of calculating the physicians' remuneration. In the beginning the rules for dividing the total sum available varied from one association to another. But more and more associations started to use an official list of medical services in the calculation of individual payment. The individual physicians charged their services to the association on the basis of the fees provided in the list. These fees were subject to some controls and limitations and were finally paid at a certain rate, determined by the relation between the total claims by physicians and the total sum paid by the fund (120).

A number of sickness funds, called 'Ersatzkassen', remained outside the control of public authorities and were not obliged to agree on global remuneration by the funds according to the legal rules. The 'Ersatzkassen' used a system of fee per item of service on the basis of their own tariff of medical services. Each physician charged his services to the association and the association charged them to the 'Ersatzkassen'.

It seems that this latter system was more favoured by physicians than the former. So after a while the principle was adopted that all funds were free to calculate the total remuneration for the supply of medical care, either as a lump sum or along the fee-for-service system. In recent years more and more funds have dropped lump sum calculation and joined the 'Ersatzkassen' in their over-all application of fee-for-service. Nowadays this way of calculating physicians' income has become more or less general in Germany (121).

There was a period when German physicians accepted from the social insurance other methods of payment. This was when insured patients only constituted a small minority and insurance practice was equated with care for the poor. But when it became clear that social insurance was going to be extended generally among the population the physicians insisted on fee-for-service. They have been putting this into practice since the 1930s, when they received the right to decide among themselves on the method of calculating their individual payments. Changes in the method of calculation, either directly by changes in the basic rates, or indirectly by changes in the method of calculating the total sum paid by sickness funds, were accepted by physicians without much difficulty, as long as the actual payment to the individual was by fee-per-item-of-service.

A similar conclusion can be drawn from events in Belgium and France. Here, also, before the introduction of compulsory insurance, many sickness funds were active. These '*Mutualités*' paid their physicians in many different ways; yet it is clear that in Belgium and France the classical fee-for-service type was used much more than the lump sum type so common in the Netherlands and Germany (122).

In France the legislator has never dreamed of imposing a system of lump sum payment on physicians. The first project for compulsory health insurance, proposed in 1921, included a method of remuneration similar to the German one. The health insurance funds would pay to the physicians' professional association a total amount which would be calculated as a yearly sum per insured; this money would have to be divided by the association among individual physicians, according to the nature and the number of their services. The mere presence of a lump sum element was sufficient to raise a storm from physicians. They insisted upon a fee-for-service payment which would be, as Dr Chaveau put it: 'un paiement à l'acte médical, à la visite, à la consultation, lequel assure aux practiciens une rétribution exactement proportionnée à l'effort fourni' (123). This requirement was as basic for French physicians as the '*entente directe*', direct negotiation of the fee between physician and patient, one of the principles of the free practice of medicine, and seen as the opposite of '*tiers payant*', the payment by the sickness funds. Lump sum payment was considered absurd.

It is this 'tiers payant', this direct payment of the physician by the sickness funds, which physicians in France have so violently opposed during the last fifty years, despite the fact that it had existed for a long time in certain areas, such as the care of industrial accidents, medical care for the poor, and health insurance schemes for coal-mines and the railways. Until now French physicians, with few exceptions, have not accepted payments other than by the patient himself and per item of service.

At the same time they have accepted in place of the 'entente directe' a collective agreement, determining the rates of fees under the control of a national commission.

The attitude of Luxemburg physicians has changed in the same way. There, under compulsory insurance since 1902, complete freedom of contracts between funds and physicians existed in the same way as in Germany at the same time. But after the First World War Luxemburg physicians came more and more under the influence of the French. They sought fee-for-service payment, and payment by the insured patient and not by sickness funds. In 1933 they received satisfaction, and the same rules were confirmed in 1957: the fees were to be paid by the insured himself, who would receive reimbursement from the sickness funds, except in hospital care where direct payment by funds ('tiers payant') was the rule. Yet in the system for blue-collar workers, the articles of association of the sickness funds generally provide for payment to the physician where the insured would find it difficult to advance the money (124).

Belgian physicians have always held the same position as the French, without making as many concessions as their Luxemburg colleagues. After a long struggle they have accepted the principle of collective agreements on fees (such a system was first applied to the whole country only in 1970) but they always refused any form of direct payment from sickness funds. A royal decree of September 1955, which tried to reorganize the supply of medical care under health insurance, with a view to reducing the financial deficit of the insurance, provided for general application of direct payment of fees by funds. The very sharp reaction of the physicians prevented this decree from being applied. Later, the attitude of the medical profession in this respect softened. In 1961 they concluded a settlement with the Minister of Social Security which allowed exceptions to the rule of payment of fees by the patient himself. The agreements with sickness funds would have to state in which cases direct payment by the sickness funds could be organized; the physicians were prepared to accept it at least for expensive treatment. But the settlement was not accepted by members of the General Association of Belgian Physicians.

Shortly afterwards this Association was replaced by a National Union of Physicians' Trade Societies (*Syndikale Kamers*), which took a much more radical position (125).

In the first draft agreement for the application of the Reform Act of 1963, proposed by the new National Institute of Health Insurance, an attempt was made to reintroduce the text of the 1961 settlement. Article 7 of this draft-agreement provided that as a rule, fees would have to be paid by patients, but that for sums exceeding 300 BF the physician, with the consent of the patient, could apply for direct payment from the funds. The physicians did not accept this draft-agreement; a strike followed and was concluded by a national agreement in which no mention of direct payment by funds was made. The legislator has left open the opportunity of making special arrangements for direct payment by funds. But very little use is made of this opportunity.

In Italy and the Netherlands also at the time of the introduction of compulsory health insurance there existed many sickness funds which paid their physicians in their own way. But the situation was different from that in Belgium and France and closer to Germany and Luxemburg. Capitation payment largely prevailed.

After 1926, when in Italy compulsory insurance was gradually introduced, two types of organization coexisted: the indirect type is associated with fee-for-service paid by the patient himself, the direct system pays the GP generally by capitation and the specialist by salary.

This situation gave rise to few difficulties and remained unchanged even after the Reform Act of 1943. From 1949 however, physicians were no longer satisfied and a period of struggle began, ending in a national agreement in 1955. This agreement made general capitation payment for GPs in direct benefit systems, and extended the direct benefit system throughout health insurance. At the same time it allowed all insured persons to choose indirect benefits if they wished.

The agreement was altered very frequently and finally was replaced by the national agreement of August 1966. This new text softened the rule for general application of capitation payment; for attendance at the patient's home the GP receives a special fee, the capitation payment covering only work in the surgery. Moreover, in every local community physicians can preserve fee per item of service paid by the patient if they make a statement to that effect to the INAM. But it appears that very little use is made of this option except in the cities and nearly all GPs are under the capitation system (126).

For specialist care the INAM has always run its own dispensaries and clinics in which specialists are salaried. This rule was confirmed by the 1966 agreement. Specialist care outside dispensaries and clinics is paid for in the traditional fee-for-service method under special agreements.

Similarly with evolution in the Netherlands. At the time of the unification of sickness funds insurance into one partly compulsory and partly voluntary system (1941) nothing was changed in the system of relations between sickness funds and physicians. Individual contracts in their wide diversity remained in existence and even today legislation has not touched the problem of the payment.

The earliest national agreement on remuneration was concluded in 1942 with the dentists. The 'National Society for the Promotion of Dentistry' and the National Unions of Sickness Funds agreed that in all individual contracts the system of remuneration should be the same: a simplified fee-for-service, supplemented by certain payments by the patient himself.

After the war similar national agreements were concluded for other groups of suppliers of care. For GPs it was agreed that capitation payment was to be general; for specialists a type of simplified fee per item of service such as for the dentists was used. Notwithstanding evolution in the method of calculating actual remuneration, these arrangements are still maintained. However, contracts between specialists and hospitals provide more and more for payment by salary. Proposals to replace direct payment by a system of fees per item of service paid by the patient and proposals to introduce fees per item of service for all cases have been rejected by the majority of Dutch physicians (127), even though certain groups are in favour of such arrangements.

In general coming events in the six countries lead first of all to the conclusion that there is no convergence as far as the method of payment of the physician is concerned; the only converging trend can be shown in the method of fixing the type of remuneration, and this could be better described as a parallel evolution with large shifts in time. It concerns especially the evolution from freely fixed fees (known in France as: 'entente directe') to individual and later collective agreements with the funds on the amount of the fees.

Otherwise the conclusion must be that for at least half a century there have existed, both in theory and practice, three types of remuneration. The first of these is the simple fee per service, paid by the patient and reimbursed by the insuring institution. It is deeply rooted in the minds of French, Belgian, and Luxemburg physicians. The second is fee per service paid by the sickness funds through the association of fund physicians: this has for generations been the standard method in Germany. The third type is capitation payment, paid of course by the insuring institution. This has already existed for a long time as a method of payment to GPs in Italy and in the Netherlands. Specialists in these countries receive a fee per item of service or a salary, paid directly in each case by the health insurance institutions.

It has, however, to be pointed out that physicians show a distinct preference for fee-for-service. Physicians who receive a salary tend to keep partial private practice in which they can charge fees to the patient, thus avoiding over-all control of the amount of their income by the sickness insurance institutions. The Italian physicians claimed and obtained in 1955 the right for all insured persons to opt for the indirect benefit system, which uses freely fixed fees for service. For the same reason Dutch physicians claim that the income ceiling for membership of the social sickness funds should be maintained and not increased; this permits them to keep about 30 per cent as private patients to whom they can charge any fees they like. This can be said also about German physicians. The conclusion is that if direct payment of physicians by sickness funds were generalized, it seems unlikely that a lump sum system of payment would be accepted by physicians, unless they were allowed to maintain some private practice.

A different tendency appears in the method of payment to hospital physicians. In hospitals there exists a strong tendency to change the method of calculating remuneration in favour of the salary, which is the most functional and simple way of payment. This is a logical result of the growing integration of the physician into the structure of the hospital. The future hospital physician will receive a salary for his work in the hospital including the outpatient department, and limited private practice will be permitted, where he will be entitled to charge his own fees (128).

Past development shows that physicians are very conservative in their method of calculating payment and regarding the source from where it is paid. They may accept changes in the method of calculation and in the method of fixing the amount, but they want it to remain the same type of payment and to be paid by the traditional person or institution. The one exception to this could be that they will gladly accept a shift from lump sum payment to payment per item of service, as this latter type of payment is greatly favoured.

BUDGETING OF THE PAYMENTS

Should we therefore expect little change in the method of calculation and the channels for paying physicians? For the answer to this question one should take into account the structural problems of financing health insurance, which will have to be faced in future, increases in expenditure exceeding the increase in wages, prices, and national income. Every year on the presentation of the budget the need for additional finance will be felt. Insurance administrators will have to think every year of increasing contribution rates or seek higher government subsidies, or increase personal payment by the insured at the time of service. It is foreseen that these increases will no longer be accepted by the public if they are not accompanied by efficient controls on expenditure.

In the present structure of the insurance the insured, the employers, and the taxpayers could feel they are throwing their money into a bottomless pit. What is the use of fixing the tariffs of fees if physicians are entirely free to decide on the nature and number of services? It may be that the day price in hospitals is fixed by government regulations but physicians decide freely how long a patient must stay in hospital. The prices of drugs, prostheses, and appliances are kept under strict control, but their nature and the number to be used are prescribed freely by the physician. So the payers of contributions and taxes have in fact very little control over the way their money is spent.

Two measures are absolutely necessary to keep expenditure on health care under control. The first is a budgeting of the total amount to be spent: the amount provided in the budget should be strictly limited to payments in a given year and should only be exceeded for very special and imperative reasons. The second is efficient control over the individual physician's practice, with regard to diagnosis and treatment as well as prescribing.

There is only one country in the six with a type of budgeting for health insurance expenditure: Germany. By paying to the association of funds' physicians the total amount fixed by agreement the sickness fund is freed of all financial obligations with respect to the supply of medical care to its members. So the fund knows in advance how much it is going to spend on medical care in a given year, and it can fix its premium rates accordingly. Strictly speaking this is only true of the agreement called 'Pauschalhonorierungsverfahren' (PHV) and not for the 'Einzelleistungshonorierungsverfahren' (EHV). In this latter case there is also a total amount paid by the fund to the association, but this is based on fees charged by the physicians; it does not limit them. In both cases, however, the association exerts control so as to avoid unnecessary services and prescriptions. One may conclude from this that strict budgeting of medical care expenditure by the sickness funds is possible. It has been in application in Germany for more than forty years.

We foresee that in all European countries agreements will have to be concluded between the insurance institutions and the associations of suppliers, in which the rate of growth of expenditure will be fixed on as objective grounds as possible. To achieve budgeting the collective contracts for direct payment of physicians by funds should include rules so that in the final account over each year the total amount of the fees of all physicians will have to be compared to the agreed growth-rate and that fees will be adapted accordingly. In the same way some normal rate of increase for hospital care, medicine, and prostheses and appliances will have to be determined.

This will give medical control bodies the opportunity of checking the activity of every physician. Eventually an unjustified excess over normal expenditure caused by a physician in the matter of services and prescriptions will lead to a reduction of his fees. In that case, of course, the physician must have the opportunity to justify his unusually expensive practice. This opportunity is fully guaranteed in the present German system by the control committees of the associations. Similarly, in all systems, democratically elected committees of physicians will have to be established for that purpose.

This could be a compromise which gives to both parties, the physicians and the health insurance, sufficient guarantees for protection of their interests. The health insurance will know in due time how much it is going to spend on health care. It discusses the level of this expenditure with suppliers, and these have equal power with health insurance to decide the amount which is going to be spent; they hold complete control of the application of the agreement. Of all the possible solutions to the problem of health insurance this technique will probably meet with the least opposition on the physicians' side. Indeed, the payment of physicians can be maintained on the largely preferred form of fees-for-service, fixed according to agreed rates as in the past. The only change, for a number of countries, would be that the payment will have to be made directly by the sickness fund. But this is not a strong objection, since the generalization of the direct payment rule is the tendency to be expected in future. Of course one will have to wait longer for this generalization in such countries as Belgium and France, and to a lesser degree Luxemburg, where most of the physicians still think along the lines of the liberal 'entente directe'.

Some will consider these proposals unacceptable for physicians. They should remember two things: first a similar system has already existed for a long time in Germany, long enough to prove that it is practicable, otherwise the physicians would have obtained its abolition long ago; and the only alternative solution to budgeting is to make lump sum remuneration general. This may be possible in hospitals, but certainly not in individual practice. When physicians have the choice between budgeted fees per item of service, limited by the budget but at the same time guaranteed at a certain level, and general lump sum payments, there is little doubt that they will prefer the first solution.

## Agreements between insurance and suppliers

The history of agreements between suppliers and social health insurance institutions is mainly an enumeration of conflicts, negotiations, and compromises. The relationship with the medical profession especially has always been difficult; the other suppliers of care, such as hospitals, pharmacists, and medical auxiliaries, have caused much less trouble (129). Here we deal particularly with agreements between sickness funds and physicians under three headings: their legal status, the role of public authorities, and the measures to be taken in the absence of sufficient agreement.

### THE LEGAL STATUS OF AGREEMENTS

There are, at the moment, three types of agreement with physicians (and the same applies to other suppliers): individual contracts, collective agreements, and combinations of both.

A fourth form of agreement, the contract of employment, had some importance in the past. Employment contracts covering special groups of workers were fairly generally applied particularly by the oldest of social health insurances. This was the case in France for the coal-mines and the railways, in Germany for the coal-mines, and in the Italian insurance against tuberculosis. It is still a matter of dispute if these contracts were and are of the same nature as in private industry, or whether they are contracts *sui generis* (130). The legal dispute has not yet been settled, but it cannot be considered as very important nowadays.

Before the introduction of compulsory insurance a large number of sickness funds, and especially the stronger funds created or supported by the trade unions, employed their own physicians to supply care to their members. A number of firms which had created private sickness funds for their own personnel, provided a proper medical service by engaging under contract of employment physicians who would also deal with industrial accidents in the plant. From the physicians' side strong protest has arisen against these situations. Since the establishment of generalized compulsory insurance systems it has always been official policy to conclude free agreements without an employment relationship with the medical profession (131). Yet contracts of employment between certain funds and their medical personnel are still found today. In the Netherlands the Sickness Funds Act of 1941 permitted funds which practised this system before the Act to continue it. A few of them have maintained such contracts until today. In a decreasing number of sickness schemes in Italy they are also still found.

One should not conclude that in a general way the physicians are now working less under contracts of employment than they did before. Here we are discussing only the relationship between the physicians and the insurance institutions. On the contrary, it should be said that more and more physicians work under contracts of employment—with the hospitals. As most hospitals are independent of the insurance institutions this does not create an employment relationship between the physician and the insurance institution.

In the oldest system of compulsory national health insurance, the German system of 1883, the relations between physicians and sickness funds originally were based upon individual contracts. This situation proved not to the advantage of physicians. Of both parties the sickness funds were clearly the stronger (132). After a number of attempts to simplify and improve the contracts it became increasingly clear that only collective agreements between two equally mandatory associations could lead to well-balanced relations. In 1931 an agreement was reached between the funds and the physicians, which created associations of funds' physicians, considered as public institutions, membership of which was compulsory for all physicians who wanted to work under insurance. The physicians continued to sign individual contracts with sickness funds, but their content was more and more determined by the collective agreements between the funds and the associations. Already by 1933 relations were ruled only by collective agreements.

One finds a similar evolution in Luxemburg. In 1902 a compulsory system of health insurance was introduced which very much resembled the German model. And in 1933 Luxemburg also imitated Germany by introducing a system of collective agreements with physicians. These were somewhat different from the German ones. No compulsory associations of funds' physicians were created and the choice was left between individual and collective agreements.

In the same period (1928–30) in France an attempt was made to establish a national system of compulsory health insurance for employed workers (133). This legislation was proposed under the influence of the German system which France learned of through the districts of Alsace and Lorraine, won back from Germany after the First World War. The government proposal dated from 1921. It provided for a collective agreement between physicians and sickness funds, in which a total amount of pay for the supply of medical care would be calculated according to a yearly lump sum per insured; the individual physicians would be paid by their professional association on the basis of the nature and number of their services. This was in fact an imitation of the German system. The violent reaction of physicians compelled the government to abandon this plan, but the government succeeded in making parliament enact a law in 1928 containing at least a system of collective agreements in which, however, the association of physicians played no particular role. The decree of 30 March 1929, meant to execute this law, weakened the position of the government further still by stating in Article 37, paragraph 2, that the agreement would only be binding for the members of the undersigning association and for the other physicians who would personally adhere to the agreement. The collective agreement finally lost all practical importance with the subsequent Act of 1930, which brought peace with the medical profession by degrading the tariffs agreed upon in the collective agreement to the rank of *'tarifs de responsabilité'*, which means that they were not binding for physicians but only constituted the basis for the financial intervention of the insurance.

In the same period again (after 1927) compulsory health insurance schemes were gradually introduced in Italy. There were two different types: in systems with direct benefits the German device of collective agreements with physicians was used, with the amendment that the agreements only applied to those physicians who had shown their individual willingness to co-operate with the insurance schemes; it has been said of this system that it did not give rise to many difficulties, mainly because the number of physicians taking part in the system was not so large as not to guarantee each of them a sufficient number of patients and also 'because the general conditions for the concluding of agreements were fixed by the public authorities' (134). In the systems with indirect benefits the relations with the medical profession are based on the principles dear to the French physicians: free fees and nonbinding insurance tariffs.

The Second World War brought a new step in the evolution of relations between sickness insurance and the medical profession. First there was the introduction of compulsory health insurance in the Netherlands. Here the relations with physicians were managed in a different way. An old device was used: individual contracts. The Compulsory Health Insurance Act of 1941 realized in fact a large part of the proposals of the so-called 'Unification Report' which had been issued in 1925 by a commission 'to bring more unity in the sickness funds system of the country' (135). One of these proposals was to generalize the system of individual contracts, already practised by a number of funds and suppliers of care, and to add for all suppliers the legal right to contract with each sickness fund in the district and the obligation for each supplier to contract with all other funds in his district who ask this, if he has done so with one of them.

In reality these individual contracts are hidden collective agreements. Already before 1941 the contents of the individual contracts were in fact determined by agreements between professional associations of suppliers (which is for physicians the Royal Society for the Promotion of Medicine, a society which has always been very active in the field of health insurance) and the associations of sickness funds. These agreements have taken the form of model contracts, which have to be followed by all members of the association (136). This arrangement was maintained under compulsory insurance which consequently organized a mixed system of collective and individual agreements.

The Belgian compulsory health insurance was introduced shortly afterwards in 1945. Little seems to have been learned from the experience of neighbouring countries, since the decree of 1945 provided for a system of individual contracts with physicians. The contents of these contracts would be determined by the Minister of Labour and Social Affairs on the advice of a technical committee which would include representatives of the suppliers of care. It is not surprising to learn that the physicians required and obtained the amendment of this text—they did so at the time without a strike—in line with the French arrangement: the insurance tariffs would not be binding on the physicians. It must be said that the General Association of Physicians at that time was prepared to advise its members to sign for binding tariffs of fees for the lower income classes, on condition that an exact criterion would be fixed to limit the number of patients counted as lower income class and also on condition that this would lead to certain advantages in the application of income tax regulations to physicians. This second point could not be given and both parties disagree about the level of agreement tariffs. The negotiations were broken off on 28 September 1947 (137).

In France the reform of 1945 constituted a new attempt to introduce real collective agreements. By the *Ordonnance* no. 45-2454 of 19 October 1945 it was said that the rates of fees were to be determined by agreements between insurance institutions and associations of physicians in each *département*; they had to be approved afterwards by a *'Commission Nationale Tripartite'*. If no agreement was reached, this commission would fix the rates itself. The associations of physicians took the same view as the Belgian: they were prepared to co-operate under this system but only with respect to those insured whose income would not exceed a certain upper limit and also on condition that these fees would bring income tax advantages. But even when the government accepted these conditions, this did not satisfy the associations: they wanted no agreements at all and the text was not applied (138).

In the years after 1955, in the various countries, very important changes in the system of agreements with physicians occurred. Only in the Netherlands has it remained fundamentally the same as it was in 1941. The first new act was the German act of August 1955, named '*Gesetz über Kassenarztrecht*'. This act did not, in fact, bring very many new elements in the relationship between the medical profession and sickness funds. It was more an amalgamation of existing rules, which were built into the Social Security Code.

The year 1955 was an important one for relations between physicians and insurance institutions in Italy with the national agreement in 1955 between the government (which had taken up the negotiations instead of the insurance institutions) and the physicians. By this agreement the right to choose between direct and indirect benefits for patients was extended to all types of insurance; this spread, much to the astonishment of physicians, the system of direct benefit more and more (139). In this system of insurance the relations with physicians remained ruled by collective agreements, which were now concluded in a uniform way on a national level. The agreement tariffs would only be binding on physicians who had individually adhered to the system; it was established that all physicians would have the right to do so. In the system of indirect benefits the physicians remained free to fix their own fees in the traditional way; but its importance in the supply of health care has been considerably reduced.

At about the same time, in Luxemburg, relations with the medical profession were reformed by the decree of 11 May 1957. This decree abolished the right of option for individual contracts, which appears never to have been used (140); only collective agreements could now legally regulate these relations. The decree otherwise changed very little in the content of the agreements and nothing in their form.

The 1960 reform in France is much more important. Somewhat earlier a proposal of Minister Gazier for collective agreements with fixed tariffs under the control of the public authorities had failed. The decree no. 60-451 of 12 May 1960 introduced a system of collective agreements, with an important new characteristic:

physicians could, if they wished, adhere individually to a model agreement if, in their department, no collective agreement had been concluded. So this system is a combination of collective agreement and individual contract.

The French reform inspired the Belgian reform of health insurance in 1961–3. But the Belgian physicians did not like the French idea of collective agreements, binding also for physicians who were not members of signing associations. Already in the draft agreement of 20 October 1961 between the General Association of Physicians of Belgium and the Minister of Social Security it had been provided that national agreements would only be binding on those who adhered individually to them. And so was the rule enacted in August 1963: an agreement committee concludes an agreement on the national or on the regional level, but it is binding only on the individual adherents. An amending act of December 1963 added another limitation: the agreement as a whole will only come into force in those districts where at least 60 per cent of all physicians (and at least 50 per cent of the GPs and 50 per cent of the specialists) have individually adhered to the agreement. In 1965 the collective agreement was replaced by a National Settlement and individual adherence by an Individual Obligation. But there was no real change in the system, the change was merely in terminology (141).

A new step in the development in Belgium occurred in 1970 at the time of the difficult renewal of the national settlement. An Act of 26 March 1970 introduced the so-called 'inverted obligation'. It states that the agreement will be in force in a certain district from the moment of its conclusion, unless more than 40 per cent of physicians (or more than 50 per cent of GPs or specialists) have explicitly refused their co-operation. The agreement will then be binding directly upon all physicians who have not explicitly refused. This reform was meant to secure for the public authorities a sufficient number of individual adherents from among the physicians by gambling on the inertia and the resistance of the individual physicians against filling in official documents. Yet it means in fact a complete change in the legal position of the physicians *vis-à-vis* health insurance. Before the new act a physician was obliged to respect the insurance tariffs because he had signed an individual contract with the insurance to that effect on condition that a sufficient number of other physicians in the same district would also do this. The national agreement or national settlement only conditioned the contents of this contract. But now the obligation of the physician to respect the insurance tariffs is based upon the law itself; the collective agreement or settlement is an instrument to actualize the legal obligation. The fact that the physician can escape his obligation by using a specific legal procedure does not change the legal nature of his obligation.

The Belgian example was soon followed in France, where the association of physicians itself promoted the idea of a national settlement (instead of the existing regional ones), with a possibility for individual withdrawal within a certain period after its conclusion (142). This was an inverted obligation, compared with the situation in regions without an agreement, where individual physicians would join the system by signing an individual contract.

But the French went further. The 'convention nationale' of 28 October 1971 has introduced an enablement for the funds to exclude from the agreement any physician who persistently exceeds reasonable standards in his prescriptions. It has been said that this rule in fact extends *ad infinitum* the possibility of individual withdrawal from the agreement, as it is sufficient for a practitioner to ignore the computer profiles, put before him by the medical section of the regional *'commission médico-sociale paritaire'*, to become excluded (143).

Very few physicians have chosen to withdraw from the agreement; the anti-agreement centres (Paris, Lyons) have largely disappeared, but the system is still very unstable, as it is endangered every year by the necessity to conclude agreements on the tariffs (144).

What are the conclusions one may draw from this development? The individual contracts in Germany and Luxemburg were put aside in 1933 in favour of collective agreements binding on all physicians who have been accepted to treat funds' members. In the same period the same system applied to Italy: collective agreements were in force for all physicians who enlisted as funds' physicians or who concluded contracts with the insurance. *De facto* in the Netherlands the same situation prevailed: collective agreements determined (but without legal obligation) the contents of the individual contracts between physicians and sickness funds. In all these countries, except Luxemburg, this formula has been conserved until the present day. No plans are in progress to change in the foreseeable future.

For a long time in the two remaining countries no agreement could be concluded. The French have tried since 1928 to introduce real collective agreements, binding on all physicians of a *département*. Only after 1960 have these attempts been successful, especially with the introduction of complementary individual agreements in the *départements*, where no collective agreement was reached. The national convention of 28 October 1971 has demonstrated the nearly unanimous acceptance of the collective agreements system by the physicians; it could permit individual physicians to withdraw and it could abolish the 'threat' of individual agreements. Luxemburg has shifted from the German to the French system: it has introduced collective agreements binding upon all physicians, but without the possibility of individual contracts in the absence of collective agreements. The Belgian system of 1961-3 consisted originally of collective agreements with individual adherence, but after 1970 it has become a system of real collective agreements, binding by law on all physicians who have no legal excuse.

So the development may be called fundamentally divergent. One group of countries seems to have an orientation towards collective agreements binding for all practitioners by force of the law (Belgium, Luxemburg, France). Another group of countries has already maintained for a long time collective agreements which are binding only on those physicians who have voluntarily adhered to the system, by signing some kind of contract with the insurance (the Netherlands, Germany, Italy). One will notice that the division of the countries on this basis coincides with that between direct and indirect benefits.

Will agreements continue to exist in the future or will the relationship with the suppliers of care be managed in a different way? One thinks in that respect, of nationalization. But it is to be observed that outside the socialist countries no nationalization of the medical profession is known in modern history. Even in a National Health Service such as the British, medicine is not nationalized. Each physician in Great Britain has the right to work in his own way and no physician co-operates with the National Health Service unless he has voluntarily accepted to do so (145). So it seems very unlikely that in future medical care in Europe will be nationalized. Great Britain has nationalized the majority of its hospitals, the government regulations are very strict on hospitals in all other European countries. The financial reasons which brought the British to nationalization of the hospitals seem to exist and to be increasing in other European countries also. So it may seem likely that hospitals will be nationalized and the hospital physicians will become civil servants. But for all other physicians it is most probable that in the future as in the past their relationship with the health insurance will be managed by a system of agreements. The question then is what these agreements will look like.

In the first place the question will arise whether these agreements will include contracts of employment or not. From the evolution described above it may be concluded that a decreasing number of physicians work under a contract of employment with a sickness fund or another insurance institution but that on the other hand more and more physicians work under a contract of employment with a hospital or a similar institution of care, which in its turn may conclude an agreement for co-operation with the insurance. It may be expected that in the future the hospital physicians will be generally integrated into the organizational structure of the hospital, by means of contract of employment or a statutory position (146). There will be no direct relationship between the hospital physician and the health insurance, the hospital acting as an intermediary.

From what has been said above one may conclude that agreements between the health insurance and the physicians outside hospitals will certainly not be contracts of employment in the future. They will be special contracts that may be called contracts of co-operation. Legally they will be contracts *sui generis* between equal partners.

The important question then is: will these contracts take the form of real collective agreements, will they be individual contracts, or will they have a mixed structure? In all countries nowadays individual contracts as such have been dropped. Only in the Netherlands do they legally exist, but their content is mainly derived from unofficial but generally applied collective agreements.

If they are to be collective agreements, the question remains whether they will be pure collective agreements or mixed agreements on a collective basis with individual application. Our historical survey shows that two groups of countries have had divergent development: France, Belgium, and Luxemburg towards pure collective agreements based on the law and the Netherlands, Germany, and Italy towards collective agreements applied only through individual contracts.

On the basis of the general social evolution, which seems to be directed towards more government responsibility (147) one may suppose that the tendency will be in favour of pure collective agreements, binding on all concerned by force of law. Past developments point that way. Remember too that the application of collective agreements through individual contracts has problems. The associations of physicians see their position in the negotiations weakened if public authorities can test their strength by putting the question to individual physicians, on the other hand the insurance will have to face a lack of stability in the number and the spread of physicians working under the agreement, a problem which will become crucial at every renewal of the agreement.

These problems do not occur with collective agreement enforced by law. Here, of course, the problem is the loss of individual freedom of choice to co-operate with social insurance or not. But this cannot really be interpreted as a threat to the medical profession as the contents of the collective agreements will have to be approved by the association of the physicians themselves. Physicians who do not agree with certain elements can persuade their colleagues by the usual democratic methods, so that their association will refuse to sign the agreement.

Of course the general binding power of the collective agreement can be weakened. It is possible that the law will permit physicians to refuse their co-operation individually, on condition that enough physicians work under the agreement to meet the needs of the insured. Another possibility is to associate all physicians who are willing to co-operate with insurance into an association of funds' physicians, which will directly conclude the collective agreement with the funds. The practitioners who do not approve the terms of the agreement can resign from the association.

It is possible that relations between the medical profession and the funds will lean towards such a compromise in future, but it is by no means certain. The legal rules on industrial relations in their evolution certainly point in the opposite direction: increasingly collective contracts prevail for all employers and workers without exception. But then it is a matter of dispute whether industrial relations can be considered as a prefiguration of the future relations between the medical profession and society (148).

THE ROLE OF PUBLIC AUTHORITIES
Public authorities can play an important role in two aspects of the relationship between the medical profession and social health insurance. Both relate to the procedure for concluding agreements. First is approval of the agreement reached between the parties; second is the implementation of necessary measures when no agreement can be reached.

**Approval of agreements.** The contents of any agreement are of extreme importance to the public authorities because of their financial consequences. An apparently small concession in the matter of remuneration may cause a big increase in expenditure on social insurance. It is not surprising that in all countries public authorities have secured for themselves a form of control over the agreements.

It is easy to show a general tendency towards strengthening the role of public authorities in this field. In the period before 1926, only Germany and Luxemburg had a comprehensive compulsory health insurance system, and neither here nor in the other countries did public authorities interfere with contracts between sickness funds and suppliers of care. When compulsory insurance came in Italy in 1926 the 'Legge syndacale' gave rise to collective agreements with physicians, but in these agreements the public authorities played no role at all, according to the principles of collective labour agreements which prevailed at the time (149). In France compulsory health insurance for wage-earners was realized to some extent in 1930. The text does not make it clear if public authorities had to play a role in the conclusion or in the approval of collective agreements with physicians. But from the written correspondence between Minister Loucheur and Dr Cibrie before the enactment of the final text of the law one can deduce that the public authorities did not interfere in what was considered as the free conclusion of contracts between private associations (150). The reform of the law on the funds' physicians in Germany in 1923–33 equally abstained from introducing control by the public authorities; and this attitude was imitated in Luxemburg where the 1933 reform left the public authorities outside the relations between health insurance funds and suppliers of care.

Real government control is found for the first time in the Netherlands. The sickness funds' decree of 1941, which introduced compulsory health insurance, made it a condition for the validity of the agreements that they should be approved by the commissioner whose function was control over the sickness funds and who was appointed by the Minister. After the war, the commissioner, who had been considered as a creation of the German occupiers, was replaced by a sickness funds' council (151). This council took over the responsibility of approving the contents of agreements. It was composed of a president and thirty-five members, appointed by the Minister, and its decisions are subject to the veto of the Minister himself: so the approval by this council may be called an approval by the public authorities.

The French 1945 reform was directed towards substantial government control in social health insurance, particularly in the field of relations with suppliers of care. The agreements between funds and physicians had to be approved by a *'Commission Nationale des Tarifs*'. This commission was composed of representatives of the funds, physicians, and the ministers concerned. In 1950 government control was intensified by a decree which gave the Minister of Labour authority to suspend the decision of approval by this commission if it might endanger the financial balance of the health insurance funds. This CNT moreover had authority to impose official tariffs where no acceptable agreement was reached.

The Belgian compulsory health insurance system, introduced in 1945, conferred on the public authorities a role which they had not played in any health insurance system before: Article 60 of the decree of 21 March 1945 authorized the Minister of Labour and Social Security to fix the rates of physicians' fees after taking the advice of the professional organizations. This arrangement was not received with enthusiasm by the physicians. In fact it never was applied but it gave a certain orientation to the relations with the medical profession: these would from then on be managed between the physicians and the Minister and not, or to a very limited extent, between the physicians and the sickness funds. So, when the royal decree of 1955 left it to associations of sickness funds and physicians to agree on tariffs of fees, these had to be approved by the Minister before coming into operation (152).

In 1955 Italy saw the first national agreement with physicians. Formally the partner to the agreement with the physicians was the INAM, but in fact the negotiations had been conducted by the physicians and the Minister of Labour; one can practically speak of an agreement between the physicians and the government (153). And also in 1955 in Germany the law on the relations between physicians and health insurance funds was reformed in such a way that the public authorities (albeit in an indirect way) have the possibility of control. Under the new rules the association of funds' physicians and the sickness funds are obliged to provide in their articles of constitution the obligation to follow directions given by the Federal and State Committees, committees of negotiation comprising equal representatives of funds and physicians, whose decisions have to be approved in their turn by the Minister of Labour. And in 1957 in Luxemburg the relations with the physicians were reformed by way of a compromise between the

German and the French conceptions. The commission of arbitration according to the German model is maintained, but its function is to approve the agreement and possibly to fix official rates in the absence of agreement; its decisions have also to be approved by the Minister of Labour and Social Security.

The role of the public authorities will become still more strongly marked in France with the 1960 reform. In the first place the representative CNT commission was replaced by a *'Commission Interministérielle des Tarifs'* (CIT) which was composed only of representatives of the ministers concerned. In the second place the rates under the agreements could not exceed certain maxima, fixed by decree of the ministers concerned; and naturally the agreements fixed immediately their rates at the level of these maxima, with the result that in reality they were fixed directly by the ministers and not by agreement. Later this radical reform was softened by the decree no. 66-21 of January 1966, which shifted the approval of the agreement back to a representative committee, called *'Commission Nationale Tripartite'* (CNT, again). But still, the decisions of this committee had to be approved by the representatives of the ministers on it, or else by a special interministerial committee. The Act of 3 July 1971 has taken the next step. It has made compulsory national agreements for the physicians, to be approved directly by *'arrêté interministériel'* (by joint decision of several ministers); such formulas are also possible for the other suppliers of care, but they can choose to maintain their old conventions.

A few reforms of lesser importance have also occurred. The Belgian Act of 1963 maintained the principle of approval of the agreement (later called the settlement) by the Minister of Social Security. In the Netherlands the new Sickness Funds' Act of 1964 concedes to a special committee of the sickness funds' council control and approval of agreements with suppliers; it was felt that the council itself could not do this, because it included representatives of the parties concerned (154). This commission only has members appointed by the Minister, by the employers, and by the employees. Approval by the Minister is still required.

To conclude, it can be observed that government control over the agreements with the suppliers of care is a recent phenomenon.

It appears that only since the Second World War have the economic and financial consequences of these agreements reached such importance for the public authorities, that they should keep a vigilant eye upon them. In a few cases the government has gone so far as to fix fees; it has done so with success in France (for physicians until 1971), without success in Belgium; but this can certainly not be called a general tendency. Yet it is clear that for the future in all systems the public authorities will want to have at least a right of veto over the rates.

There seems to be one exception to this rule: in Germany control by public authorities is limited to the general rules for the negotiation of agreements, it does not extend to the agreements themselves. These are concluded between the sickness funds and the association of funds' physicians in full freedom of contract. This exception can be explained. The sickness funds are responsible for their financial balance; they must cover their possible deficit either out of their reserves or by increases in the premium rates. But the premium rate is limited by a legal maximum, which may only be exceeded with the approval of the Minister. All funds have reached and exceeded this maximum (155). So there is control by public authorities over the rates, albeit in a very indirect way.

In a general way it can be concluded that in future the role of public authorities in the conclusion of the agreement with suppliers of care will increase.

The tendency, moreover, is sustained by the fact that the sickness funds, with a few exceptions, are no longer real insurance institutions, but have become executive offices for state insurance or a public service. This means that the sickness funds are in reality very weak partners in the negotiations with suppliers of care. While the physicians, hospitals, and other suppliers defend their own direct interests, the sickness funds bear no real financial responsibility, which makes them incline to concessions in the interest of their insured. More and more the true partner in the negotiations with suppliers is not the sickness fund but the government (156).

**Measures in the absence of agreements.** If no agreement has been reached different measures can be taken by several authorities to protect the operation of insurance. The simplest way is fixing rates of health care benefits by the sickness funds themselves without control of the fees and price charged by suppliers of care. This can only be done in a system which reimburses the patients for their medical expenses, and not in a system with direct benefits. Such a system always needs rates for the payment of suppliers: these can be fixed by a procedure of arbitration, by a special commission of conciliation, or by the public authorities themselves.

We have seen that in the actual situation various systems are used. We attempt here to ascertain how far the opinions and the rules in this field have developed with time and if in this development some convergent or divergent trends can be established.

For a number of countries, such as Germany, there is little evolution to be noticed in this matter. The Committees of Arbitration which determine the contents of the agreements if the parties themselves cannot come to a conclusion had already been introduced by the Berlin Agreement of 1913. At the time individual contracts between physician and sickness fund were kept in mind, but the technique used was the same as the one in present-day Germany.

Luxemburg legislation has followed the German example with some delay: in 1933 it charged a Conciliation and Arbitration Commission with the task of deciding on conflict between physicians and sickness funds if no agreement could be reached; the commission had to take the advice of the *'Collège Médical'*, highest authority of the medical profession and of the authority controlling social insurance. Its decision took the place of the absent agreement. In 1957 the decision of the commission of arbitration was subjected to approval by the Minister of Labour and Social Security.

Another example of relative immobility in this field is given by the Netherlands. Before 1941 in this country no action could be taken by the public authorities in the case of absence of agreements with suppliers of care, because social insurance for health care was of a voluntary nature. Free negotiations between funds and suppliers had to provide for a sufficient number of contracts for the supply of care to members of the sickness funds. After the introduction of compulsory insurance in 1941 little changed in this direction. The Netherlands still rely very much on free negotiations between funds and suppliers. If an insufficient number of individual suppliers want to conclude agreements, the Minister can only issue guiding rules to be proposed to both parties in order to promote that conclusion of a national agreement. If his action is unsuccessful the patients will have to pay their physicians themselves, and the Minister may decide which sums the funds can pay to their members who incur such expenses. It is true that the Minister has also power to fix binding maximum rates for all physicians, hospitals, and other suppliers of care in the framework of general price regulations; this rule, however, is not specific for the health care field, and it is very doubtful if it will ever be used in this field.

Little can be said on this point as far as Italy is concerned. In the regulations which deal with the relationship to the medical care suppliers there is no mention of a procedure to be followed in the case of insufficient co-operation by physicians with the insurance. We cannot find any evidence of public action having been taken on such occasions, even though such situations have occurred frequently in the history of Italian health insurance.

There have been a number of interesting developments in this field in France and in Belgium. The French project of 1921 provided for a procedure of the same type as was introduced in Germany in 1913; this, however, was rejected by the French physicians. When finally the compulsory health insurance legislation came into operation in 1930, the agreement system had lost all of its binding power. The agreements only served to make the whole system work more easily; if no agreement could be reached, the rates would be fixed by the insurance institutions themselves; in no case could they be imposed on suppliers of care.

In 1945 an attempt was made to change this situation. The collective agreements would arrange for rates of fees which could be imposed; where no agreement could be reached the CNT, which also had to approve agreement tariffs, would itself fix the fees. Yet this system never really applied especially because the sanctions against excess fees were weak.

Only the reform of 1960 would finally realize a true system of collective agreements where rates were imposed. Under this legislation an interministerial commission would fix two types of rates if no agreement could be reached on a national level or in certain regions: a higher rate, to be applied to the physicians who voluntarily agreed to conclude an individual agreement, and the lower, a non-imposable rate for all services by other physicians. In 1966 a *Commission National Tripartite* replaced the commission for approval of the agreement rates, but the rates in the absence of agreement remained within the competence of the Minister; they are now fixed by interministerial decrees.

Of particular importance is the rule, introduced in 1960, that in regions without a collective agreement individual doctors can sign a proposed agreement to work under the health insurance system. The large majority of the physicians in most regions signed such agreements. Only for the others would the (ridiculously low) official tariffs apply (157).

The new regulations concerning the national settlements (Act of 3 July 1971) have abolished the possibility of individual agreements if no national collective settlement can be reached for physicians. Tariffs, in such case, will generally be fixed by the government.

In Belgium in 1945 an attempt was made to introduce a system of rates of fees, binding on the physicians. These rates would not be fixed by way of agreement but directly by the public authorities; every year each individual physician would have to notify the health insurance institution if he was going to respect the official rates or not. With this system there would be no need to provide for absence of agreement. We have already mentioned that this system did not work at all. In 1955 a system of agreements was enacted, but it never took effect. Only by the Act of 1963 was a workable system finally organized. It would by way of agreements fix rates of fees which were imposable on the medical profession. In the original act it was foreseen that, in the case of absence of national agreements, the government would have authority to impose official maximum rates of fees for all physicians and for all patients.

The strong sanction was weakened by the modifying act of December 1963, which introduced the possibility of regional agreements if no national agreement could be obtained and which considered it sufficient that 60 per cent of the physicians would commit themselves to respecting the agreement rates. This compromise was maintained in later modifications of the legislation, with the explicit consent of the medical profession.

A divergent development can be observed in the European systems on this point. In the first group of countries no coercive measures are taken in the case of absence of agreements with the medical profession: both in the Netherlands and in Italy public authorities leave both parties to negotiate a solution to any conflict without neglecting the interests of insured patients.

In another group of countries a conflict between the partners to the agreement is solved by way of compulsory arbitration. This is necessary, for the health insurance system could not work without agreements. In these countries (Germany and Luxemburg) there has practically been no evolution on this point: they both have possessed this system for a long time and only in Luxemburg has it suffered certain modifications during its existence.

In a third group (France and Belgium) rules in the absence of agreement have been very controversial for a long time. In these countries the solution arrived at is that if no collective agreements exist (France) or if too large a number of individual physicians have withdrawn from the agreement (Belgium) the public authorities will impose official rates of fees on all physicians on all occasions.

Will this divergence continue in future, or are we to suppose that in all systems evolution will necessarily go in one direction? To answer this question we should consider that the agreements with the physicians are not only a device to ease the operation of insurance systems, but that they are an essential condition to guarantee protection of the insured. This is all the more true in systems where the suppliers are paid directly by the insurance institutions. But also if the insurance benefits consist of reimbursements to the patient, the agreements are of essential value: without such agreements a necessary link is lost between the reimbursement and the fee or the price paid by the insured. This leaves the insured ignorant about the part of the expense which will not be reimbursed.

As it is probable that in future all suppliers of care under social health insurance will be paid directly by the health insurance institutions, it follows that public authorities in all countries will have to take measures to protect the insured in the absence of agreement. The *laissez-faire* attitude of the Italian and Dutch governments in this respect will not last for long.

Yet, the nature of the measures to be taken is difficult to decide. Will the other countries imitate the compulsory arbitration system of Germany and Luxemburg, or will they copy the imposition of official rates as in Belgium and France?

Closer observation shows that the system of official rates imposed by public authorities, seems typical for insurance systems where benefits consist of reimbursements to the patients. In such systems suppliers charge fees which indeed should be regulated by the public authorities if the suppliers do not agree to respect certain limitations. Arbitration, on the other hand, seems more appropriate where suppliers are paid directly by the funds; payment is a matter for direct relation between suppliers and insurance institutions, which in the case of conflict can best be solved by way of arbitration. And as in future suppliers will be paid directly by the funds, it seems that arbitration will be used by public authorities.

REFERENCES

1. DUPEYROUX, J. J., *Evolution et tendances des régimes de sécurité sociale des pays membres des Communautés Européennes et de la Grande-Bretagne* (Luxemburg, ECSA, 1966), pp. 40 ff.
2. LEDEBOER, L. V., *Heden en verleden van de ziekenfondsverzekering en de verzekering voor bijzondere ziektekosten* ('s Gravenhage, 1973), pp. 11-12.
3. CHERUBINI, A., 'Introduzione storica alle assicurazioni sociali in Italia (Il Ventennio fascista 1923-1943)', *Rivista degli infortuni e delle malattie professionali*, 5 (1969), 737.

4. VELDKAMP, G. M. J., *Sociale triptiek. Verantwoording en achtergronden van een beleid* ('s Gravenhage, 1968), pp. 56-57.
5. *Disegno di legge relativo all'istituzione del Servizio Sanitario Nazionale*, presented to the Italian Parliament, 13 August 1974.
6. MANNOURY, J., *Enige aspekten van de gedachte aan een nationale gezondheidsdienst* (Alphen a.d. Rijn, 1967); MONTES, F. 'Pour un service national de santé', *Droit Social*, 2 (1969), 97-135; GRANDJEAT, P., *La Santé gratuite* (Paris, Seuil, 1965); etc.
7. *Health Services Financing* (London, BMA, 1970), pp. 149-50; MONTES, F., *Vers l'harmonisation de la sécurité sociale des pays de la communauté européenne?* (Paris, 1963); HERDER-DORNEICH, PH., and SCHREIBER, W., *Einkommensgrenzen und Kassensanierung in der Gesetzlichen Krankenversicherung* (Berlin, 1969), pp. 10-12; *Soins médicaux individuels et sécurité sociale* (Geneva, WHO, 1971), pp. 40-41; etc.
8. See F.I. DE HUSZAR, G. B., *Fundamentals of Voluntary Health Care* (Caldwell [Idaho], 1962).
9. BURNS, E., *Social Security and Public Policy* (New York, 1956), p. 129; DUPEYROUX, J. J., op. cit., pp. 49-50.
10. SOMERS, H., and SOMERS, A. R., 'Major issues in national health insurance', *Milbank Meml Fund Q.* 2 (New York, 1972), 209.
11. BURNS, E., op. cit., p. 127.
12. PERRIN, G., 'Avenir de la sécurité sociale', *Revue Internationale de Sécurité sociale*, 1 (Geneva, 1969), 14-15.
13. COMMISSION DE LA CE, *Rapport sur la situation sociale dans la Communauté en 1967* (Brussels, EEC, 1968), pp. 175-6.
14. EUROPEAN INSTITUTE OF SOCIAL SECURITY, *Complementary Systems of Social Security* (Leuven, EISS, 1973).
15. BREMME, G., *Freiheit und Soziale Sicherheit* (Stuttgart, 1961), p. 39.
16. ZELENKA, A., 'Les Tendances de la sécurité sociale dans le monde', *Conférence Européenne sur la Sécurité Sociale* (Brussels, sd), Part II, p. 10; HEISE, B., *Sozialpolitik in der E.W.G.* (Göttingen, 1966), p. 236; MONTES, F., op. cit., p. 20; COMMISSION DES CE, *Rapport sur la situation sociale dans la Communauté en 1960* (Brussels, 1961), p. 170.
17. CHIAPPELLI, U., *L'Assicurazione sociale di malattia* (Milan, 1969), p. 55.
18. Act of 17 August 1974, no. 286, art. 13.
19. HERDER-DORNEICH, PH., and SCHREIBER, W., op. cit., pp. 53-74.
20. SOCIAAL-ECONOMISCHE RAAD, *Advies inzake een strukturele verhoging van de loongrens, en van de maximumdagloongrens in de verplichte ziekenfondsverzekering voor 1970* ('s Gravenhage, 1969), Annexe IV.
21. Struktuurnota gezondheidszorg.
22. DUPEYROUX, J. J., op. cit., pp. 186-7.

23. ASSOCIATION INTERNATIONALE DE LA SECURITE SOCIALE, *Evolution et tendances de la sécurité sociale, Italie* (Geneva, 1959), pp. 25–29; CHIAPPELLI, U., op. cit., pp. 63–64, 77–82.
24. DUPEYROUX, J. J., op. cit., pp. 169–71.
25. RIBAS, J. J., *La Politique sociale des communautés européennes* (Paris, 1969), p. 396.
26. DE WIT, J., 'Geschiedenis van de ziekenfonds- en algemene ziektekostenverzekering', *De groei van de sociale verzekering in Nederland* (Amsterdam, 1969), pp. 134–5.
27. ENGELS, J., *De evolutie van de verplichte ziekte- en invaliditeitsverzekering* (Brussels, 1970), p. 22.
28. MANNOURY, J., *Hoofdtrekken van de sociale verzekering* (Alphen ad Rijn, 1967), p. 190.
29. 'La Sécurité sociale aux Pays-Bas', *Revue Internationale de Sécurité Sociale*, 1 (1970), 36–37.
30. ASSOCIATION INTERNATIONALE DE LA SECURITE SOCIALE, op. cit., p. 30.
31. —— *Evolution et tendances de la sécurité sociale* (Geneva, 1959), **9**, 25–26.
32. DILLEMANS, R., 'Het statuut van de instellingen der sociale verzekering in Frankrijk', *Album Van Goethem* (Antwerp, 1964), pp. 305–16.
33. DUPEYROUX, J. J., *Securité Sociale* (Paris, 5th edn, 1973), pp. 793–5 and 828–9.
34. *De Sociale Verzekeringswetten, Ziekenfondswet* (Deventer, sd), p. 197.
35. BUREAU INTERNATIONAL DU TRAVAIL, *Le Coût des soins médicaux* (Geneva, 1959); ASSOCIATION INTERNATIONALE DE LA SECURITE SOCIALE, *Le Volume et le coût des prestations de maladie en nature et en espèces* (Geneva, periodically); ABEL-SMITH, B., *An International Study of Health Expenditure* (Geneva, WHO, 1967); EUROPEAN INSTITUTE FOR SOCIAL SECURITY, *Evolution and Financing of the Cost of Medical Care* (Leuven, EISS, 1972); etc.
36. —— *Aspects sociaux de la coopération économique européenne* (Geneva, 1956), p. 45; COPPINI, M. A., *Les Incidences économiques de la sécurité sociale* (Brussels, EEC, 1971), pp. 83–132.
37. FISCHWASSER, G., 'Lohnfortzahlung und erste Stufe der Neuordnung der gesetzlichen Krankenversicherung', *Die Ersatzkasse*, **9** (1969), 328–9.
38. Act of 2 May 1974, art. I, 61–66 in *Mémorial*, **33** (1974), 596–7.
39. ASSOCIATION INTERNATIONALE DE SECURITE SOCIALE, *Evolution et tendances de la sécurité sociale, France* (Geneva, 1959), p. 52.
40. *Sozialbericht 1973* (Bonn, Bundesminister für Arbeit und Sozialordnung, 1973), p. 91.
41. Act of 2 May 1974, art. I, in *Mémorial*, **33** (1974), 597.
42. Act of 20 December 1974, art. 51.

43. DE WIT, J., op. cit., p. 131; LEDEBOER, L. V., op. cit., p. 7.
44. ENGELS, J., op. cit., p. 45; DUPEYROUX, J. J., *Sécurité Sociale* (5th edn, 1973), pp. 32–36.
45. FULCHER, D., *Health Care Systems* (Geneva, 1974), pp. 11–12.
46. ENGELS, J., op. cit., pp. 91–99.
47. COMMISSION DES COMMUNAUTES EUROPEENNES, *Rapport sur l'évolution de la situation sociale dans la Communauté en 1967* (Brussels, EEC, 1968), pp. 175–84.
48. DUPEYROUX, J. J., *Evolution des systèmes de sécurité sociale des pays membres de la C.E.E. et de la Grande-Bretagne*, pp. 169–71.
49. VAN BUGGENHOUT, A., *L'Impact macro-économique de la sécurité sociale* (Geneva, BIT, 1970), Table XIII, no. 84, pp. 74–75.
50. BURNS, E., op. cit., p. 34.
51. *Health Services Financing* (London, BMA, 1970).
52. COMMISSION DES PRESTATIONS SOCIALES, *Rapport sur les options du VIe Plan* (sl, febr. 1970), pp. 56 and 62–63; DELEECK, H., *Maatschappelijke zekerheid en inkomensherverdeling in België* (Antwerp, 1966), pp. 170–5.
53. BUREAU INTERNATIONAL DU TRAVAIL, *Les Aspects sociaux de la coopération économique européenne*, p. 45.
54. VELDKAMP, G. M. J., 'De Harmonisatie van de Sociale Zekerheid in E.E.G.-verband', *Rechtskundig Weekblad* (Antwerpen, 1967–8), p. 16.
55. INTERNATIONALE VEREINIGUNG FÜR SOZIALE SICHERHEIT, *Entwicklung und Tendenzen der sozialen Sicherheit, Deutschland* (Geneva, 1959), p. 61.
56. INTERNATIONALE VERENIGING VOOR SOCIALE ZEKERHEID, *Ontwikkeling en tendensen van de sociale zekerheid: Nederland* (Geneva, 1959), Part II, p. 24.
57. ILLUMINATI, F., and COPPINI, M. A., 'Les Relations entre les institutions de sécurité sociale et le corps médical', *Revue Internationale de Sécurité Sociale*, 2 (1968), 252.
58. RIBETTES-TILHET, J., 'Médecine et sécurité sociale dans quelques pays d'Europe', *Droit Social*, 12 (1964), 640-4.
59. ASSOCIATION INTERNATIONALE DE SECURITE SOCIALE, *Développement et tendances de la sécurité sociale: Belgique* (Geneva, 1959), Part I, pp. 74, 82; idem., *France*, pp. 44–46.
60. DOUBLET, J., *Sécurité Sociale* (Paris, 1967), pp. 115–16.
61. NASCHOLD, F., *Kassenärzte und Krankenversicherungsreform* (Freiburg im Breisgau, 1967), pp. 47–55.
62. HATZFELD, H., *Le Grand Tournant de la médecine libérale* (Paris, 1963), pp. 46–68.
63. GILDER, S. S. B., 'The World Medical Association and medical care', *International Medical Care* (Oxford, Lancaster, 1972). pp. 316–25.

## References

64. GLASER, W. A., *Paying the Doctor* (Baltimore, London, 1970), p. 25.
65. ROEMER, M. I., *L'Organisation des soins médicaux dans le cadre de la sécurité sociale* (Geneva, BIT, 1969), pp. 18–19.
66. INTERNATIONALE VERENIGING VOOR SOCIALE ZEKERHEID, op. cit., Part II, pp. 46, 56–57.
67. 'Sozialversicherungsanordnung no. 30 des Präsidenten des Zentralamts für Arbeit', 5 December 1947, *Arbeitsblatt Britischer Zone* (1947), p. 425.
68. LEËN, W., DELPEREE, A., and DUCHATELET, L., 'Rapport belge, L'Efficacité de la sécurité sociale', EUROPEAN INSTITUTE FOR SOCIAL SECURITY, *Yearbook 1970* (Leuven, 1970), pp. 82–83.
69. RIBAS, J. J., *La Politique sociale des communautés européennes* (Paris, 1969), pp. 406; VELDKAMP, G. M. J., *De sociale zekerheid opnieuw beschouwd in perspektief* (Alphen ad Rijn, 1967), p. 18.
70. PEQUIGNOT, H. and RÖSCH, G., 'Qu'est-ce que le petit risque?', *Droit social*, 3 (1970), 68–74.
71. *Soins médicaux individuels et sécurité sociale* (Geneva, OMS, 1971), pp. 25–26.
72. PREVOST, J., 'Action sanitaire et sociale', *Répertoire de droit social et du travail* (Paris, Dalloz, sd).
73. ENGELS, J., op. cit., p. 15.
74. COMMISSION DE LA CEE, *Conférence Européenne sur la sécurité sociale* (Brussels, EEC, 1962), part I, p. 764.
75. HATZFELD, H., op. cit., pp. 177–96.
76. DOUBLET, J., *Sécurité sociale, Mise-à-jour 1969* (Paris, 1969), p. 16.
77. ENGELS, J., op. cit., pp. 172–88.
78. Declaration of the Prime Minister in Parliament, 21 April 1964, p. 22.
79. GOSSERIES, PH. P., 'La Collaboration du corps médical à l'assurance maladie-invalidité obligatoire en droit belge', *Revue belge de Sécurité Sociale*, 3 (1967), 431.
80. VELDKAMP, G. M. J., *Sociale triptiek*, p. 178.
81. RICHTER, M., *Die Sozialreform, Dokumente und Stellungnahmen* (Bad Godesberg, sd), Part 8, pp. 9–100.
82. SOZIALENQUETE-KOMMISSION, *Soziale Sicherung in der Bundesrepublik Deutschland* (Stuttgart, sd), p. 220.
83. FULCHER, D., op. cit., p. 73.
84. Act of 2 May 1974, art. I, 10, in *Mémorial*, 33 (1974), 587.
85. SOZIALENQUETE-KOMMISSION, op. cit., pp. 217–20.
86. VELDKAMP, G. M. J., *De sociale zekerheid opnieuw beschouwd in perspektief*, p. 18.
87. ENGELS, J., op. cit., p. 390; HATZFELD, H., op. cit., pp. 61–62; contra: RANG, J. F., 'Het eigen risico in de ziekenfondsverzekering', *Tijdschrift voor Sociale Geneeskunde*, 44 (1966), 373; RICHTER, M., op. cit., Part 7, p. 24.

88. HEISE, B., in COMMISSION DE LA CEE, *Conférence Européenne sur la sécurité sociale*, Part I, p. 271.
89. WANNAGAT, G., op. cit., p. 9; *Sécurité sociale: évolution ou révolution?* (Paris, 1968), pp. 178-9, 183-4.
90. HATZFELD, H., op. cit., p. 46.
91. PRICE, L., 'Les Principes revisés sur la sécurité sociale adoptés par l'association médicale mondiale', *Bulletin de l'AISS*, 2 (Geneva, ISSA, 1964), 210-11.
92. DOUBLET, J., *Sécurité sociale* (Paris, 1967), pp. 14-15.
93. DE WIT, J., op. cit., p. 130; ECKSTEIN, H., *The English Health Service* (Cambridge [Mass.], 1958), pp. 17-19; HOGARTH, J., *The Payment of the General Practitioner* (Oxford, 1963), pp. 14-15.
94. DUPEYROUX, J. J., *Sécurité sociale* (5th edn.), pp. 32-33.
95. HATZFELD, H., op. cit., p. 32.
96. NASCHOLD, F., op. cit., pp. 56-57.
97. LYNCH, M. J., and RAPHAEL, S. S., *Medicine and the State* (Springfield [Ill.], 1963), pp. 36-41.
98. DE WIT, J., op. cit., p. 132.
99. LYNCH, M. J., and RAPHAEL, S. S., op. cit., pp. 37-50; GLASER, W. A., op. cit., pp. 123-4.
100. INTERNATIONALE VERENIGING VOOR SOCIALE ZEKERHEID, op. cit., Part II, p. 35; DE WIT, J., op. cit., p. 133.
101. ASSOCIATION INTERNATIONALE DE LA SECURITE SOCIALE, *Evolution et tendances de la sécurité sociale, Italie*, pp. 57, 65.
102. HATZFELD, H., op. cit., pp. 183-4.
103. —— op. cit., pp. 155-6, 179.
104. ROEMER, M. I., op. cit., p. 56.
105. DUPEYROUX, J. J., 'La Sécurité sociale et les médecins', *Recueil Dalloz*, 31 (1960), 189.
106. RIBETTES-TILHET, J., 'Médecins et sécurité sociale dans quelques pays d'Europe', *Droit Social*, 12 (1964), 640-1.
107. COPPINI, M. A., and ILLUMINATI, F., 'Les Relations entre les institutions de sécurité sociale et le corps médical', *Revue Internationale de Sécurité Sociale*, 2 (1968), 219, 270-3.
108. GLASER, W. A., op. cit., pp. 299-300.
109. MAIWALD, D., 'Krankenversicherung und Effektivitätssteigerung der freien Praxis', *Deutsche Versicherungszeitschrift*, 9 (1968), 215-24; SEPPILLI, A., 'I medici e la reforma sanitaria', *I problemi della sicurezza sociale*, 5 (1969),

825–36; 'Etude conjointe de la F.N.O.S.S. et de la C.S.M.F. sur les modalités d'aide financière des Caisses de sécurité sociale à la médecine de groupe', *Notes et Documents*, F.N.O.S.S. (1962), p. 7.
110. PEQUIGNOT, H., 'Illusions et réalités', *Cahiers Laënnec*, 1 (1967), 30–39.
111. HOGARTH, J., op. cit., pp. 23–26.
112. BING, J., 'Commentaire du décret no. 69–505 du 24 mai 1969', *Questions de Sécurité Sociale*, 8 (1969), 175; SCHUTYSER, K., *De geneeskundige controle in de sociale zekerheid* (Gent, 1974).
113. LEDEBOER, L. V., *Heden en verleden*, pp. 58–64.
114. INTERNATIONALE VERENIGING VOOR SOCIALE ZEKERHEID, op. cit., Part II, pp. 50–51.
115. SAVATIER, R., *Traité de Droit Médical*, pp. 279–81.
116. *Reform des Vertrauenärzlichen Dienstes*, (Deutsche forenschafts-bund, Bad Godesberg, sd); SCHUTYSER, K., op. cit.; POULIZAC, H., 'Du Médecin contrôleur ou conseiller médico-social', *Droit social*, 4 (1968), 251–9.
117. BACHELET, M., 'Influence des organismes de sécurité sociale sur le développement de l'industrie pharmaceutique dans les pays de la CEE' (Thesis, Grenoble, 1963).
118. WANNAGAT, G., *Lehrbuch des Sozialversicherungsrechts* (Tübingen, 1965), Part I, pp. 55–60, 131.
119. LYNCH, M. J., and RAPHAEL, S. S., op. cit., pp. 38–41.
120. HOGARTH, J., op. cit., pp. 242–7.
121. ASSOCIATION INTERNATIONALE DE LA MUTUALITE, *Les Relations avec le corps médical* (Geneva, July 1971), p. iv.
122. HATZFELD, H., op. cit., pp. 32–33; PANNIER, R., *Mens, geneeskunde, gemeenschap* (Brussels, 1970), pp. 41–42.
123. Cited in HATZFELD, H., op. cit., p. 41.
124. KAYSER, A., 'Les Relations entre les médecins et la sécurité sociale au Grand Duché de Luxembourg', *Le Corps médical*, 8 (Luxemburg, 1966), 581.
125. ENGELS, J., op. cit., pp. 294–385.
126. ASSOCIATION INTERNATIONALE DE LA SECURITE SOCIALE, *Evolution et tendances de la sécurité sociale, Italie* (Geneva, 1959), pp. 58–65; COPPINI, M. A., and ILLUMINATI, F., op. cit., pp. 254–7.
127. VAN DE VEN, A. C. M., 'Les Médecins et les assurances sociales aux Pays-Bas', *Revue Française du Travail*, 1 (1965), 51–53.
128. QUAETHOVEN, P., *Het statuut van de ziekenhuisgeneesheer in de E.E.G.* (Leuven, 1969), p. 445.
129. RIBETTES-TILHET, J., op. cit., p. 640.
130. BONNET, R., 'Le Statut professionel des médecins de la sécurité sociale minière', *Droit Social* (1965), 11.

131. LEDEBOER, L. V., op. cit., p. 4; WANNAGAT, G., op. cit., p. 57.
132. HERDER-DORNEICH, PH., *Honorarreform und Krankenhaussanierung* (Berlin, 1970), p. 76; LYNCH, M. J., and RAPHAEL, S. S., op. cit., pp. 37-38.
133. HATZFELD, H., op. cit., pp. 41-43.
134. ASSOCIATION INTERNATIONALE DE LA SECURITE SOCIALE, *Evolution et tendances de la sécurité sociale, Italie*, p. 58.
135. LEDEBOER, L. V., op. cit., p. 5; DE WIT, J., op. cit., pp. 132-3.
136. VELDKAMP, G. M. J., 'De plaats van de geneesheer in de wettelijke struktuur van de sociale gezondheidszorg', *De geneesheer en het recht* (Deventer, 1968), pp. 31-33.
137. ENGELS, J., op. cit., pp. 291-311.
138. HATZFELD, H., op. cit., pp. 72-74.
139. CARAPEZZA, G., *Les Rapports entre les médecins et l'assurance contre les maladies dans la République Italienne* (Brussels, 1965), pp. 8-9.
140. KAYSER, A., op. cit., p. 579.
141. DILLEMANS, R., 'De nieuwe wetgeving inzake ziekteverzekering', *Actuele problemen van sociaal recht* (Antwerp, 1966), pp. 164-5.
142. MONIER, J., 'La Convention nationale entre la sécurité sociale et le corps médical', *Droit Social*, 9-10 (1971) (no. spécial), 567.
143. FARINE, CH., 'La Convention nationale entre la sécurité sociale et le corps médical', ibid., p. 574.
144. DUPEYROUX, J. J., *Sécurité sociale* (5th edn.), p. 367.
145. ECKSTEIN, H., *The English Health Service* (Cambridge [Mass.], 1958), pp. 194-9.
146. DELIEGE-ROTT, D., *Le Médecin face au Marché Commun* (Leuven, 1968), pp. 194-5.
147. PERRIN, G., 'L'Avenir de la sécurité sociale', *Revue Internationale de Sécurité Sociale*, 1 (Geneva, 1969).
148. HATZFELD, H., op. cit., pp. 297-8.
149. ASSOCIATION INTERNATIONALE DE LA SECURITE SOCIALE, op. cit., pp. 57-58.
150. Cited in HATZFELD, H., op. cit., p. 42.
151. DE WIT, J., op. cit., pp. 138-9.
152. ENGELS, J., op. cit., pp. 290-329.
153. CARAPEZZA, G., op. cit., pp. 20-22.
154. VELDKAMP, G. M. J., op. cit., pp. 33-34.
155. SOZIALENQUETE-KOMMISSION, *Soziale Sicherung in der Bundesrepublik Deutschland* (Stuttgart, sd), p. 233.

156. BARJOT, A., 'Les Relations entre les médecins et la Sécurité Sociale en France', *Revue Française du Travail*, **1** (1965), 13; DUPEYROUX, J. J., 'Introduction', 'La Convention nationale entre la sécurité sociale et le corps médical', *Droit Social*, **9-10** (1971) (no. spécial), pp. 555–6.

# PART FOUR

## TOWARDS HARMONIZATION

# 13
# *Proposals*

## Nature, field of application, structure

INSURANCE OR HEALTH SERVICE?

In the previous part we concluded that the future social financing system of medical care in Europe would be compulsory insurance complemented by voluntary insurance for special services or at least with possibilities for private insurance.

Is this the situation now in the various European countries? To a great extent, yes. In all countries concerned there is an almost complete range of medical services offered in social circumstances by compulsory insurance. In various countries basic voluntary insurance still exists for some categories, but this is bound to disappear so that not too much importance should be attached to it. Important however is the presence of additional and private insurance in all countries, which will continue to exist.

Only one element of discord is to be found: in Italy the imminent establishment of a public health service. Together with Great Britain's this will mean two national health services within the European community.

Is this a disharmony which has to be eliminated? We do not think so. What ultimately is the difference between compulsory insurance and a national health service (1)? The difference cannot lie in the scope of application, because public health services exist which only apply to a limited group (for instance, the military) while compulsory insurance may cover all inhabitants of a country (for instance, the Dutch AWBZ). Nor does it lie in the extension of the services, since a public health service may only be organized for certain sectors (for example, intramural care), while compulsory insurance may cover all sectors and vice-versa. Financing is not a criterion either: a national health service can also be financed with premiums (this is partly the case in Great Britain), while compulsory insurance may be funded by the government (to a great extent this is the case in Belgium).

Only one criterion is valid, viz. that in compulsory insurance the beneficiary has always to fulfil certain conditions to qualify for services, while in a public health service system the need for care alone is enough. There is also a difference in content. In a public health service the government is explicitly responsible for the availability of sufficiently and adequately spread medical services, whereas this does not belong to the legal obligations of social insurance (2).

What is the practical importance of these differences? There is a tendency everywhere to limit restricting conditions for obtaining insurance benefits. It is also established that the compulsory insurance systems, although this does not belong to their primary task, try to organize their medical services in such a way that there is a sufficient, adequate, and rational supply. Governments also take responsibility in many instances (control of medical practice, of medical studies, of medicine, of building, and rates of hospitals, etc.), and this will soon have to apply to all countries in the shape of an over-all plan for health and social insurance.

The distinctive differences between a national health service and compulsory insurance are therefore not so important; the actual differences may well be smaller than those between two different systems of compulsory insurance. The future development discussed in this study can just as well take place in the framework of a national health service as in the form of a generalized compulsory insurance.

FIELD OF APPLICATION

Our future view of social health insurance in Europe anticipates for the health care sector an extension of protection to the entire population. In some countries the present situation is still quite far removed from this.

In Germany there is a wage limit for compulsory insurance for employees (not for workers) and state employees and self-employed (except farmers) are not compulsorily insured, and even excluded from subscription to voluntary insurance if their income exceeds the wage limit. In the Netherlands there is a wage limit for compulsory insurance for all employees: state officials and self-employed have a similar system to Germany, except that for heavy medical risks all inhabitants are insured. In Germany there is pressure to eliminate the salary limit for employees, although not in the immediate future, but in the Netherlands strong opposition is still against even a structural increase in its level (3).

This is a significant deviation from the common goal of EEC countries for their future development. The restriction of protection to employees and persons below a certain level of income indicates a completely different concept of social insurance: it is considered a protective measure for economically weaker groups, or at least not for economically strong groups. The risk of illness is therefore not viewed as a social risk for *all* citizens (4).

From a social standpoint this causes painful repercussions. People on one side of the frontier do not benefit from social protection which others in exactly the same circumstances enjoy. For European co-ordination this presents difficulties: insurance in two countries for one person can only be co-ordinated when he qualifies in both countries.

As for financing, the consequences are obvious: the wage limit excludes a complete national solidarity, to which the systems in most countries are necessarily orientated. Economic distortions (5) may also be expected: on the one hand the pressure of financing of health care on labour costs in enterprises will be different in the absence of such a national solidarity and on the other hand the competitive position of private health insurance is artificially favoured, since social health insurance takes care of the bad risks. This happens for instance in the old-age insurance in the Netherlands and with the retired insured in Germany. We would conclude that if there is one disharmony which has definitely to be eliminated, it is this one.

We may not forget, however, that in other countries also the final stage of the evolution has not yet been achieved. In no single country does the system apply to the entire population (except the Dutch scheme for heavy risks). There remains always at least a small group who depend on voluntary insurance. What is more: to qualify, the insured are still, in the old manner, indicated through enumeration of compulsorily insured categories, based on their professional activities, to which is added the right of obtaining medical services for certain family members or dependants.

Once more than 98 per cent of the population is brought under mandatory insurance, even if the range of the service is not the same for all groups (for the self-employed insurance is sometimes limited to the so-called serious risks), it cannot cause many problems to let the systems apply to the entire population, at least for the minimum guaranteed protection. This would have the advantage of preventing a number of disputes on the obligation to take insurance and would also to a great extent bring an end to complicated regulations on protection of members of the family and dependants.

## SPECIAL SYSTEMS

There is a tendency towards national coverage of the financial risks in medical care. Obviously the future image of social health insurance in the European countries is seen as a regrouping of national systems; with possibly more favourable conditions for certain groups. However this does not correspond with the present situation, not even with the prevailing trend.

The disadvantages connected with a dispersion among numerous particular systems do seem important enough to justify a categoric reversal of the evolution and to pursue the course of harmonization through establishing national systems.

National solidarity is not only a beautiful slogan, it is also a requirement of social justice for those groups in society whose financial means are limited or whose health risks are high. In isolating these groups within special systems, the general systems of social health insurance act as group insurances who want to exploit the advanatages of their relatively favourable risk-situation on the one hand, while on the other hand they benefit from the advantage of belonging to the social security system (the state guarantee and the compulsory membership) (6). This forces special groups with a less favourable situation into a system of part social insurance part assistance. Also the general systems can be unfavourably influenced by the exclusion of certain more prosperous or low-risk groups, who can build up a flourishing mutual, voluntary, or private insurance.

The risk of needing medical care threatens all people in the same way. And since individuals can not generally cope with it alone, it has to be carried in solidarity by all together.

Still other disadvantages are connected with classification into special systems: high administration costs, an insufficient actuarial basis for covering of risks in small systems, curbing of social mobility through particular advantages for some sectors and through difficulties when switching from one system to another (7).

This point is closely connected with the previous one. As a first element of a plan towards harmonization of health care insurance we put forward the implementation of one national insurance (national service) for all inhabitants of each country. In order to achieve this, opposition will have to be overcome from the existing multitude of organizations, which cannot all be preserved, and from the particularism of the various strata of society, who do not want to pay more towards social security than they can get out of it. But the reform will be pressed by the financial instability built into the system, which continuously raises issues of general reform and rationalization.

## Financing

Here we deal only with the part of financing that concerns the raising of funds. Budgeting of expenditure is discussed later, in relation with payments to suppliers of care.

For a number of reasons the method of financing the Dutch national insurance has been chosen as the means for financing social health care insurance in future. The essential point of it is that a premium is paid by all who earn an income exceeding a certain minimum level, and that the premium is fixed at a percentage of this income, equal for everyone or preferably progressive. Besides governments would grant rather flexible subsidies in the framework of public health policy.

In this manner there would exist two complementary sources of financing (possibly to be supplemented by the insured through some kind of cost-sharing) which would supplement each other in order to guarantee a sufficient provision of funds.

What is suggested here can only be one proposal of many. It is crucial however that a way of financing is found which works out a just distribution of costs and provides for sufficient and adequate financial means over a more or less extended period in order to avoid the present ever-recurring deficits. The choice is, of course, also influenced by the economic and social side-effects, which are still insufficiently known (8).

However, it should be an object of harmonization, as far as premiums are concerned, to eliminate wage ceilings for their calculation. In the social insurance schemes which provide substitute incomes a calculation ceiling can be justified as a restricted solidarity, in as far as the benefits are tied to the same ceiling as the contributions. In health insurance, however, in which all insured without discrimination qualify for the same kind of health care, a calculation ceiling initiates adverse income redistribution, since higher income classes usually make better and more frequent use of health services (9). The breaking down of the wage-ceilings for premium calculation has hardly started. Only Italy has been preserved from this disastrous system. Belgium just proposed to abolish it. In all other countries it should be destroyed as soon as possible.

The harmonization of government contributions according to specific criteria has more economic importance. Partial government subsidies, aimed at alleviating one or other sector (for example, agriculture, mining, navigation, railways, . . .) actually result in subsidies to the enterprises of that particular sector and therefore threaten to create a distortion in international competition. This would not be the case with global government subsidies, from which all sectors benefit equally. In the European Coal and Steel Community it is a rule that subsidies to social security systems in one sector should be authorized by the high authority (10).

Just how the financing of social security for health care should proceed in the future except for the above-mentioned points, is hard to determine.

An isolated harmonization policy only aiming at health care cannot have many favourable results in this respect. The harmonization of financing should be considered within the complete framework of financing social security and government expenditure. If one harmonizes the pressure on enterprises through social changes but leaves the differences in fiscal pressure unchanged one can create an even larger divergency than before. On the other side social advantages are often offset or improved by fiscal measures. Whether such a broad harmonization, which almost means a uniformity of public finance on the income side, will soon be attained, is a question which cannot be answered here.

## Services

EXTENT OF SERVICES

From our historic review it appears that in all systems of the European countries until around 1950 a similar range of services was provided, resulting more or less in the most complete medical care available. But from 1952 a divergent development started: newly established systems (mainly for self-employed) only covered serious risks.

The future of social health care as we see it will not show such differences: for various reasons we suppose that all systems will provide the same services for all inhabitants, viz. complete medical care as required and possible in each illness.

Two important reasons can be given for eliminating existing differences by bringing the systems for self-employed up to the level of those for salaried people. First of all there is national solidarity and the extension to the entire population of one system of health care insurance; it is very difficult to achieve this goal when the object of the insurance itself is more limited for certain groups than for others. But secondly and equally important is the social argument: some people soon feel discriminated against when having to pay high premiums in proportion to smaller benefits available to them. Particularly telling is the example of the French independents whose violent protest actions a few years ago were inspired by this feeling (11).

Indeed it appears to us that adjustment in this direction will not cause too many difficulties. The population seems rather attached to coverage of the small risk—the large majority of self-employed take additional insurance for the small risk—so that every extension in this area will be welcome.

## DEGREE OF PROTECTION

Earlier we arrived at the conclusion that the health insurance of the future would in principle give full basic protection. This basic protection would comprise all medical techniques, but only in their social form, excluding unnecessary services or services given under particularly luxurious conditions. What is considered luxury will of course be subject to change. This basic protection would be offered without additional payment by the patient at the time of service, except for drugs, prostheses, and appliances.

At present this situation has not yet been achieved in any single country. In the Netherlands and in Italy there is direct medical service without additional payment by the insured at the time of service for most of the insured, but the range of services is not yet complete everywhere (viz. self-employed have to be satisfied with coverage of serious risks only). In Belgium, France, and for the greater part also in Luxemburg, medical services are not fully taken care of by the government: part of the cost is left to the insured. Germany has largely achieved complete basic protection for those (about 90 per cent of the population) who fall within social security, either mandatorily or voluntarily. There is only an additional payment requested for pharmaceutical supplies and medical aids. German insured have also to pay supplements when admitted to a private room, as is the case in all countries.

The Dutch, German, and Italian socially insured (some 70 per cent of the population) do not pay extra for consultation by appointment or for 'out-of-hours' house-calls. In the Netherlands and Italy the idea of 'basic' protection is reflected in the fact that they may not (at the expense of the insurance) consult a specialist unless upon referral by the GP.

In Belgium, France, and Luxemburg the insured has to pay extra whenever he wants more than the basic protection by making 'special demands': consultations outside hours, house-calls without medical necessity, hospital care in private room, etc. Moreover, in France an additional payment is due when the patient requests a physician who is well known or very competent (according to a special list, kept for each *département*).

In which direction should harmonization be advocated? In the first place, full basic protection should be recognized in all countries as a distinct goal. France, Belgium, and Luxemburg, and also (in the indirect services) Italy are still quite far removed from this goal. The resistance of physicians to abolition of cost-sharing by the insured is well known (12), even if not *all* physicians think likewise. But one's sense of justice is offended when insured persons on one side of a border, who pay practically the same premiums for medical care, have to pay extra for such and such a service while those on the other side do not. The very small impact of co-insurance on consumption, and also the small financial proceeds prove sufficiently that there is no valid economic motivation to oppose to this equity motive (13).

In our proposal, co-insurance is maintained for pharmaceutical supplies and for prostheses and appliances. In all countries concerned there appears to be agreement along these lines. Only in the Netherlands is this not the case.

The exclusion of de-luxe care (with the understanding that this concept has to be flexible) is viewed as a general feature of any future system, but is, however, not to be considered as the essential goal of harmonization policy. If certain countries (the Netherlands, Germany, Italy) want to provide more than basic protection, one can hardly demand that they give it up. This would completely contradict the principle of *'rapprochement dans le progrès'* (progressive convergence) (14).

Still one definite form of limitation to basic protection has to be considered for extension to all countries: the refusal of insurance benefits (or the demand for additional payment) if some basic rules of organization and rationalization are not complied with. A good example is treatment by a specialist when the insured has not been referred by his family doctor (as in the Netherlands and Italy). In countries where this is not a rule yet, such a clause could in more than one respect have a very favourable effect (15). Public health would be served by a closer relationship between every insured and his family doctor. But also the financial situation of the insurance would benefit from the elimination of many useless or duplicate specialist examinations, being a result of inexpert shopping for specialists by the insured.

We would certainly like to see this point incorporated into a harmonization programme. However we must bear in mind the unwillingness of the physicians' associations, which are predominantly controlled by specialists.

TYPE OF BENEFITS

We have already explained why we believe that in future basic protection in medical care will be provided directly, ie that all providers of care will be paid directly by the insurance organization, without the insured having to advance the money first. These direct medical services would not exclude a residual sector of private medicine, on the one hand for services by sickness fund physicians which are considered as de-luxe care, and on the other in all those cases where the insured consults a non-health fund physician or where he explicitly declares to his health fund physician that he does not want to be treated under insurance conditions.

Such a situation has already been achieved for all socially insured in the Netherlands and in Germany; only it has to be extended, with compulsory insurance, to the entire population. In Italy the greater part of the population has the right to choose direct services or indirect services; this option can be exercised at the beginning of every year and upon each hospital admission. Once the system of direct services is open to all inhabitants, the European level we advocate will have been attained.

However in Belgium, France, and Luxemburg there is an entirely different form of benefit. Fees are advanced by the insured and (fully or partially) repaid by the insurance. Sometimes even fees are fixed freely by the supplier of care and paid out by the patient who later receives benefit from the insurance. But in these three countries there are to a large extent direct services for hospital expenses, sometimes even for physicians' fees in the hospitals and in Belgium and Luxemburg for drug expenses.

We are fully aware of the fact that a transition from one to the other form of benefit will encounter fierce opposition from the physicians' associations. This opposition is mainly based on the fear of arbitrary rule and excessive demand or 'over-consumption'. However, from objective studies it appears very doubtful that prepayment of fees would exercise much influence on consumption (16).

Conquering this opposition will be difficult but worthwhile. First of all medical services are becoming more and more expensive, so that it is becoming ever more objectionable to advance the money. It makes even less sense since in the general evolution of social security in the European countries simplification and rationalization are pursued, which means cutting out detours in financing. When medical services are partly or fully funded by social security, it is neither logical nor rational that payment is made via the insured when it can also be done directly. There is also the financial argument that administration costs of the system can be reduced quite a lot if the agencies do not have to intervene for payment of every individual service or small group of services, and the accounts over a certain period can be settled with the physicians, which allows mechanization and automation. And the large majority of the population seem to prefer direct benefit (17).

Many will view the above considerations as useless, because they are of the opinion that physicians in Belgium and in France will never in principle accept the *'tiers payant'*. To these sceptics it can be replied that they underestimate the flexibility of opinions among physicians. It is true though that physicians everywhere are greatly attached to the traditional ways of practising their profession but in the course of history they have also given evidence of considerable capacity to adjust themselves to the ideas and necessities of a new care. See, for example, the adoption in 1963 of the principles concerning co-operation with social security by the World Medical Association, because the principles of 1948 were not in accordance with development social security took in some countries.

The history of relations between physicians and social security in Belgium and France shows that often quite a long time, sometimes even a generation, elapsed before physicians stopped stubbornly clinging to outmoded principles; and that this painful operation was only possible at the expense of a split in the medical syndical front. This happened in France where the physicians, in the period after the decree of May 1960, agreed to conclude agreements. They had fought this since 1927 and had sworn to defend the '*entente directe*'; similarly Belgian physicians approved agreements with health insurance after June 1964 having refused to do so since the beginning of compulsory health insurance in 1945. On this matter a longer period is necessary, but this should not prevent us from putting it on the harmonization list as one of the most important elements.

LIMITATIONS IMPOSED ON BENEFITS
Apart from the limitation of the degree of protection which has been discussed above, various legislations have imposed specific limitations with respect to the services themselves. The principal limitations are: limitation in duration of the service and limitation to the services or products included on a specific list.

**Limitation in duration.** In the future European system there is no room for limitation in duration of health services. This opinion is based on the already established tendencies.

This tendency appears to be justified. Often social consequences of a prolonged illness are much worse than those of short illnesses, so that there would be ample reason to provide better services after a certain duration, instead of stopping them at a certain point. This was the philososphy behind the special French arrangement for lengthy illnesses, in force from 1945 to 1955 (and in some aspects even afterwards) (18). Too much weight should not be given to financial considerations, because the cases of illness exceeding a certain time limit only constitute a small percentage of the total number.

In Italy alone there still exists a general time limit for health services, albeit with some exceptions already. This limit should be lifted. In Germany and in Luxemburg there existed an indirect time limit for hospital treatment, which is still considered as a substitute for sickness benefits and was therefore subject to the same limits as the sickness benefit itself. This archaic view is without any foundation today and is being abandoned.

**List of medical services and official list of drugs.** In the comparative part of this study we were able to determine that all countries use a list of medical services (at least for specialist services, less so for GP services). Besides, all countries with the exception of one (Germany) have an official list of drugs which may be supplied at the expense of the insurance.

It is difficult to claim that it is better or worse to practise health care with or without a list of services, with or without a list of drugs. This is a technical aspect of medical care, which has to be judged within the entire health system.

Yet it can be predicted with some certainty that in future social insurance systems in Europe, both these elements will be present. As to the list of services, it has to be remembered that physicians (outside the hospitals) will be paid per item of service. This requires that a tariff list be maintained in the form of a description of the medical services. And with respect to a list of drugs attention has to be drawn to the fact that in all countries rationalization of the manufacturing and consumption of medicine is being demanded. Everywhere it is being established that the market is submerged by thousands of pharmaceutical specialties, the therapeutic value of which is often identical. More specifically it has been noticed that in Germany, in the absence of an official list, there are at least three times and according to some sources almost twenty times more registered medical specialties than in other countries (19). The possibility that such a list be introduced in Germany is therefore not to be excluded.

Looking at medical and pharmaceutical care as an industry offering goods and services, with quite a considerable market we are faced with the remarkable phenomenon that in the Common Market this group of services and goods maintains a completely heterogeneous structure, which hampers all comparison and makes competition impossible. Where one succeeds in comparing products and medical services, enormous price differences seem to exist: very often relativities between prices amount to no less than from one to ten. At this moment there exists no common market in this sector whatsoever. If one wants to overcome national limitations, it is obvious that first of all the structure of prices and rates has to be adapted and harmonized, in order to make it possible gradually to level prices at a later stage.

Such unification of the lists of medical services is an elementary requirement. Is medicine so different from country to country that the list of medical services need be long in one country and short in another? Are bones in one country harder than in another, so that setting of a leg fracture costs more here than somewhere else?

So too with pharmaceutical products. It seems a remote possibility that medicines with a specific therapeutic value exist in some countries of the EEC and not in others. Rather it should be accepted that in fact similar or highly equivalent products are marketed under different names. So here also harmonization is indicated.

Unification of lists of services and of recognized drugs is necessarily the work of specialists. It will not be an easy task, if one looks at the difficulties already encountered on the national level to draft acceptable lists. It would seem fully justified for the EEC to take the initiative in this field. Once the experts have obtained a result, the common list could be issued to the member-countries, by way of recommendation, such as has taken place for the common list of occupational diseases. It could even be argued that this be done by means of a directive, in application of article 100 of the Treaty, since it concerns a matter which directly influences the institution of the Common Market (20).

CONDITIONS REQUIRED FOR OBTAINING SERVICES

In the previous chapter it was established that *waiting periods and minimum premiums* for entitlement to health care benefits are considered as an outdated remnant of the old voluntary health insurance and doomed to become extinct.

Yet such waiting periods still exist in various systems. In Belgian health insurance there is in principle a six-month waiting period in which 120 working days should be completed; in France this is in general three months, with the exception of agricultural workers, for whom another calculation is in force and for farmers, who are not subject to it; in Italy rather shorter waiting periods are applied, equal to the normal probation period at the beginning of insurance for employers, but the self-employed are in the same situation as in France; in Germany and in Luxemburg the health funds can impose waiting periods up to six months on the voluntary insured; only in the Netherlands are waiting periods totally unknown.

It was established that the use of waiting periods has still further increased over the last years. In 1952 Italian domestic workers were given a waiting period of six months, and the newly set-up systems for trades-people (1956) and small businessmen (1960) also made provision for waiting periods; in France the new system for the self-employed too required waiting periods (1966) and in 1968 the regulations in this respect were strengthened within the general system. Minimum premiums are still to be found in Belgium (in principle for all insured, with exceptions), in Italy (only for domestic personnel), and in France (for independents).

It is worth including within a harmonization programme the elimination of waiting periods and minimum premiums. First of all because waiting periods are incompatible with the idea of shared responsibility which dominates the financing of health care in our society. A waiting period creates the impression that the right to health care benefits is granted the insured because of his premium payment.

In reality this is not quite so: the insured is entitled to services because he falls under compulsory insurance: the premium obligation is not relevant and can in some cases be dropped (21). In addition it should be mentioned that the consequences of a waiting period of for example three months can be quite serious for the insured, if in that period he should suffer a serious illness, the more so because private insurance coverage for that period would be quite unlikely as he would at the same time be paying the premiums for compulsory insurance. Such conditions are not in line with the basic sense of justice, particularly when such a waiting period does not exist for other groups of the population or across the border.

On top of that one has to consider that in the long run waiting periods will become entirely superfluous and superseded, when insurance is broadened to cover the whole population.

## Relations with the care suppliers

FREE CHOICE OF SUPPLIER

We suggested earlier that the European systems of social health insurance will in future concentrate on a better guarantee of free choice of supplier of care; this will not necessarily lead to a refinement of formal freedom of choice, but to a realization of actual freedom of choice, through the elimination of time and space barriers between patient and physician, assuming that the financial barrier has already been eliminated.

It appears that this should be done through rationalization in the delivery of medical care, ie through measures to achieve a more balanced infrastructure of institutions, chemists, and consulting rooms, by stimulating co-operation in medical practice, and by an efficient streaming of the patient towards appropriate services, in which the GP can play an important role.

In most countries measures have already been taken by the minister of public health or by professional organizations to achieve a more adequate distribution of the medical infrastructure, mainly for hospitals and pharmacies. Social security can, although it falls beyond its task, be active in this area, for instance by providing better pay for physicians located in unattractive areas. It has, however, few opportunities to be active in the rationalization of medical services. The only exception seems to be the authority that was given to the French health funds for participating in the financing of medical group practices.

Where would there be room for a harmonization policy?

We do not suggest promoting an efficient infrastructure or an organizational rationalization in medical services as a legal task of the insurance institutions everywhere. We have been able to establish that in the European countries it was a common characteristic that the providers of services remained independent from social security.

Nevertheless we believe that two roads towards harmonization are open. The first one would provide the health funds in all countries with the legal chance of working towards an efficient infrastructure. This would not be necessary for promoting a better distribution: such action might emanate from the payment system; all systems are in any case largely free to proceed in this direction through agreements with the medical profession. With respect to support to medical group practice in its various forms it appears desirable that in countries other than France the legislation should authorize the use of their reserves by social security funds for such purposes. And in any case legislation should everywhere sanction the role of the GP who advises the patient and co-ordinates any special examinations and treatment he may need; this could easily be done by making referral by the GP a condition for reimbursing such services. As of now this is only a general rule in the Netherlands and Italy.

The second approach would consist of an agreement on the European level, between the social insurance institutions and the medical associations in order to promote in the agreements between health insurance and medical profession the goals of an efficient spread, appropriate streaming and an organizational rationalization, viz. by adjusting the type and the calculation of payment accordingly.

CLINICAL FREEDOM AND MEDICAL CONTROL

Few will challenge the view that in future physicians will have freedom to examine and treat as well as freedom to prescribe as is now the case in all systems. Nor will anybody deny that in order to safeguard this freedom measures have to be taken to check abuses or that the use of this freedom should be regulated so that it remains within budgetary limits.

There are essentially two ways to regulate this freedom: a special department for medical control in the health insurance institutions and the mutual control by representatives of the physicians; each of them dominates in one group of countries and there does not seem to be an evolution in a converging sense.

In our view of social health insurance we predict, though, that both forms of control will undergo change, through which they will in fact become complementary. This will mean eventually harmonization of control mechanisms in Europe.

Through this development the medical control services will gradually be freed from the strict interdiction against participation in medical treatment and will advise, not only the insurance institutions, but also physicians and all kinds of health institutions (for example, preventive services). At the same time committees of physicians for mutual control will less exclusively be directed towards discovering abuses, and will more positively promote the quality of medical services.

The first form seems better suited for all circumstances where physicians have an isolated practice, while the second form of control will find acceptance where physicians are working in group practice or are connected with institutions, and where the body of physicians is responsible for efficiency and quality of medical care. More specifically one thinks of hospitals, but it is also to be noticed that this is indeed the case with the German *Kassenärtzliche Vereinigungen,* where such mutual professional control has existed for a long time.

From one standpoint there is little urgency about a reform of controlling devices on these lines. It will not make much difference to organizational efficiency or to financial results. On the other hand we have to take into account the crisis in medical control, which for a long time has existed in all countries in practically the same, now outdated form (22). One has to think about the difficulties which the medical control officers experience in carrying out their task, as long as they are not considered by other physicians as real physicians. One has to keep in mind the unpopular aspect of a control which is purely negative. And one has to think of the waste involved in maintaining a large team of highly qualified physicians, or in the operating of numerous well-equipped control committees of physicians, who have access to statistical data, who gain experience, who can compare and evaluate as nobody else can, without making use of it for prevention, therapy, or quality improvement. A European agreement or a recommendation of the EEC on this could mean an extraordinary step forward in medical care in Europe.

There is of course more involved in clinical freedom than medical control systems. Also relevant are the list of services and the list of drugs and especially payment systems for suppliers of care.

## PAYING THE SUPPLIER

Physicians can be compensated for their medical work for insured patients in numerous ways, but the two basic forms are: fee per item of service and lump sum payment.

It appears now that the existing forms of payment vary considerably between the countries, and that everywhere the physicians hold on to their present form of compensation. There can be seen a slight tendency in the hospitals to move towards a generalization of salary-type payment, while in individual forms of medical practice there is always a certain preference for fees per item of service.

Therefore there are not too many conclusions to be drawn with respect to a harmonization policy on this point. The form of compensation does in principle not interest the insured nor the insurance organizations, unless because of side-effects present in each form. In so far as they are undesirable these effects have to be fought against by specific means rather than abolishing the form of payment itself. The best form of payment is ultimately that which is preferred by the person receiving the payment and at the same time acceptable to those who have to pay.

What is important for the insurance (and therefore also indirectly for the insured, in so far as he pays a premium) is the level of remuneration. If the insurance wants to offer its members real protection against the cost of medical care, its financial situation is closely linked with the general level of physicians' fees and with the compensation of other suppliers of services, no matter what its form.

Above it was pointed out that the repeated, and probably in the future even worse, financial difficulties of health insurance will lead in all countries to recommendations that medical expenses be tied to a certain budget (23); for that purpose it is not sufficient to fix rates of medical fees and prices for drugs, hospital care, and auxilliary services, but budgetary restrictions should also be put on the use of drugs and on hospital care and on the nature, number, and frequency of medical services.

It was assumed that in all European countries agreements between physicians and health funds would be concluded in which the rate of increase of the medical care expenses would be determined each year. Based upon this a certain limit would be set in individual or collective agreements to the total remuneration of the physicians, together with a limit to the total amount of drugs and hospital care to be prescribed. These limits could only be exceeded after rigorous justification.

At present such a mechanism exists only in one country of the EEC, Germany, where for a long time now it has rendered excellent service, although it is less strict in its structure now than it was before (24). Harmonization would mean no less than the introduction of such budgetary limits in the payment of physicians and in their freedom of prescription. Such measures would not be popular with doctors generally.

It will certainly require time and effort to introduce it. It will even be strenuous to maintain and improve it in Germany. But it seems essential to the substance of social health insurance. Without such measures, periodic, even yearly, financial crises will continue to threaten the systems, reorganization measures will be taken in panic every year, which threaten to make hollow the protection offered by the system. The development of legislation will remain unco-ordinated because of an accumulation of short-sighted settlements and solutions. Only programming the budget of medical expenses will provide adequate financing for health insurance. If one knows which expenses to expect one can determine what premiums will have to be demanded and what services will be provided. Only when health insurance is rid of its chronic underfinancing, will it have real meaning as a central instrument of public health policy.

Whether the difficulties facing such budgeting would be so insurmountable as some people like to pretend, is questionable. If a proposal is worked out in the way explained earlier, then we believe physicians as well as social security institutions will find it practicable, without fear of compromising their basic demands. Indeed it is not to be overlooked that because of the continuous financial difficulties of health insurance, the idea of nationalization of medicine keeps recurring. If physicians do not co-operate in keeping health insurance in financial balance, then, as some authors are convinced, they are heading for nationalization. We do not believe this ourselves, however we think an alternative solution would be a generalized lump sum payment system. And faced with this choice, the physicians would undoubtedly choose the fee per item of service, with budgetary limitation on the global sum available to them collectively.

## The system of agreements

FORM OF THE AGREEMENT

Based on a number of general considerations, rather than on the historical development of systems, it was held above that in the future the relations between insurance and physicians would most likely be controlled through collective agreements, which would be binding on all physicians of a certain group or in a certain area by force of law and therefore not by virtue of individual joining.

In any case it seems desirable to guide evolution along these lines. Indeed these agreements do not only have to offer physicians and other medical providers an adequate reward, but they should also supply the insurance organizations with a sufficient number of competent associates in order to offer medical care to the insured. To a great extent this provision of sufficient associates would lose its stability, if the operation of the agreements systems, as is sometimes the case, rested upon voluntary joining or resigning by individual suppliers of care. Besides, individual agreements might well reveal the weak cohesion of the physicians' associations, by acting as some kind of referendum on the viewpoints adopted by the association. It is therefore in the interest of the physicians' associations that collective agreements directly apply to individual physicians. In the legislation on collective labour agreements between employers and employees, those who are in no way a party to the agreement cannot refuse its application, certainly not if it is ratified by the government.

Developments in the various countries, however, indicate that a certain flexibility in this rule seems desirable. Two exceptions to the rule of direct universal application could be allowed. In the first place individual suppliers and insured patients can agree, explicitly or implicitly, that their relationship will not be ruled by the terms of the general agreement. And secondly, individual suppliers will be free to opt for entirely private practice, if they believe their patients need no financial support from health insurance.

In this respect no adaptation is necessary in the German and Luxemburg legislations. The evolution of Belgian legislation has to continue in its present direction; the rule should be cancelled which requires, for an agreement to become effective, that less than a set number of physicians have refused to co-operate, preferably by removing the possibility of refusal and at any rate by cutting out reimbursement for suppliers who refuse the agreement. Similar to the Belgian legislation, the Italian legislation is close to the proposed ideal: here the condition of applicability which is the registration of the physician on the lists of the health funds can be maintained if the option for indirect benefits is removed. The legal situation should be entirely reversed in the Netherlands, since the physicians are legally tied to the health funds by individual contracts, which are merely a reflection of a non-committing collective basic text.

Such reforms should be considered as not attainable in the near future. Much more time will have to elapse and the application of social health insurance should have been extended to the entire population beforehand. For the time being it would suffice if in all countries collective agreements could be negotiated, the implementation of which would be subject to individual adherence or at least to a right of refusal. Therefore it would suffice if the Dutch legislation would ratify *de jure* the actual binding effect of collective agreements.

APPROVAL BY GOVERNMENT

We came to the conclusion that the trend indicates that governments' role will become increasingly more important in the negotiation of agreements with physicians and that the agreements always should be subject to government approval, at least as far as fees are concerned.

When all individual agreements are reformed into collective agreements which *ex lege* apply to all individual physicians, then the need for government approval will become more obvious, as is the case with collective labour agreements, when they are ratified by the government.

At present government approval exists already in most countries. In order to harmonize it would suffice that in Germany agreements become subject to direct government control and that in the Netherlands and Luxemburg such control become more direct than is currently the case.

MEASURES IN THE ABSENCE OF AGREEMENTS

Assuming there will be an evolution towards an arrangement for direct payment by the funds for both medical fees and hospital and drug costs in all European countries, we believe that in the absence of agreements all countries will organize mandatory arbitration, the ruling of which will have the same legal force as a regular agreement. If it is agreed that a cancelled agreement should remain in effect until the arbitration ruling has been approved by government, this system would constitute a guarantee for continuous implementation.

At present such a structure only exists in Germany and Luxemburg; in France and Belgium maximum rates are imposed by government in the absence of agreements, and in the Netherlands and Italy, no coercive measure whatsoever is taken.

In order to arrive at harmonization in the four countries (France, Belgium, the Netherlands, and Italy) a delicate arbitration procedure has to be established. It will not be easy to constitute the arbitration committee or to indicate the arbiters with full approval of all parties concerned. But the German and Luxemburg experience demonstrates that it is possible.

Nevertheless it appears as though the effort will be worthwhile. For if a stage can be reached when all social medical care is directly granted at the expense of the funds, payment for these medical services will be made in a centralized manner, by specialized payment services. This, however, can only operate if clear and accepted agreements with the physicians have been made. Failing such agreement the system would seriously be disturbed. For one would have to revert to the system of refunding the insured for the prices and fees paid by them. But there would be a lack of the necessary administrative infrastructure to refund each insured individually. Moreover, one has to keep in mind that the imposition of mandatory fee rates by government, even if this can be tolerated for pharmaceutical products and hospital services, always creates real trauma in physicians. This is reflected by feelings of dissatisfaction and resistance against health insurance and against the government.

And yet this is the only alternative to mandatory arbitration unless in case of disagreement between the funds and physicians the protection of the insured is left entirely at the mercy of the physicians, which in our civilization can no longer be accepted.

# 14

## *The way ahead*

### Action nationally

BELGIUM

To implement the harmonization plan outlined above, Belgium should make the field of application of its system cover the total residing population and consequently entirely dissociate the right to health care from premium payment or from a certain family tie or relation with a premium payer. The same applies to all European countries, except for the Netherlands.

All special systems (seamen, railways) would automatically cease to be effective. Also the differences in extent of coverage would disappear: this means mainly that the restriction of insurance for the self-employed to serious risks should be abandoned.

This should go along with complete national solidarity in financing. Any discrimination should be abolished.

In financing health care the employers need no special role. It would be desirable to calculate the premium on a uniform—preferably progressive—basis on all personal incomes. The wage and income ceiling for premium calculation should disappear and be replaced by a minimum ceiling below which no premium would be due.

It appears important that the medical services should no longer be paid for in an indirect form (reimbursement of medical expenses to the insured) but in a direct form (payment of medical services directly by the insurance). In the case of services by physicians this would require a special effort. The tools exist already: the special agreement of 'third-payer'. One should attempt to introduce this system gradually, starting with the most expensive services.

Contrary to the current trend the co-insurance system should gradually be abandoned. This implies that charging unrestricted fees to patients with an income above a certain level would be dropped (although this measure does not seem to be the most urgent one). On the contrary the insurance would not intervene in matters which are to be considered as de-luxe care: treatment outside the framework of the insurance by physicians who do not co-operate with the insurance or for private patients.

A certain personal contribution for pharmaceutical supplies seems to be socially accepted in Europe. This should only be adapted to the European level. The same applies for prostheses and appliances.

But specialist care under insurance should be subject to referral by the family physician.

On the other hand waiting periods and minimum premiums for the right of services should go entirely.

Furthermore relations with the physicians should be developed according to the principles of existing collective agreements, approved by the government and applicable to all individual practitioners. The possibility of keeping oneself exclusively outside the system of agreements should be eliminated with time, or at least be sanctioned by complete refusal of insurance finance.

The agreements should be set within a programming of medical costs at medium-term. The rate of increase should be established by mutual agreement each year. In this rate of increase, certain amounts should be included for the signing of prescriptions by physicians. If they unjustifiably exceed an average for their type of practice they should face curtailment of fees by a commission of colleagues or of equal representation.

The payment of fees itself should be subject to a yearly final settlement, with a certain payment quota, set through comparison of the over-all bills for all physicians with the agreed rate of increase over the same period. Here also the individual who unjustifiably exceeds a certain average would be punished with a curtailment of fees.

Long before this stage were reached, it would be necessary to organize mandatory arbitration for occasions when differences arise between the insurance and certain groups of suppliers. The ruling of such mandatory arbitration would be binding as an actual agreement.

## GERMANY

The first priority in Germany is to extend mandatory health insurance to the entire resident population. Not only should mandatory insurance be extended to self-employed and even to all categories of non-active persons, but all ties between right to services and premium-obligation should be severed. Immediately the idea of 'taking care of family members' ('*Familienhilfe*') would disappear.

Such an organizational pattern would no longer permit the financial autonomy of the health funds. Since no direct link would exist between those who pay a premium and those who benefit from the services, it would not be possible any more to permit groups of insured in their own health fund to balance out assets and liabilities by establishing a proper premium rate. It would rather seem that financing should be based on a nationally shared solidarity without subdivisions: there would be one health fund with one premium system. The old health funds would only be in charge of providing medical services (and possibly of collecting the premiums).

As in Belgium it should be added that employers do not seem to have any special task in financing health care, and therefore the premiums should be imposed on all personal incomes. The calculation limit should be lifted, but a minimum-limit below which no premium would be due, should be maintained.

As to the form of services and the degree of financing by the insurance, Germany has already reached the future European goal. Small changes still remain to be made. An end should be put to the old-fashioned opinion which considers hospital care as a substitute for sickness benefits. Perhaps as time passes an official medicine list will have to be introduced; let us hope it will be a European list. And probably also the various tariff-lists for medical services will have to be unified, preferably in the form of a European list of services.

In our opinion, the relations with the physicians are at present better organized in Germany than in any of the six countries. The associations of health fund physicians (*Kassenärztliche Vereinigungen*) are too useful as an institution for their disappearance even to be considered. A certain adaptation to change will of course be necessary. Budgeting of medical fees, included in the PHV system, has to be maintained and there should be a reaction against the tendency to abandon this system for a larger use of the EHV (see Chapter 12). However this system has to be extended in four ways. First of all it has to be transferred from the regional level to the national level; the role of the *Kassenärtzliche Bundesvereinigung* will become more important. Secondly it will not only cover all physicians' fees but all medical costs. Thirdly it can be extended in time: instead of determining each year the global expenditure level, it would programme the increase of expenditures at medium term. And fourthly one can go beyond the narrow lump sum *per capita* calculation of the over-all expenditure when during the negotiations all relevant elements are considered.

FRANCE

As in Belgium, France has mandatory insurance for health care which covers almost the entire population. Our harmonization programme would now require and it is the declared intention of the government anyway that this insurance apply to the entire residing population, *qua tale*. Qualifying for health care would depend on residence, without any relation to the obligation of premium payment.

Obviously financing would also have to be based on nationally shared solidarity: the form and amount of premiums would have to be organized in one system for the benefit of one national fund. This would mean the end for numerous special systems (self-employed, farmers, agricultural workers, seamen, miners, various transportation workers, etc.), which could at most offer additional voluntary insurance.

As in the other countries the employers' contribution, which cannot be generalized for the entire population, will have to be abolished and a premium for every one will have to be calculated as a progressive percentage of all personal incomes. A calculation limit could very well be dispensed with, a minimum limit below which no premium is due (such as now in the system for self-employed) should be generalized.

What will be difficult for France, if it wants to follow our harmonization plan, is the switch from indirect care, ie reimbursement to the insured, to direct care, the dreaded *'tiers-payant'*. Thanks to the public hospitals, this is applied to a great extent in the hospital sector, pharmacists apply it more and more, but up to now physicians are very resistant to this system.

Third-party payment would apply to all medical services in their social form, with exclusion of de-luxe care, ie when the insured states that he wants to be treated as a private patient or when he wants to see a physician who does not respect the agreements (as long as this possibility exists). In this case all payments by the insurance should be refused. This can be done rather easily, since the existing tariffs for such cases are already unchanged since 1960, and of very little significance.

Existing co-insurance would be eliminated, with the exception of the pharmaceutical sector and artificial aids for which in the future cost-sharing would continue to be usual all over Europe.

It would specifically imply that the *dépassements d'honoraires* by physicians who because of fame or competence are on a special list would disappear. The more so as the fee increases based on the financial status of the insured have already gone, and this was less urgent.

Likewise waiting periods and minimum premiums for entitlement to services would have no place in the system of the future. However specialist care and hospital care would have to be subject to referral by the family physician and possibly to subsequent referral by the appropriate specialist.

The form of agreements with the physicians and the way of determining the tariffs could be kept unchanged, and has even to be considered as progressive. But mandatory arbitration should be organized in place of the unpopular, and also ineffective, rates imposition by the government in case of absence of agreement.

These agreements and possibly the replacing arbitration rulings should be incorporated in programmed expenditures for medical care. There should be a calculation of the balance of fees at the end of each period, calculated on the ratio between total claims for fees and the agreed increase of expenditures. This would offer to the already introduced peer review the possibility of curtailing fees in cases of unjustifiable excess.

## ITALY

For Italy also the first objective is to extend the application of mandatory health insurance to the entire resident population. The present plans for creation of a national health service point in this direction. Hopefully the old dream will be achieved of a real fusion of all large and small systems into one organization, where national solidarity can be expressed.

Obviously the raising of funds for medical care would have to be completely revised, in such a national health service. Based on our harmonization plan we would like to see it as a premium calculated as a progressive percentage of all personal income exceeding a certain minimum. Using taxation amounts essentially to the same thing, although psychologically it has another effect.

As to the services there is one immediate goal to be noted for Italy: lifting the time limit for providing services in general. The form of the health care benefits could be maintained, provided there is an adaptation for some smaller groups, which still have indirect care. For the time being a generalized option between direct and indirect care would be sufficient; as time goes by there will be a tendency to maintain only direct provision of care.

Where waiting periods and minimum premiums are still required, they have naturally to be eliminated. A limitation of the services to serious medical risks only for some categories of non-agrarian self-employed will also not survive the creation of a national health service.

The relations with the physicians will in the future also be settled by national collective agreements. Italy will only have to see that this applies directly to all physicians, without having to be registered on a list. If there have to be exceptions, they will be sanctioned by complete withdrawal of insurance financing for care given or prescribed by these suppliers.

For payment of physicians as for the total expenditures for medical services, a programming of costs should be drawn up preferably by separate agreement. This should somehow, perhaps in the manner suggested for Belgium and France, put a budgetary ceiling on the fees of physicians and on their prescriptions for drugs and hospital care.

With such a structure it will obviously be necessary to take care of the permanent character of this system of agreements. In other words, when disagreement arises between the parties, the existing agreement should be binding until a new one has been reached or until an arbitral ruling has taken its place.

LUXEMBURG

For Luxemburg the same applies as for most European countries: it should try to extend the application of health insurance to all inhabitants irrespective of professional activity or of premium payment. The present field of application is large enough to warrant the supposition that action in this matter can easily be taken.

The financing of the system would likewise have to be organized on a national level. The separate existence of special systems (employees and state officials, self-employed and farmers) would thus come to an end.

We suggest a reorganization of financing based on the previously described model: deduction of a progressive premium percentage on all personal incomes without calculation limit, but with exemption for the low income groups. The government would also grant subsidies based on certain criteria; the employers would not participate in financing.

As in Belgium and France, Luxemburg also maintains the indirect form of medical benefits through reimbursements to the insured, although this is being dropped in the case of hospital expenses and fees related to surgical interventions. Further efforts should be made in order to generalize the direct system ('*tierspayant*'). Then one could more readily switch over to complete financing of socially provided medical care, with the elimination of cost-sharing where it exists. Only for pharmaceutical supplies and for medical aids would a personal contribution by the insured be required in future.

Limitations on the duration of hospital care are already being removed. Another restriction though would be advisable, viz.

making the right to specialist care dependent upon referral by the family physician.

Besides the usual collective agreements with the physicians, which now already follow completely the line of the expected European evolution, special programming agreements should be concluded with all parties concerned, including the government, in order to determine a yearly figure for the rate of increase in medical expenditure at medium term. These agreements would act as budgetary limits for payment of physicians and for their prescription activity. In which way it would function was already explained for Italy, France, and Belgium.

NETHERLANDS

For the Netherlands to comply with the European standards of the future, it would suffice to merge the health fund insurance with the 'General Act Special Medical Costs' (AWBZ) in such a way that the services of the health insurance funds would be extended to all AWBZ insured and would be financed in the same way as the AWBZ, except that contributions should be a progressive percentage on all income, without a ceiling.

More has to be said though on the relations with physicians. First of all the existing informal agreements between health fund associations and physicians' associations should be raised to the level of collective agreements with direct legal authority, in a first stage for all those who would be willing to co-operate with the funds and in a further stage for all suppliers. These collective agreements should be approved by the government (possibly via the agreement commission of the health insurance council).

These agreements should be incorporated in a system for programming medical expenditure as a whole, which would place a budgetary limit on medical expenditure and on prescriptions by physicians. How this system would operate can be seen in the present German system and has already been sufficiently explained in the previous pages.

This would imply reviving an old form of medical control: peer review by physicians mutually. It would be advisable that this control, and likewise also the control services of the health funds should develop to be more involved in improving the quality of medical services than in discovering abuses.

BRITAIN

For British readers it will be obvious that the British national health services are entirely in line with our future model of health insurance in Europe.

We have already mentioned why we see no fundamental difference between a national health service and general national health insurance. Reintroducing an insurance element in the NHS would certainly be contrary to the established trends in health insurance and in social security in general.

Field of application, benefits, conditions for benefits and relationship with the suppliers of care are organized exactly as we are proposing for the other European countries for the future. There are only two exceptions, one apparent, the other a real one.

The apparent exception is to be found in the way of payment of the GP: by capitation fee instead of the continental fee per service. It certainly would not enter my mind to propose a change from the first to the second system. In my opinion capitation payment is a much superior type of remuneration than fee-for-service, in the interest of the physician, the patient, and health insurance. But I believe that in future physicians who work outside a hospital or a similar organization will press for more fee-for-service payment, which serves their financial interests best. The part of this type of payment in the remuneration of the British GP is certainly increasing.

The real exception is in the way of establishing and carrying out the budget of the service at all levels. We propose that the budget for medical care of all types be fixed in agreement with the suppliers of care, who will then have to take their responsibility for the good use of the money. Only if they have a personal interest in it and if they know at the same time that they are serving the interests of the community will physicians and other health professionals look closely at the work of their colleagues. This is the primary condition for 'peer review' to be implemented, and indeed for the realization of an efficient control of quality and quantity of health care provided at the public expense.

## Requirements at the European level

The European treaties offer certain possibilities for introducing a harmonized policy. Apart from these treaty procedures, other means could be employed by the community organizations. But European social policy is not solely the work of community organizations: national organizations could also be active on the European level. What could be done on these three levels in order to achieve what we have proposed will briefly be illustrated.

PROCEDURES STIPULATED IN THE TREATIES

It is not likely that social harmonization will give rise to *decrees* by the Council.

**Directives,** binding for the member countries, can be adopted in two cases.

First of all in application of Article 101 of the EEC Treaty, when certain legal measures are necessary in order to eliminate the differences which 'are of direct influence on the institution or the operation of the Common Market'. This is undoubtedly the case of the differences in structure and content of the range of medical services and of the list of pharmaceutical supplies, since these would simply make unification of the market for medical services impossible. A directive of the Council could therefore oblige the member countries to adapt their legislation to a European range of services and a European list of medicine. In view of the precedent of the European list of occupational illnesses it is more probable that this will happen in the form of a recommendation. A commission of experts should first make a thorough study of this problem.

Secondly in application of Article 57 of the EEC Treaty, the Council may issue directives for the co-ordination of laws and regulations regarding admission and practice conditions for the liberal professions. For medical professions the third paragraph of this article even requires that such co-ordination must have taken place before the right of free movement within the community can be put into practice.

## The way ahead

We have nevertheless to view the organization of relations with physicians under social health security with some realism: it is the most important area for regulating the practice of health professions. Directives could be issued about admission to health fund practice and on the application of collective agreements to foreign physicians. The cause of harmonization as we see it could be furthered a great deal if such directives could stipulate that collective agreements between health insurance and physicians would directly apply to all physicians.

By virtue of Article 155 of the EEC Treaty *recommendations* can be given on subjects stipulated in the Treaty of the Commission, whenever it is deemed necessary.

In order to implement our harmonization programme it would be advisable that the Commission should first of all send a recommendation to the member states with the purpose of expanding their health insurance system to the entire population as such and of tying the right to services to the qualification of residence, free from every premium payment or mandatory contribution. This would automatically lead to the unification of financing and free it from the premium system of social security for employees.

It further appears that a recommendation could be prepared on the degree of financing of medical expenditure, in which all countries would be requested to guarantee full medical care for all citizens under a system of agreements with the suppliers of care. At the same time they should be recommended to use the direct form, ie to pay the physicians directly through insurance organizations, possibly with supplements to be charged to the insured for pharmaceutical supplies, artificial aids, and appliances. And they should certainly be advised to refuse all insurance financing in the case of care given or prescribed by suppliers who keep themselves outside the agreements.

Finally it seems to us that a recommendation could be formulated on the improvement and rationalization of medical care in general. It could be recommended to reform medical control in the way explained earlier, so that it would seek improvement in the quality of medical care rather than curb abuses. It could also be demanded that the national legislations should give some leeway to the insurance organizations so that they might provide organizational and financial support to forms of rationalizing medical practice such as group practice and investments in equipment and personnel.

In form and in content these recommendations have obviously to be the product of consultation on the community level between all parties concerned, based on studies by government experts, with the initiative and the help of the services of the Commission.

A real application seems possible here of the 'Co-operation in the social field between member-states', stipulated in Article 118 of the EEC Treaty. The latter could probably be stressed even better by replacing the recommendation by *advice*, as is provided in Article 118.

**Action of the community organizations outside the procedures stipulated in the treaties.** Article 118 of the EEC Treaty states that the Commission will promote close co-operation between the member states in the social field by studies, advice, and organizing consultation. We do not consider this as a real *procedure* stipulated in the treaty, but as part of the general activity of community organization.

The *studies*, carried out at present by the Commission, are mainly concerned with finding common definitions for terms and concepts, with costs and financing, and with examination of the possibility of ratification of existing international treaties. Naturally these studies are geared to harmonization. For our harmonization programme it would be advisable to pay special attention to studies on the cost and financing of health care, and in a more prognostic perspective than has yet been the case. In the study on common definitions and concepts it appears very important to us that the concept *illness, which entitles to medical care through health insurance*, be investigated, as well as the concept *medical services*, with its subconcepts *general medical services, pharmaceutical services, hospital services, etc.*

It also appears important that the commission should *consult* with the proper authorities of the member states, including the social partners, the insurance organizations, and the medical corps, about the development and financial problems of social insurance for future health care.

Such consultation would undoubtedly lead to certain ideas concerning the generalization and unification of insurance for health care in each country concerning provision of medical services and relations with the medical side. This consultation should precede the recommendations to be issued by the commission. The effectiveness of recommendations and advice appears to consist of the fact that they express and mould a consensus of opinion. Failing that consensus, the recommendations and advice will remain inoperative anyway.

On the other hand use should be made of an entirely different activity of community organizations, which has developed in recent years only: *programming at medium term*. It appears that in such programming a gradual implementation of the Common Market for health care (including the pharmaceutical sector) should be adopted. This should include the study of the supply of services with its economic implications, the gradual unification of the list of services and medicines, of the pricing of pharmaceutical products and of costs of hospital services, and the continuing standardization of documents and forms for obtaining and receiving such services and products. Also provision should be made for the free establishment of medical practice. This calls for standardization of diplomas and licence conditions for physicians, pharmacists, and for the paramedical sector; and also for harmonization of the extent of applicability of collective agreements between the insurance organizations and the medical profession.

Another procedure beyond the treaty can give important results here. The ministers in the Council can make unanimously *special agreements*. Here opportunities are offered for social harmonization, which is not given much elbow-room within the community treaties.

Several points out of the harmonization programme so far suggested appear sufficiently important to be subject to special agreements. Member states could adopt the obligation to guarantee health care for each inhabitant of their countries, regardless of premium payment. This way it could also be accomplished that for all insured the services would be the same: the complete range of currently existing medical care techniques, and that they are provided in the same way: direct payment to physicians by the insurance. If the member states could come to an agreement about the financing system of health care insurance, a special treaty on this would certainly be a great success for common social policy. Even a restricted agreement, dealing only with government subsidy to insurance, would be a fine achievement.

Possibly these elements, and particularly those dealing with the applicability and the services of health insurance, would find their place in a treaty about European minimum standards of social security which would not be based on the greatest common denominator of the current system, but would aim at the desired future social protection of the population of the member states.

ACTION BY NATIONAL AUTHORITIES
Also nationally we should expect (or hope for) action on various levels in order to implement the desired progressive development of social health insurance.

The first level is that of government where a start is made of programming of social expenditures at medium term. This practice is on its way to be expanded to all countries of the Common Market.

In this programming obviously an important place is reserved for projecting expenditure on medical services. It would be desirable in each country for forecasts to lead to multilateral consultation between all parties concerned (government, insurance organizations, medical profession, and possibly also the social partners in as far as they participate in financing) in order to determine a programming of increase in costs for total health services as well as for the large subdivisions. This programming would then demonstrate the need for a system in paying physicians and in the provision of services which would permit adherence to such programming, ie by indicating on an annual basis the budget for health care, not to be exceeded.

An important part of the agreements on health care systems would not find its origin in laws and regulations, but in *collective agreements* between the insurance and the medical profession. Unfortunately, but unavoidably in the current legislative framework, this consultation is presently being conducted within narrow national borders.

First of all a European representative body should function within the borders of the European community as a whole, and preferably sponsored by community institutions both for insurance organizations and for the medical profession. The already existing contact bodies of physicians' and hospitals' associations at the EEC can possibly offer a starting point for such development.

These European organizations of providers and insurers of health care could direct their efforts towards smoothing the way for European collective agreements concerning the provision of health care and the payment of the medical sector.

To that effect it is naturally required that the method by which services are given is the same everywhere, and that the method of calculating remuneration (description, tariff structure, price control) if not the same at least should be compatible. All of this will not be accomplished in the near future, but it appears that European organizations of the medical sector and the insurers of health care can make an important contribution. If they can show to the community organizations and to the individual national governments that they mutually agree about a specific system of services or a specific method of calculating medical fees, the prices of pharmaceutical services or hospital costs, then there is a good chance that such a recommendation will be received successfully by all governments and authorities concerned.

Once this point has been reached specific European collective agreements could be negotiated between insurance and the medical sector, under which could be determined how services would be provided to all inhabitants of the European Common Market and how the medical sector of the EEC will be paid. As a result of these agreements direct payment could be implemented, the proper contribution of the insured for pharmaceutical services and for medical aids could be determined, and the forms and documents that would have to be used (specifically referral notes from GPs and service notes) could be agreed upon.

Within the framework of this European agreement national collective agreements could form the link between the programming of medical expenditure and the actual level of the physicians' fee, taking into account the amount of prescribed medicine and hospital care. These national agreements could also institute democratic interdoctor control for meeting the budgetary ceilings, both collectively and individually.

In this way one could finally (but after what an arduous journey!) come to a settlement arrived at by those concerned, within the broad framework of legislation that guarantees the public interest, and in which both the national and the community aspect would be equally represented. Such a settlement would guarantee for all inhabitants of the community full health care in a *social* manner without personal extra payment (except for pharmaceutical services and medical aids) and in which ample attention is given to the promotion of quality care. This settlement would be such that the interest of both the insurance and the medical sector would be secured, as on the one hand both parties freely agree on the extent of costs and how the personal fees have to be calculated, but on the other hand it is guaranteed that the budgetary ceiling will be met. In addition a just and flexible financing with a responsible government intervention would make an end to the ever-recurring deficits in this sector.

REFERENCES

1. BURNS, E., *Social Security and Social Policy* (New York, 1956), pp. 130–3.
2. *Soins Médicaux individuels et sécurité sociale* (Geneva, WHO, 1971), p. 14.
3. SOCIAAL-ECONOMISCHE RAAD, *Advies inzake een structurele verhoging van de loongrens en van de maximum-dagloongrens in de verplichte ziekenfondsverzekering* ('s Gravenhage, 1969), p. 7, annexe.
4. PERRIN, G., 'La Sécurité sociale comme mythe et comme réalité', *Revue Belge de Sécurité Sociale*, **10** (1966), 1069–80.
5. TINBERGEN, J., 'Les Distorsions et leur correction', *Revue d'Economie Politique (Paris)*, **1-2** (1958), 256–63.
6. NETTER, F., *La Sécurité sociale et ses principes* (Paris, 1959), pp. 192–3.
7. RIBAS, J. J., *La Politique sociale des communautés européennes* (Paris, 1969), p. 396.

# References

8. COPPINI, M. A., *Les Incidences économiques de la sécurité sociale* (Brussels, EEC, 1971).
9. DELEECK, H., *Maatschappelijke zekerheid en inkomensherverdeling in België* (Antwerp, 1966), p. 170.
10. 'L'Influence de l'intégration et de la coopération internationales sur l'économie belge', *Chronique de politique étrangère*, 5 (Brussels, 1969), 590-1.
11. 'L'Assurance maladie des travailleurs non salariés des professions non agricoles', *Droit Social* (no. spécial) (1970), p. 3.
12. MALLET, H., and CARRE, L., *Médecine et Traité de Rome* (Paris, 1963), pp. 105-6.
13. VELDKAMP, G. M. J., *Sociale Triptiek* ('s Gravenhage, 1968), p. 178; MICHEL, CL., 'La Consommation médicale des Français', *Notes et Etudes Documentaires*, 3584 (Paris, La Documentation Française, 1969), 55; EUROPEAN INSTITUTE OF SOCIAL SECURITY, *Evolution and Financing of the Cost of Medical Care* (Leuven, 1972), pp. 210-13, 434-7.
14. Art. 117, Treaty of Rome.
15. DEJARDIN, J., 'L'Organisation des soins médicaux dans la sécurité sociale', *Revue Internationale de Sécurité Sociale*, 3 (Geneva, 1968), 384.
16. MICHEL, CL., 'Les Causes générales de l'accroissement des dépenses de l'assurance maladie en matière de soins de santé', *Revue Internationale de Sécurité Sociale*, 1 (1974), 7-8; SANDIER, S., 'L'Influence des facteurs économiques sur la consommation médicale', *Consommation*, 2 (1966), 71-94; ROSCH, G., 'The economics of medical care in France', *Health Services Financing* (London, BMA, 1970), pp. 378-9.
17. EUROPEAN INSTITUTE FOR SOCIAL SECURITY, op. cit., pp. 214-15, 437-8.
18. *Sécurité sociale: évolution ou révolution?* (Paris, 1968), pp. 128-33.
19. KASTNER, F., *Monograph on the Organization of Medical Care within the Framework of Social Security* (Geneva, ILO, 1968), pp. 29-30.
20. VAN LANGENDONCK, J., *De harmonisatie van de sociale zekerheid in de E.E.G.* (Leuven, Rechtsfakulteit, 1971).
21. CREMER, R., *Traité de l'assurance-maladie* (Leuven, 1966), p. 168; WANNAGAT, G., *Lehrbuch des Sozialversicherungsrechts* (Tübingen, 1965), pp. 299-300; NETTER, F., op. cit., p. 196.
22. SCHUTYSER, K., *De geneeskundige controle in de sociale zekerheid* (Ghent, 1974).
23. GLASER, W. A., *Paying the Doctor* (Baltimore, London, 1970), pp. 304-5.
24. KASTNER, F., op. cit., p. 56.